Our Kind Of Work

*The Glory Days and Difficult Times
of the 25th Street Theatre*

Dwayne Brenna

For Kara

Thank you for a lovely
scene (we've got to
get you back to the
theatre!)

thistledown press

All the best, Dwayne

Thistledown Press Ltd.
118 - 20th Street West
Saskatoon, Saskatchewan, S7M oW6
www.thistledownpress.com

Library and Archives Canada Cataloguing in Publication

Brenna, Dwayne, 1955-
Our kind of work : the glory days and difficult times of
the 25th Street Theatre / Dwayne Brenna.

Includes bibliographical references.
ISBN 978-1-897235-95-9

1. 25th Street Theatre Centre–History. 2. Theater–
Saskatchewan–Saskatoon–History. I. Title.

PN2306.S37B74 2011   792.097124'25   C2011-905334-9

Cover photograph by Larry James Fillo
Cover and book design by Jackie Forrie
Printed and bound in Canada

Thistledown Press gratefully acknowledges the financial assistance of the Canada Council for the Arts, the Saskatchewan Arts Board, and the Government of Canada through the Canada Book Fund for its publishing program.

ACKNOWLEDGEMENTS

The author would like to acknowledge the University of Saskatchewan Library Special Collections which houses a compendious collection of 25th Street Theatre materials dating back to 1973. Special Collections Librarian David Bindle and staff members Rita Chillak, Kulwant Singh, and Joel Salt were particularly selfless in their efforts to see that I had the proper information at my fingertips.

The University of Alberta Rutherford Special Collections was also very helpful in allowing me to view a copy of *Targya* which I could find nowhere else in the world.

I would also like to thank those who agreed to be interviewed for the book. Andy Tahn, Layne Coleman, and Irene Blum were exceptionally candid and extremely generous with their time through a series of long interviews and emailings afterwards. This book would not have been possible without them.

The Research Office at the University of Saskatchewan was very helpful in awarding this project a Publications Fund grant.

Thank you, also, to the Dean's Office at the College of Arts and Science which allocated a Researcher of Tomorrow Fellowship to allow an undergraduate student to work as research assistant on this project. And a very special thank you to my trusty research assistant Ashley Gerling, who worked with great proficiency on a multitude of tasks which included checking my sources, making initial contact with interview candidates, and organizing my endnotes.

Patrick Close and Larry James Fillo were exceptionally generous in allowing me to use their excellent photographs in this book. Thank you, also, to Robert Wyma and the Board at 25th Street Theatre for permitting me to use several photographs that were in their possession.

To Al and Jackie at Thistledown Press, a special thank you for taking on this project, and also to my editor Rod MacIntyre, who provided many helpful suggestions and made this a better book.

As always, I would like to thank my wife Beverley Brenna and sons Wilson, Eric, and Connor, who were unswervingly supportive during the creation of this manuscript.

For Don and Dave and John and Tom,
who helped me on the way

CONTENTS

INTRODUCTION

MOOSE JAW, SPRING 1983. The snow had begun to disappear along Railroad Avenue. The long hard winter was melting off the shoulders of the shop girls and the railroad men as they walked home at the end of the workday. They didn't have far to go, for Moose Jaw was still a small city in 1983. Fewer than thirty-thousand people lived there. By no means the cultural hub of Saskatchewan, it boasted no professional theatre troupe, no dance company, and no symphony. There were school auditoriums in which to stage plays, but on this night 25th Street Theatre would be performing in the Union Centre in Palliser Heights.

The haunt of workingmen and women of all stripes, Union Centre looked a lot like a school auditorium. Its stage was a raised proscenium, inset into the back of the building, with a large flat floor space in front of it. There weren't dressing rooms for the actors, only a series of basement rooms in which to change into their costumes. Union Centre was not really a theatre after all; standing in the auditorium, it was easier to imagine a fiery union man delivering a tirade against the capitalist bosses than it was to imagine a group of actors performing a play about a country-and-western singer in decline.

I was one of six actors in that production of a play called *The Laffin' Jack Rivers Show*. We had been travelling across southern Saskatchewan in a van outfitted with a makeshift stereo system wired into the fuse box by an enterprising John Leclair moments before leaving our point of origin in Saskatoon. All of us, with the exception of Denise Kennedy who came from Ontario, were residents of Saskatchewan. Several of us had worked in other provinces: Ian Black had appeared in the Toronto production of *Tamara*, but he was never able to showcase his talents more completely than in *Laffin' Jack* where he acted, sang and played guitar with a level of virtuosity befitting both actor and musician; Leclair had performed as bassist for Duck Donald in Calgary; I had returned to Saskatchewan after a stint with the Stratford Festival and some CBC productions in Toronto. The group also included seventeen-year-old Colin Munn, from Regina, who later changed his name to Colin James and would become a well-known blues singer and guitarist. Our director, not on tour with us, was Janet Wright, who had made for herself a prosperous career as an actor and director across Canada. (She would later become famous playing opposite Eric Peterson in the television program *Corner Gas*.) We were a rough-and-tumble crew, living out of each other's pockets and sleeping in turns on hotel beds and floors. I was paid the Canadian Actors' Equity (CAE) minimum wage for touring as were most of the other actors (CAE is the union of professional stage actors). We frequently borrowed money from each other two or three days after our weekly pay cheques had been delivered.

Twenty-Fifth Street Theatre was undergoing financial hardship, which didn't bother the actors much because the theatre always seemed to be undergoing financial hardship. Almost every theatre in the country, with the exception perhaps of the National Arts Centre (NAC) and the Stratford Festival, seemed to be in financial ruin. It might have worried some, in other occupations, that our lead publicity car had been stopped by police outside Melfort after its owner had reported it stolen. (In fact, the owner had lent it to the theatre company for an indefinite period of time but had grown antsy when the vehicle was not returned after a month.) We actors had heard rumblings that this time the financial situation was indeed dire, so it was not entirely surprising when we were informed (some time after performing in Moose Jaw) that there would be no hope of holding over the tour after its final date in Prince Albert. The playwrights Ken Mitchell and Michael Taylor suggested to the actors that we continue with the tour as a cooperative, independent of 25th Street Theatre, sharing the profits along the way, but this idea seemed too risky to some of the actors and was later scrapped.

Ken Mitchell had grown up in Moose Jaw and had become a professor in the English Department at the University of Regina. Mitchell was, and continues to be, well known as a playwright, novelist, short story writer and, latterly, as a cowboy poet. His play *Cruel Tears*, set in a Saskatchewan truck yard but based on *Othello*, had been an instant success at Persephone Theatre and had involved Mitchell in a collaboration with Saskatoon folk band Humphrey and the Dumptrucks. Mitchell had continued to collaborate with Michael Taylor, one of the original Dumptrucks, and the result had been *The Laffin' Jack Rivers Show*, for which Mitchell composed the book and Taylor composed the songs.

About the demoralization of a country-and-western singer, the play is set in an obscure small town beer parlour, owned by the anti-artist Armbruster, in which Laffin' Jack and his band have been contracted to play. Over the course of an evening, Laffin' Jack has to endure the catcalls of a patron as well as the immoral financial dealings of the bar's owner and infighting in the band. Alcohol helps him cope, but his music suffers. Michael Taylor's songs, about lost love and pickup trucks, provide a vehicle for the actor playing Laffin' Jack to show the character's artistic disintegration. The play did not resemble anything well-made (in the Scribean sense) or anything you might see in London and New York City at the time; it was a curious mixture of songs and dialogue with a few moments of intense physical action thrown in for good measure. Nothing that happened onstage would have been foreign to an audience of working men. They could certainly recognize a skin-flint bar owner when they saw one; they'd seen people ejected from bar rooms kicking and screaming (as happens in the play); they knew the heart-felt pleasures of country-and-western music and appreciated the inclusion of a beautiful female singer in the band. When, on other occasions, we'd performed the play in actual barrooms and nightclubs, it had been quite common for audience members to stroll into the acting area and order a beer at the realistic-looking bar.

On this night in Moose Jaw, though, the audience was almost entirely union men and workers. Some were still wearing hardhats after a day on the job. There were no suits around. They cheered heartily for the female singer, they chuckled familiarly about the bar owner's wily ways, they commiserated as they watched Laffin' Jack succumb to alcoholism. In the middle of the evening, and while a scene was going on, the local Fire Marshall wandered out on stage and asked me (I was playing Armbruster) if we could keep our set out of the way of the fire exits. The Fire Marshall's appearance didn't phase the audience, however; they might have been used to agit-prop theatre which is portable and ready for interruption. At the end of the evening, the roof was raised with a resounding ovation. Hardhats were tossed in the air. So enthusiastic was the response that I could not help glancing at my fellow actors during the curtain call. And then it struck me, in a way in which I had not been struck during the rehearsals and the early part of the tour: I was involved in the dissemination of popular culture.

A definition of the term 'popular culture' has to include the adjectives "populist" and "grassroots." Popular culture refers to that which is practiced and enjoyed by the broadest cross-section of society. Proponents of popular culture seek to understand and articulate the viewpoints of the masses and to do so in a manner that is intelligible to the masses. In the case of theatre, they might explore the tropes and stories, the literary and dramaturgical forms, which are popular across a wide spectrum of the population. They might examine the language of theatre — not simply the words of the playwright but also the equally important language of music, set construction, dance, and physical action — from the point of view of the grassroots audience.

In his book *A Good Night Out*, John McGrath equates popular culture in England with the working class, noting that "the so-called 'traditional values' of English literature are . . . an indirect cultural expression of the dominance over the whole of Britain of the ruling class of the south-east of England."[1] McGrath offers a quotation from Brecht, who provided a succinct definition of what is popular in a polemic written in 1938: "Popular means: intelligible to the broad masses, adopting and enriching their forms of expression/assuming their standpoint, confirming and correcting it/representing the most progressive section of the people so that it can assume leadership . . . "[2] While McGrath's book has more to do with class-conscious England than with the linear society of Saskatchewan (he was writing largely about his experience with 7:84, an English left-wing agitprop theatre group), some of the statements made in his book still resonate with the inception of 25th Street Theatre.

The creation of a theatre of popular culture is, in essence, a political act. It assumes that there are other valuable forms of entertainment besides those which appeal to an educated elite. It gives power to the grassroots population by giving it a voice. There are many ways of telling a story, as McGrath writes, and simply by choosing what story to tell and how to tell it, the artist exerts power over us. Furthermore, the artist employs devices which are themselves loaded with class-based significance. McGrath notes, for example, that Tom Stoppard's play *Every Good Boy Deserves Favour* requires a small symphony orchestra in its performance. The inclusion of this type of orchestra makes it clear that Stoppard is writing for a middle-class audience, and in McGrath's view, reinforces the play's implicit right-wing message that socialism can drive one mad.[3] For McGrath, the creation of a working class theatre is a step in the direction of a classless (and possibly Utopian) society:

> This area of social, political and cultural development of the
> working class towards maturity and hegemony, leading to the
> possibility of a classless society at some time in the future, is
> that in which an oppositional form of theatre can, and does,

play its part. It is, in my opinion, a form of theatre which is searching, through the experience and forms of the working class, for those elements which point forward in the direction of a future, rational, non-exploitative, classless society, in which all struggle together to resolve humanity's conflict with nature, and to allow all to grow to the fullest possible experience of life on earth.[4]

Theatre can be used to change the social, political and cultural landscapes and, while 25th Street Theatre had been founded to promote no particular political stance, its mandate — particularly following the opening of *Paper Wheat* — was viewed as a socialist one.

What, then, are the characteristics of a populist, grassroots theatre? Experimentation with form seems a high priority. In *Dangerous Traditions*, Judith Rudakoff writes that Toronto's Theatre Passe Muraille, in its early years, "constructed theatre without fixed form. It conceived and created events that continued to develop even after their birth. It provided a home for people who wanted to re-define home."[5] Experimentation with form means questioning the theatrical forms which have been handed down to us and arriving at forms more suited to the subject matter at hand. It is quite possible that the three- or five-act structures do not do justice to modern working class experience. As Brecht famously said, "Petroleum resists the five-act form; today's catastrophes do not progress in a straight line but in cyclical crises . . . "[6] At the same time, artists in a theatre of popular culture must redefine their thinking about the audience for which they are writing. What are the expectations of that audience? What is, or should be, the relationship of artist and audience in such a theatre?

In his book, McGrath delineates the characteristics that separate working class audiences from the tastes of the bourgeois in England: the working class "likes to know exactly what you are trying to do or say to it" whereas the middle class prefers obliqueness; the working class likes to laugh while middle-class audiences "tend to think laughter makes the play less serious"; working class audiences like lively, popular music, unlike the middle class who see music as a threat to seriousness; working-class audiences are open to emotion on the stage while middle-class audiences are sometimes embarrassed by it; the working class prefers variety in its entertainment whereas the middle class "seems to have lost the tradition of variety round about 1630"; working-class audiences "demand more moment-by-moment effect" than their middle-class counterparts; working-class audiences are arguably more appreciative of immediacy and familiarity with on-stage events; working-class audiences enjoy localism, "characters and events with a local feel"; and, lastly, working-class audiences also enjoy a sense of identity with performers like Billy Connolly in Glasgow or Max Boyce in South Wales (or Don Harron [as Charlie Farquharson] in rural Canada.)

In Canada, we might translate the cultural hegemony that McGrath writes about in terms of a colonial dilemma. Especially in the sixties and seventies, Canadians were inundated with the theatrical entertainments of their colonial masters in Europe and the United States. Not only were they in the grip of American television programs and motion pictures; they were also given a steady diet of European and American plays in the repertoires of Canadian theatres. One has only to look at the playbills of Edmonton's Citadel Theatre, or of any of the university theatres, in 1970. The Citadel's season in 1970-71 consisted of Wilde's *The Importance of Being Earnest*, Douglas-Home's *The Secretary Bird*, Shakespeare's *Othello*, Appell's *Lullaby*, Dyer's *Staircase*, Simon's *Plaza Suite*, and Stewart Boston's *Counsellor Extraordinary*. Boston's play was the only Canadian play performed at the Citadel that winter. The University of Saskatchewan's Greystone Theatre (Saskatoon was without a professional theatre at the time) presented Appell's *Lullaby* (or *Three on a Honeymoon*), Shakespeare's *The Merry Wives of Windsor*, Thurber's *Many Moons*, Chekhov's *Uncle Vanya* and Rogers' *Flowers for Algernon* in that year. The Department's only nod to Canadian theatre was a visiting production of the Canadian Mime Theatre, entitled *Visual Delights*, which was performed for two nights in October. In the seventies, there was an explosion of alternate theatre in Canada, which came about as a means of redressing this longstanding colonial hegemony. Twenty-Fifth Street Theatre was part of that movement.

At its beginning, 25th Street Theatre bore the earmarks of an iconoclastic theatre of popular culture, a theatre, like Passe Muraille, without walls. It was to be collectively-run; no one person was to be in control of all facets of the operation. Its founders envisioned an artistic enterprise which spanned many art forms and synthesized them. The troupe was to include directors, actors, dancers, musicians, photographers, and set designers. It was to have its own journal, chronicling new developments in all of the arts. It was to bring a new audience into the theatre, an audience of students and the working class, of farmers and labourers. And it was to bring new theatrical voices and forms to the stage, voices and forms which weren't being witnessed on any stage until that time. In its heyday, 25th Street Theatre accomplished many of these goals. The theatre's eventual decline from a producing and touring organization in the seventies and eighties to an organization which today harbours the Saskatoon Fringe Festival, but little else, might be attributed to a lack of sympathy and support for those original, lofty goals — and their increased costs over time.

Publicity shot for *The Sibyl* at Castle Theatre, 1974

Cast of *The Sibyl*, 1973

Covent Garden, with Andy Tahn, 1973

The editorial team of *Targya*, in interview, 1973

Patrick Close

)on'tcha Know — *The North Wind and You in My Hair,* with Ruth Smillie and
haron Stearns, 1978

Don'tcha Know — The North Wind and You in My Hair, with John Agius and Lisa Reitapple, 1978

ONE:
"A NICE GROUP OF CHILDREN" (1972-73)

THE UNIVERSITY OF SASKATCHEWAN had not been a hotbed of political activism in the politically vibrant sixties. There had been little in the way of marches and protests against the Viet Nam War, or any other war, as there had been at almost every major university in the rest of Canada and in the United States. There were certainly American draft dodgers present on campus at that time, and even when I arrived on the scene in 1973, I encountered a long-haired fellow standing in front of Marquis Hall selling copies of the Georgia Strait. Many of the other remnants of the sixties were there on campus, as well, including pot-smokers and drug busts, but aside from a muted sit-in or two, the campus had come through that period without much political demonstration.

Though not of an overtly political nature, there had been dissatis-faction among students in the Drama Department at the University of Saskatchewan in the late sixties and early seventies. The aging, crusty and autocratic Department Head, Emrys Jones, was seen by some of his students as being too traditional and relentlessly in the past with his anniversary productions of *Candida* and with his view of theatre in education as a training ground for other professions as opposed to a training ground for actors. Dissatisfaction boiled over in the winter of 1965 when students protested the town-and-gown policy of casting on the Department's mainstage, an event which led to the re-casting of Professor Walter Mills' production of *Blithe Spirit*. Saskatoon's major amateur theatre company, Gateway Theatre, was founded in 1966 partly as a result of that protest, for the large cadre of local amateur actors had found themselves without a company in which to perform after the university's town-and-gown policy was lifted. In 1972, with Jones near the end of his tenure as Head of the Drama Department, students were again protesting departmental policy. They were unhappy about Jones' insistence that university theatre training be viewed as part of a liberal education, not as pre-professional training. The students wanted a program which would allow them to concentrate in a more focused manner on actor-training. Despite having taught several great acting talents, including Frances Hyland and Eric Peterson, the Department clearly was not providing concentrated actor-training for the majority of its students.

As a student at E.D. Feehan High School in Saskatoon in the late sixties, Andras (or Andy as he was then known) Tahn had displayed talents both for writing and for drama. As a performer, he was featured in the Feehan Follies of 1969, along with the Klaasen Trumpet Trio and folk singer Randy Cloak. Included in Tahn's personal scrapbook is an editorial which he wrote for the *Saskatoon Star-Phoenix* in April 1968, calling for a lowering of the voting age in Canada. His diatribe is steeped in the cult of youth that grew to prominence in North America in the sixties but also in the involvement of youth in the Hungarian Revolution and in protests in Soviet Czechoslovakia and Poland. Tahn saw injustice in the fact that a young Canadian of nineteen could become a soldier and die for his country but that he could not vote until he was twenty-one. "Who is better informed if not the young who is constantly confronted with various types of media blaring and blasting current situations and happenings to him?" Tahn wrote. "Who is more involved, who is more concerned if not the young, for isn't it his life, his future, his elders are toying with? What freedom or liberty does he enjoy — living as a puppet?"[7] Perhaps his high regard for youth is what kept Tahn young during his career with 25th Street Theatre; he always seemed to be younger than he was, and he always approached his theatrical projects with an unbending zeal that brimmed with youthful petulance. A month after the *Saskatoon Star-Phoenix* published his editorial, it announced publicly that two students from E.D. Feehan had been selected to attend a creative writing course, sponsored by the Saskatchewan Arts Board, at the Summer School of the Arts in the Qu'Appelle Valley. One of those two was Andy Tahn.

Upon graduating high school that spring, Tahn enrolled in Drama at the University of Saskatchewan. He took Jones' playwriting course, frequently locking horns with Jones about the fundaments of writing. According to Tahn, Jones was a conservative teacher, "but in a good way." He was forever extolling the virtues of Aeschylus and Shakespeare, but Tahn thirsted for a more modern approach to playwriting. In a moment of exasperation, Jones exhorted Tahn, "If you know so much, why don't you just go off and write a play?" Jones went further than that, showing Tahn a newspaper article about the Beck family in Blucher and their struggles with the federal government over non-payment of taxes. Tahn claims that the germ of that idea eventually became the storyline for his play *Jakob Kepp*, which was successfully produced at 25th Street Theatre several years later. "I instantly saw the dramatic possibilities in the story," Tahn said in a 2009 interview.[8]

Tahn found the mix of faculty interests stimulating, and he picked up new knowledge from various members of the Drama Department. From Walter Mills, who became a mentor, Tahn learned the value of entertaining an audience. "Plays are not essays," Mills would say. "It's not enough to make your audience think. You also have to make them feel." Raymond Clark and others were interested in the avant-garde; they taught their students to create in their own way, "to cut their own swath." According to Tahn, the eclecticism of the Drama Department was an elixir to young minds. "So when I put it all together," Tahn said later, "you get Emrys Jones telling me to write a play. Then you get injected with these fantastic hormones of creativity and the avant-garde — do it your way, just get out there and do it! Put that with a young man, put that energy together and what do you get? You get your own little theatre company."[9]

During Tahn's first year as a student at the university, a group of Robert Hinitt's former students from Aden Bowman Collegiate decided to mount an experimental production of Georg Büchner's famous play *Woyzeck*. The group included Irene Blum, Carol Greenhouse, Brenda Anderson, Peter Roberts, Rick Roberts, Wayne Arcus, Allan Youngson, and Cathyjane Crandell, each contributing a ten-dollar membership fee in order to bankroll the production. Dissatisfied with the local theatre scene, and with little desire to work for Gateway Theatre, they had decided to create their own theatrical entity and to produce work that interested them. Brenda Anderson, a student in the university's Drama Department at the time, was influenced by the experimentalism of faculty member Carl Hare, and it was Anderson who suggested that the company create of production of Büchner's play. "We were radical youth," said Irene Blum in an interview on April 16, 2009. "What could we do? If you go into Gateway, you have to deal with the structure of it. The same with the university. We knew we couldn't do this play at Gateway." Blum contacted Professor Konrad Haderlein at the University of Saskatchewan, and asked him to create a new translation of the play. According to Blum, Haderlein was not confident in his command of vernacular English at the time, so Blum, Anderson, and Greenhouse worked with him, in committee. Together, they plodded through the play line by line, listening as Haderlein translated from the German and then supplying their own Canadianized and modernized version of Büchner's language. They met with Haderlein three or four times, pounding together the translation, and then Anderson typed the English version from her notes.

The group elected their own board of directors, with Wayne Arcus as administrative director, in December 1968 and called themselves

Theatre Project (according to Blum, who hosted the first organizational meeting, Rick Roberts saw a record album entitled "Blues Project" on his stereo and suggested that the company name themselves Theatre Project, similar to the album). They reserved a space at the Frances Morrison Public Library in which to hold auditions and placed a classified advertisement, announcing the open audition and interview, in the *Saskatoon Star-Phoenix*. Among the seventy or so actors from high schools, the university, and the general community who answered the advertisement was a young Andy Tahn. According to Blum, Tahn gave an assured audition and was selected to join the company. "I don't think he'd ever worked in the theatre before," Blum later said, "but he was very intense, and we hired him."

The company assembled a large cast to perform in the production and began rehearsing in the basement of the newly built Centennial Auditorium. Brenda Anderson directed the play which was performed by John Dunn (as Woyzeck), Peter Roberts (as the Captain), Allan Youngson (as the Idiot), Richard Epp (as the Doctor), Irene Blum (as the Grandmother), Phillip Chevaldayoff (as the Drum Major) and Cathyjane Crandell (as Maria). Others in the cast included Teresa Greenaway, Andy Tahn, Alex George, Gary Goffman, Rod Snell, Becky-Jean Purves, Valerie Berteig, Gary Berteig, Joyce Stilborn, Susan Matthews, Jacqui Presly, Margaret Roberts, Gail Homersham, and Sheila Pinkerton. The actors pitched in to create other elements of the production. Wayne Arcus and Rick Roberts built the set, which consisted of old railway ties and other raw lumber. The raw lumber was arranged to look like a spider web in which Woyzeck would eventually be caught; the climactic moment of the production had John Dunn, who played Woyzeck, receding into the vortex of the web with a tight spotlight on his face. Blum designed the costumes, looking to create a medieval feel, and Greenhouse sewed them. "It was a very expressionistic, Bergmanesque interpretation," Blum later said. "It had a medieval Everyman-look to it." When the need for production-based music arose, Blum contacted David Kaplan, in the university's Music

Department, who recommended PhD candidate Jack Johnson. It was Johnson who created the original musical score.

Rather than simply renting a theatre space and performing their play, Theatre Project entered it in the Saskatchewan Regional Competition for the Dominion Drama Festival (DDF), in the hope that they would attain national exposure in their first season. The troupe performed *Woyzeck* before DDF adjudicator Dennis Sweeting on Thursday, March 27, 1969. Sweeting had high praise for the production and its director. The *Star-Phoenix* reported that Sweeting "complimented the director's work with crowd scenes, particularly those involving choreographed dancing."[10] He admired Haderlein's new translation of the play for its flowing language and singled out actors Peter Roberts and Allan Youngson for commendations. Brenda Anderson won an award as most promising director at the festival, Allan Youngson won the Dr. A. Davis Beatty Trophy for Best Characterization, and the production won the Bessborough Award for best classical play in the Western Zone. It was not, however, picked as winner in the Best Production category and did not advance to represent Saskatchewan beyond the provincial festival. This came as a surprise to the young ensemble. As Irene Blum said later, "We were sure we were going to win, and we were absolutely shocked when we didn't."

Although Theatre Project's artistic output was limited to a single production, the company can legitimately be seen as the predecessor to 25th Street Theatre. When it did not go on to the DDF finals, as hoped, Theatre Project decided to mount the play a second time, for one night only on April 29 at the Castle Theatre in Aden Bowman Collegiate. The company had plans to produce other plays as well as children's drama lessons and adult-centred workshops. They were unhappy, however, with the state of Castle Theatre, which was only three years old at the time, and Wayne Arcus went before the Saskatoon Collegiate Board to complain about the theatre's deterioration. He argued that the backstage areas and lighting booth were in a general state of disorder, that the communications system was in disrepair, that the winch and rope system was unsafe, and that the foyer was a public safety hazard.

Theatre Project offered to assume responsibility for maintenance and management of Castle Theatre if the Collegiate Board would permit the company to use the theatre as its home base. Arcus explained to the Collegiate Board that the mandate of his company was "to provide an organized outlet for theatrical creativity among interested high school and university students."[11] On September 24, 1969, the company announced that it was planning a season and that an organizational meeting would be held in the conference rooms of the Upper Mub on the university campus. The meeting could not have gone well; shortly thereafter, the company disbanded and gave Tahn approximately three-hundred dollars — the box office receipts from their April performance — with which to start his own theatre company.

On September 26, Tahn wrote for the *Sheaf* (the university student newspaper) a belated commentary on the Theatre Project's production of *Woyzeck*; it was not so much a review as a diatribe against the sorry state of the theatre in Saskatoon. He characteristically disarmed his reader by admitting his naïveté in the initial paragraph: "Having seen only a few theatrical productions in the past year and having read no more than a dozen or so plays in my entire 'thinking' life I can safely presume I'm one of the general everyday run-of-the-mill public (if there exists such a thing) . . . " After his affinity with the general public had been clearly stated, Tahn then went on to accuse local companies of trading in exhaustion and fatigue. He asked what local theatre companies have to offer and answered that they offer "[e]xhaustion and fatigue on opening night with a spark here and there of a good performer, a few lovely lines delivered in a half sentimental mood, a salty tear shed downstage center, a façade of splendor and a glorious array of costumes, a tragedy that no man has experienced . . . " He announced, confidently and prophetically, that theatre "should partake of people and people of theater." His aspirations for local theatre were high-minded:

Theater should be living and breathing, breathing moist and heavy; eat at our guts and squeeze our dry eyes from their secure shallow sockets — it should be a theater that dances lively steps

DWAYNE BRENNA

on a young maiden's head or one that kisses fat babies with huge pink lips; a local theater that is not afraid to reveal its wide hairy nostrils or its yellowed teeth. A theater that burns the lungs, that can chuckle to itself and drink warm blood; a theater that chats with unblemished young girls who date tall handsome men whose brothers are short, fat and ugly; a theater that cuddles beside a naked audience — dynamic theater — a force.[12]

He advocated a theatre that was relevant to its audience, a theatre with dirty faces and eyes full of blood, and then worried that Theatre Project might be pursuing its mandate only to demonstrate that it was trendy and different from all the other theatre companies in Saskatoon.

Tahn's article was meant to stir up a controversy, and it succeeded. There was more than a hint, in the article, that Tahn was not only unhappy with the state of Saskatoon's theatre scene — he was also not entirely happy with his experience with Theatre Project. He characterized his brief association with the company as "an awkward run-in":

Last year I had an awkward run-in with one of the local theatre companies which turned out to be quite exciting and disappointing at the same time. Theatre Project [sic] — a theatrical company built and organized by eight young people who were selfish and honest enough to demand that theatres do away with the stale cigar smell of empty bare walled auditoriums. Since no one was providing for their desires they upped and started their "own" theatrical company. Theatre Project produced the controversial Woyzeck. The original aims and desires of Theatre Project interested me deeply but as time passed I could sense the slow loss of some of their beginning purposes brought about by the tough rehearsal schedule, financial worries, etc — worries that can destroy any vision.[13]

The young Andy Tahn was in a mood to take no prisoners, and his article was met with some rancour. Also in the Sheaf, local amateur actress Hetty Clews voiced her annoyance at Tahn's diatribe:

Having read Mr. Tahn's super-heated non-sentences, I would like to offer some return reflections. It is difficult to determine the purpose of the article "Reflections on Local Theatre". Evidently, Mr. Tahn has a commendable interest in Theatre Project, which company, I agree, has "an air of theatrical creativity about it," but then to me, so has any theatre company I know. Once this interest is understood, and its partisan denigration of other nameless companies is rejected, once, in fact, we eliminate odious comparisons, then what remains as the focal point of the attack? It could be understood to be one of three. Is Mr. Tahn angry with playwrights, for not providing us with "kick in the groin" scripts; with companies for not adapting scripts to accommodate perverted housewife reading and exposed toilet bowls; or with audiences for not obligingly agreeing to participate in a little cosy nudity?[14]

Clews disagreed vehemently with the assertion that there was a need for theatrical change of the sort Tahn envisioned. She exhorted him to begin writing his own plays if he was so dissatisfied with the theatrical fare in Saskatoon. "With his flair for imagery and rhetoric," Clews wrote, "Mr. Tahn should be able to do this quite well."

Tahn needed time to learn about the theatre and to gestate his ideas. He continued his studies in drama at the University of Saskatchewan, acting in productions of *The Visit*, *Bedtime Story*, *The Merry Wives of Windsor*, and *Uncle Vanya*. Walter Mills, a professor in the Drama Department at that time, remembers that Tahn occasionally used to work late in the Hangar Building on campus, whereupon he would spend the night on an old mattress in the Arena Theatre's backstage area. It was not until 1971 that Tahn and a group of interested university drama students decided to change the local theatrical landscape. By September of that year, Tahn had finished a three-act play, according to George Elder "a romantic trip to end all romantic trips," entitled *Miklos and Kristina*. Later reminiscing about the conception of 25th Street Theatre (then called 25th Street House Theatre) in the first issue of the company's journal, *Targya*, Elder maintained that a number of close-knit friends, including Tahn and himself, were living together at that time in the two-room basement suite of an old mansion on 25th Street East in Saskatoon. Although Elder was a folk musician, he was almost as interested in theatre as Tahn, and together they envisioned a new "type of theatre whose philosophy would be so loose and whose structure so undefined that it could operate under almost any circumstances, using almost any form of the arts (visual, audio, or both) to communicate the individual artist's ideas to his audience." How was the company name arrived at? Elder maintained that "we looked out our door, read the street sign on the corner, and came up with Twenty-Fifth Street House."

Being young and brash and seemingly invulnerable, Tahn and Elder proceeded from dreaming about the project to acting upon their dreams with extreme rapidity. According to Elder, "one night we got drunk and decided to amalgamate every available artist in Saskatoon, form a performing company, and produce publicly all the original Canadian material we could get our hands on, beginning with Andy's play and my songs." The production of Tahn's play and its venue was announced to the public in an article written by Ned Powers of the *Saskatoon Star-Phoenix* on December 17, 1971. One does not sense a great deal of optimism for the fledgling company in Powers' article; he had seen other theatre companies like Theatre at the Gallery (which had been running at the Mendel Art Gallery) come and go in Saskatoon. "Another new dramatic group, the Twenty-Fifth Street House, is taking shape in Saskatoon," he wrote, "and one of its prime concerns is to put an end to the dramatic migration to outside cities."[15] In the article, Tahn hinted at his vision for the new company. "We want to have a company writing and producing its own plays . . . ," he said in the interview, "a company with its own resident writer." The production of *Miklos and Kristina*, a play "about the Canadian artist's scene and a search for reality," was slated to be produced in April 1972 at the Centennial Auditorium.

The next order of business was to secure a volunteer secretary, "an unemployed housewife" who was immediately handed an overwhelming list of duties "of the most urgent priority." Elder would later write, when this first secretary finally crumbled under the workload, that he and Tahn learned a valuable lesson about crushing the enthusiasm of volunteers. He also noted that, among the early errors of the company, was the "high-pressure salesmanship which we used on any and every person who might have something to contribute to our cause and then handing them nothing more concrete than our ideas, which, after all, were only our ideas and not theirs." Such a method, Elder suggested, could attract the enthusiastic and inexperienced but did not attract knowledgeable and competent people. Although Elder and Tahn did not have much money between them — Elder was living on unemployment insurance and Tahn was still a student — they began to acquire various assets for the company, including a rented office space on Third Avenue with some chairs, desks, and a few borrowed typewriters. When their first secretary resigned, Tahn and Elder found two more secretaries to take her place, both of them volunteers willing to work forty hours per week. The company needed money badly, and Tahn and Elder devised a scheme — based on Theatre Project's membership plan — of charging a membership fee of two dollars for every artist who wanted to be involved. After they had amassed a group of eight or ten "highly interested" people, they decided to find a president for the organization since neither Tahn nor Elder felt they were competent to lead.

The company's first president was "intelligent, respectable, had lots of theatre experience and a good business head" but resigned within two weeks of agreeing to serve. He was overwhelmed by the fact that Tahn and Elder had already committed to produce *Miklos and Kristina* at the Centennial Auditorium and that the total anticipated cost of the project would be about $25,000. They were also getting into debt with the real estate company over their office space. They decided to seek a new president, and they soon found one with no family commitments, no outside job, plenty of enthusiasm but, according to Elder, no experience. In February 1972, under this new president, they applied for a grant from the Company of Young Canadians (CYC). Before the grant results were announced, apathy had begun to grow among the volunteer office staff. The secretaries quit. Under pressure from the real estate company, the office space was reduced to only one room. Tahn went broke, and Elder's unemployment insurance ran out. The president tried to take the company in a new artistic direction and, according to Elder, the company was reduced to two rival factions. Their second president resigned, and Tahn and Elder decided to assume control of the company themselves. They were buoyed when the CYC grant came through, allowing them to hire and pay for a coordinator for a period of twelve months. "This was pivotal," Tahn later said. "I remember the letter. It was personally signed by Pierre Elliot Trudeau . . . It was given for things that were going to change the fabric of Canada. And we fit the bill. We were going to be a populist company. We thought, we really like Saskatchewan. This is our home. Let's do plays about who we are."[16] They accepted the grant and cancelled the show at the Centennial Auditorium, moved out of the office on Third Avenue and "back to the basements of Saskatoon."[17] In April 1972, Elder left the city, looking for a paying job, and got work as a waiter on a CNR passenger train.

The remaining members of the company met on May 2, 1972 at Tahn's parents' home on 925 Trotter Crescent in order to hammer out a constitutional proposal. In attendance were Tahn, Rose Marie McSherry, Jim Watts, Dennis Gingrich, Sam Lindquist, Sharon Baker (later Bakker), and Gerry Stoll. In the proposal, the Company, which was already calling itself 25th Street House, set forth its desire to become a permanent live-theatre company. Nowhere in the document are the words "professional" or "Canadian Actors' Equity" used; the Company would be happy to remain outside the aegis of Actors' Equity if it could achieve its aims more easily by so doing. The stated objectives of the company are as follows:

1. The prime aim of 25th Street House is to organize a permanent live theatre Company in Saskatoon."

2. Twenty-Fifth Street House will work towards a capability to write, produce, and direct their own productions.

3. Twenty-Fifth Street House will emphasize the training and growth of the Company and its individual members.

4. Twenty-Fifth Street House will seek to provide and prove viable a model of organization in theatre which will ensure control by the membership without jeopardizing the artistic discipline, progress, or integrity of the Company or its individual members.

5. Twenty-Fifth Street House will strive to involve as large and varied a segment of the community as possible in its progress. We will strive to involve as participants and as spectators those people who have previously had little or no contact with live theatre.

6. Twenty-Fifth Street House will emphasize live theatre, but the Company will strive to incorporate the various art forms (dance, music, film, graphic arts, etc.) into its programs.

7. Twenty-Fifth Street House will always remain open to new members who demonstrate a willingness to actively participate in our Company and in the furtherance of its aims and programs.[18]

Several of the objectives stated in the constitutional proposal belie the youth of the company. Lacking the confidence to view themselves as a full-fledged producing organization, the signatories spoke of working "towards a capability" and of training and growth. The company's openness to new members would later prove vital to its development; invited artists like Guy Sprung and Paul Thompson would help steer the company in new directions. But the most important objectives listed in the proposal are, in my view, items four, five, and six, for they point the way for 25th Street Theatre to develop a groundbreaking new (at the time) concept in theatre-making. Item four speaks of the need to provide a new model of organization, one which ensures "control by the membership." From its beginning, 25th Street would become a model of collective growth, amidst a professional theatre community that had become increasingly dominated by the presence of the despotic director. One might infer that 25th Street's model was, from the beginning, a socialist one, but Tahn later argued that his theatre was founded to fulfill no political purpose and certainly not a Marxist one. "Politics wasn't of interest to me," he said in a 2009 interview. "You might be surprised to hear that. Politics, to me, was never the motive. And that's where I ran into conflict with Guy Sprung when he directed the second *Paper Wheat*. He injected the political."[19] Item five speaks of involving new audiences and as large and varied a segment of the population as possible, including those who have had "little or no contact with live theatre." Nowhere in the document is the call to create a populist, grassroots theatre made more clearly than in this item. The desire to experiment with new forms, which, as we have seen, is a necessary component of populist theatre, is stated graphically in item six. The company promised to "incorporate the various art forms" in its presentations.

The company began to take shape quickly after its constitutional meeting. Its second windfall came on December 8, 1972, when it received a Local Initiatives Grant from the Department of Manpower and Immigration for $45,000. "Back then," Tahn said later, "that was a lot of money. We were able to hire a full staff. It was a big story in *The Star-Phoenix* because nobody knew we even existed, and here we are getting forty-five thousand dollars."[20] This tidy sum of money was enough to employ fifteen artists (at non-Equity wages) until May 31, 1973 and through six productions. At the end of the company's first full season, George Elder, who had returned to Saskatoon in October 1972 to serve as administrator for 25th Street Theatre, maintained that the company had managed to save $1,500 of the original grant along with $3000 worth of materials.[21] 25th Street was always good at making its limited funding go a long way.

The company had found no permanent venue in which to perform for its first season. (Its studio space at the corner of Whitney Avenue and Rusholme Road, which was dubbed Whitney Place, was used for rehearsals but not as a theatre.) Because of its close ties with the university, the company was able to perform its first production, a play called "Gardens, Sketch #1" by Andy Tahn, in the new arena theatre at the Hangar Building. Produced in August 1972, before the university had begun its autumn session, for an invited audience of about forty people, "Gardens, Sketch #1" featured Madeline Stewart, Stephen Carter (who was then an anthropology student at the University of Saskatchewan), and Tahn himself in the cast. Tahn referred to the company by two names in the program, calling it both 25th Street House and New Century Theatre. According to Tahn, the addition of the second name was an attempt "to be brash, new, and bold."[22] It was dropped before long, as was the "House" in 25th Street House. The program note for "Gardens, Sketch #1" contains a mission statement for the new company:

> twenty-fifth street house/NEW CENTURY THEATRE is the result of a search for a new alternative to the successful theatres already existent in Saskatchewan. Its prime aim is to organize and prove viable a permanent theatre fixture which will enable young unestablished artists to work and experiment freely, in their own direction.[23]

Because Tahn's company could not charge for admission on shows mounted in the Drama Department, they decided to move to Knox United Church on Spadina Crescent where tickets could be sold. "Gardens, Sketch #1" was followed closely by a double bill of Strindberg's "The Stronger" and Tahn's "Bandages, or Gardens, Sketch #2", performed on September 8 in the basement of Knox United, with tickets sold for the princely sum of twenty-five cents. Sharon Bakker, a native of Aberdeen who would become a longstanding member of the company, was in the cast as well as Dennis Gingrich, and Ken Waschuk. The production of Strindberg's classic one-act, which featured Sandra Lindquist, Beverly Barry, and Birkett Bentley, was out of character for the company and is one of a handful of occasions on which non-Canadian playwrights were featured on the stage at 25th Street (Harold Pinter's *The Birthday Party* was produced there in 1973).

On November 10, the company performed in an eclectic evening at St. James Hall, with adaptations by Andy Tahn of *King Cat* and *The Magic of Cobbie Bean* as well as a choreographed dance piece entitled

Voices For Dance. King Cat was directed by Madeline Stewart and featured Doug Knott, Chris Popoff, and Neil McMillan in the cast. Sharon Bakker directed Eric Braun and Karen Wiens in *The Magic of Cobbie Bean*. *Voices For Dance* featured poems by Shakespeare, Irving Layton, Colleen Fitzgerald, and Andy Tahn, among others, and was choreographed and danced by Delphine Diakiw, Colleen Fitzgerald, Al Lake, Neil McMillan, and Gerry Stoll. An article appearing in the *Sheaf* on November 10, the day of their opening, hints at some animosity between the company and Ned Powers, then entertainment writer at the *Saskatoon Star-Phoenix*. The anonymous writer refers to Saskatoon as a "cultural wasteland of Guy Lombardo fans" and maintains that 25th Street Theatre "is hiding out in a small office downtown, desperately trying to avoid destruction at the hands of the Ned Powers Conspiracy."[24] There is an anonymous review of the November 10 performance, which appeared in the *Sheaf* on November 14, 1972 under the headline "A Grimm Evening." Despite that unhappy play-on-words, the review is generally positive, noting that the production benefited on its opening night from a full and appreciative house. The reviewer wrote that it is "not often that fairy tale theatre of this caliber presents itself" and then singles out the performance of Dundurn-born Karen Wiens, in *The Magic of Cobbie Bean*, for praise. Noting that most of the evening's characterizations "did not demand anything more than saying the lines and memorizing rudimentary actions," the reviewer maintained that Wiens' "feline grace was a contrasting performance, however, that gave a little depth to the one-dimensional action. Her movements seemed naturally cat-like and smooth . . . "[25] The theatre artists might have under-estimated their potential in this shallow evening of fairy tale theatre, but the production was nevertheless deemed delightful and entertaining.

On December 16, just one week after receiving their Local Initiatives grant, 25th Street Theatre produced Ken Mitchell's play *Pleasant Street* at the YWCA Auditorium in Saskatoon. Mitchell had already written his one-act *Heroes* by this point, but 25th Street wanted to produce a new script. The play was based on Pleasant Street in the

Dick and Jane series of primary-school readers. "It was a cute little story," said Tahn later, "it was just fun, entertaining . . . a nice little piece."[26] The one-night-only performance, directed by Stan McGaffin, had an audience of approximately eighty-five people. Two days later, Tahn embarked on a personal tour of Saskatchewan, with the promise of hiring twenty-eight artists and craftsmen for the theatre. In a press release, he stated that he was "looking for hard workers, not 'professionals', to build a new original theatre in this province."[27]

On January 26, 1973, 25th Street organized a poetry performance entitled "Art For Eyes And Ears." The advance advertising in the *Sheaf* suggested that four artists — English professor Ron Marken, poet Terrence Heath, Mendel Art Gallery employee Louise Walters, and twenty-three-year-old Andy Tahn — would "'perform' their poetry in the theatre in an attempt to escape the traditional 'poetry reading'."[28] While the reviewer for the *Sheaf*, Gayle Cardiff, does not offer much description of how the evening differed from a traditional poetry reading, she gives the impression that Marken's reading was the most well-received of the evening. She refers to Tahn's performance as "emotional tantrums before a live audience."[29] A ticket for the event, which was staged at the Mendel Art Gallery, cost a mere dollar.[30]

By March 1973, Saskatoon's newest theatre company was beginning to feel pressure to produce something more than poorly attended single-night entertainments. Tahn's play *Covent Garden* was to be performed in March, and an advance article in the *Sheaf* suggested that proof of 25th Street's ability to produce "great drama, music and dance will be put on the line" with the production.[31] The production was ambitious, featuring thirty artists from within the company, with Tahn himself playing one of the leads opposite Deborah Anderson, with Colleen Fitzgerald choreographing the dance component, and with music provided by Dennis McBride and Marti Borycki. The production was huge. "I had a full orchestra in the pit," Tahn reminisced later, "and we put on a musical based on a poem I had written, a twenty-page poem which I had sold to the CBC. And because the CBC bought it, I thought, well, let's turn this into a play. And it's basically the story of a young man who goes to England and has a love affair. It was a good little story. I acted in it, I wrote it, I directed it. I didn't think of it as an ego trip. I just did it."[32]

It was also the first performance in which Layne Coleman appeared at 25th Street Theatre. A native of North Battleford, Coleman had little previous theatre training. He and Tahn had met in a coffee house. "He had a beard," Tahn remembered later. "He was in the mountains, and he had just come out . . . There was something about Layne. He had a big beard, he was a little guy, and he was very sincere. That's what struck me. And I said, 'Why don't you come and work with us for awhile?'" Tahn and Coleman quickly became close and trusting friends. "He is the most genuine, down-to-earth, sincere, honest, truthful, hard-working person I've ever met," Tahn said later. "My association with Layne has been a blessing."[33] In *Covent Garden*, Coleman worked as a dancer although he had never received any formal dance training.

Because the multi-media show was produced at the Centennial Auditorium — Saskatoon's largest theatre venue — ticket prices were raised from $1 to $1.50 and $2. The choice of Centennial Auditorium for a venue was a poor one; the play was too small for so large a stage, and the actors had to strain to be heard in the large auditorium. Jean Macpherson of the *Saskatoon Star-Phoenix* panned the production magnificently in her review, suggesting that "it was so much like a high school play one expected to look around and see an audience of beaming teachers, admiring classmates, and proud parents." She could find no possible explanation for the presence of the dancers onstage and was incredulous at the appearance of a saxophonist who played one note and crept off the stage. The plot was hackneyed, in Macpherson's view, and she finished with the damning statement that 25th Street Theatre "seems to be a group of nice children with a long, long way to go in their chosen field."[34] Even more pointed was an article in the May issue of *Where It's At*, a publication of the Mendel Art Gallery. The commentator addressed Tahn specifically and familiarly, first expressing admiration for his talent and then taking him to task for his apparent lack of humility: "But man, how about taking that chip off your shoulder? Talking good theatre can be nothing more than a case of verbal diarrhoea. Talking good theatre and producing good theatre are two different things. I'd like to see less talk and more performance. A dash of healthy humility might help."[35] Personal criticism such as this was hard to swallow for the young Andy Tahn. "There was a lot of truth in [what Jean MacPherson wrote]," Tahn later said. "But still it hurt. The play was for one night. And we put everything into it. It was a huge stage. I wasn't a great director. Now I know better how to deal with different stages."[36]

The season limped to a halt with three further productions in the spring of 1973. *Pilk's Madhouse* by Toronto playwright Henry Pilk was presented at the Indian and Metis Friendship Centre on May 19 and 20. Directed by Stan McGaffin, the actors were Elizabeth Mudry, Layne Coleman, Ed Sutton, Tahn, and Trevor McLaine. The inaugural season ended on June 8, 1973, with a dance extravaganza entitled *Catch the Sun*, which was performed in the E.D. Feehan High School Theatre. Original music for the production was composed and performed by Bill Higbee, Bill Chelsom, and Paul Mowbray, with Elizabeth Mudry on flute. The dancers were Bill James, Jack Neimann, Colleen Fitzgerald, Lee Brady, Greg Roberts, and Delphine Diakiw.

Also in May of that year, the company began advertising for submissions for a new arts publication called *Targya*. The literary section of 25th Street Theatre published two issues of the journal, which had a polymorphous mandate. "In this, the first issue of *Targya*," the editor Bill Boyle wrote, "we hope to acquaint the people of Saskatchewan with a new concept in magazines; a concept whereby many forms of the arts may be combined, yet each individual artist's work is presented as a separate entity, complete in itself."[37] The editorial offices of *Targya* were located at 202–120 2nd Avenue North in Saskatoon. The editorial staff was listed as follows: Bill Boyle (editor), Don Ward (assistant editor), Mel Melymick (editorial), Bryson Williams (editorial), Len Taylor (photographer), Bob Whittaker (photographer), Pat Close (photographer), Ray Statham (production supervisor), and

Gord Findlater (production supervisor). Linda Vidler, Gerry Stoll, and Bryson Williams were in charge of public relations and advertising.

The first issue of *Targya*, published in loose leaf on heavy bond paper and distributed in a folder in spring 1973, featured poetry by Mel Melymick, Bill Metke, Gayle Cardiff, and Red Rock. The issue also included George Elder's tale of the founding of 25th Street Theatre, entitled "Conception," and Lorne Falk's poem "Targya and the Prairie," which situated the word "targya" in a natural setting (the word is Hungarian and means "a gift" or "a toast"):

Yellowed grey, smoothed and dry
The great old tree in a sand toned sky
Stood flat to the prairie.
Killed by lightning; while
Down, down by the bluing root gum
Eleven flower cups hummed and drummed and
Bared their tears to a sad faced sun.
Targya.
Toll and knell
As the green sheaths swell
They chopped the dead tree down.
Chimes and rhymes in the old tree lines.
The yellow flowers bell. Targya,
Targya.

The imagery of death and rebirth, in Falk's poem, is very apropos for a new theatre company and a new journal, with youthful leaders like Andy Tahn and Bill Boyle and with a mandate to replace outdated theatrical and literary practices with new innovative ones. The young people at 25th Street Theatre were in the business of clearing out deadwood and making room for green sheaths and yellow flowers.

Unfortunately, *Targya's* lifespan was brief. A second, and final, issue was published in autumn 1973, not in loose-leaf like the first issue, but spine-bound like a traditional journal. Bill Boyle had moved on to other challenges; there is no mention of him as editor in the second issue. An editorial staff, quite different from the staff in the first issue, is credited with the publication. The new staff included Jan Dawson, Gary Jahnke, Patrick Close, Don Ward, Ian Frenette, Vi Wilkinson, Martin Heavisides, and George Elder. The autumn 1973 issue featured an essay by Anthony Appleblatt on the history of the Ku Klux Klan in Saskatchewan, poems by Glen Sorestad, Ricky Magis, Terrence Heath, and Dan Poitras, and a short story by Don Ward. Local folk musician Don Freed, who had played with Johnny Cash in one of Cash's concerts in Saskatoon, contributed the lyrics of a song entitled "Learn Some Karate." Freed's song poked fun at the craze for kung fu and kung fu movies in the early seventies:

One of these days all hell's gonna break loose
— don't you be left in the caboose,
Oh ya! Learn some karate now.
Don't fill your mind up with peace and love,
— fill it with something you can make some good use of.
Oh ya! Go out and learn some karate now![38]

Freed's early involvement with 25th Street Theatre would later lead to his contribution of music for Andy Tahn's *The Ballad of Billy the Kid*, one of the theatre's first successes.

The company's first season had been too ambitious and too hastily conceived. In an effort to regroup, Tahn and his colleagues hired UBC drama instructor Raymond Clarke to provide a series of acting workshops for company members. In a press release, 25th Street Theatre explained that the company was establishing "a practical school/training ground for the unestablished artist."[39] The plan was to bring in artists of all stripes who would conduct interdisciplinary workshops. A rather unsympathetic article appeared in the *Saskatoon Star-Phoenix* on June 27, stating that members of the company "admit they haven't really known where they've been going since their formation 18 months ago." In future, the article suggests, the company was planning to move more slowly and to "make sure they are completely ready for each production rather than jumping into them as they have in the past."[40] Nevertheless, as Clarke argued, "the concept (of 25th Street Theatre) is very exciting really," but its success "depends on the professionalism they bring into it." It was time to go back to school.

Two:
"THEIR SPECIAL BRAND OF DOGGED INTREPIDITY"
(1973-75)

TWENTY-FIFTH STREET THEATRE WAS in trouble. In a too-ambitious first season of ten productions, it had ignored production values and the need for long rehearsals. The fledgling company had gambled, and lost, its reputation on one big show at the Centennial Auditorium. Critics had savaged the production and questioned the viability of the theatre. Audience numbers had not dwindled appreciably over the year, perhaps because the company had usually presented its offerings over one or two nights and were off the stage before reviews came out and also because admission prices were extremely low. Worse still, the company's most visible member (who was referred to in press releases first as "Member in Charge of Artistic Direction" and later as "Artistic Director") had come under attack. Tahn had been accused of putting himself before the company; it was difficult to argue otherwise after the opening of *Covent Garden*, which Tahn wrote and directed and in which he played one of the leads. And people were beginning to wonder if the public grants that 25th Street had acquired were taxpayers' money well-spent.

To complicate matters, a new professional theatre company began producing plays in Saskatoon in 1974. Founded by Janet and Susan Wright and Brian Richmond, the new Persephone Theatre would offer a mixed repertoire of Canadian and international plays.

In its first season, Persephone Theatre enlisted the services of Ken Mitchell, who had already worked at 25th Street Theatre (in *Pleasant Street*). With Humphrey and the Dumptrucks, Mitchell had written a Saskatchewan-based adaptation of *Othello* entitled *Cruel Tears*. The rock-opera premiered to rave reviews and eventually toured Saskatchewan and Alberta; it continues to be produced nationally and internationally. While there is reason to believe that Saskatoon's population might have supported more than one professional theatre company in 1974, it is also true that the new Persephone Theatre was cutting into 25th Street's audience, particularly when they mounted locally-written plays. There was also a question of theatre space. Outside of the Centennial Auditorium, which was far too large to accommodate a local company, no purpose-built theatre space existed in Saskatoon in 1974 aside from high school and university theatres. In its first two seasons, Persephone Theatre occupied spaces — at the Mendel Art Gallery and at the university's Drama Department — which had been occupied in one way or another by 25th Street Theatre in its inaugural season.

It was a time to rebuild, and 25th Street Theatre had decided to move cautiously. While he remained artistic director of the company, Tahn receded from acting, directing, and writing plays for a season. Only two plays were produced in the 1973-74 season, Harold Pinter's *The Birthday Party* and *The Sibyl*, adapted by Alexander Hausvater from a novel by Pär Lagerkvist. In the next two seasons, and after, artistic diversity was no longer the mandate at 25th Street Theatre; poetry readings, dance recitals, and art exhibits were no longer on the menu because the company had decided to focus specifically on theatre.

The company's choice of Harold Pinter's play as its pre-Christmas show at St. James Hall on Dufferin (it ran for three nights, December 13-15) was an odd one, necessitated most likely by the need for a sure-fire hit. The play was neither the work of a new Saskatchewan-based playwright nor particularly relevant to a Saskatchewan audience (in the way that other 25th Street shows strived to be). Several reviewers nevertheless found the choice of play entirely appropriate and were happy that 25th Street Theatre had reined itself in with a tried and tested product. In the *Star-Phoenix*, Jean Macpherson began her review with praise for the appropriateness of the play: "A little non sequitur of a play, *The Birthday Party* by Harold Pinter nevertheless proved an appropriate vehicle for Twenty-Fifth Street House, a young Saskatoon drama company now pacing itself wisely in presentations suitable to its size and scope." Macpherson praised Toronto director Ken McEvoy for getting good performances from his actors.[41] In his CBC Radio review, university Drama Professor Walter Mills was effusive about the meticulous rhythm and pacing of the production. He also raved about most of the performances:

> Sharon Bakker as Meg is radiant — every nerve is in the role. Sandy Tucker is Lulu. Don Glossop turns in one of his finest performances as Goldberg. And Layne Coleman is outstanding as McCann. Bruce Garman plays Stanley, the central character, and while I might have wished for a little more maturity in the role, no one can complain about his performance. Dennis Mazurik [who played Petey] was probably the weakest member of the cast showing primarily a lack of experience, but the play didn't suffer as a result.[42]

Julianne Labreche, in the *Sheaf*, felt the need to explain the play to her readership; she wrote, "The Birthday Party, typical of much contemporary drama, blows out its birthday candles and leaves the world in darkness. It offers no redemption, promises no hope, seeking but to expose the meaninglessness of a creed of faith in an empty land." Labreche's review was mostly complimentary; she quibbled only about lapses in dialect among the cast members. Judging from this performance, Labreche wrote, "this young professional company has shown tremendous improvements from their previous productions. Maintaining this caliber, they are quite capable of holding their own compared to the amateur and university theatre in Saskatoon."[43]

If 25th Street's production of *The Birthday Party* had been bewildering, its production of *The Sibyl* at Globe Theatre in Regina and Castle Theatre in Saskatoon was downright perplexing. The play was based on Pär Lagerkvist's novel, which intertwines the story of the Wandering Jew who was doomed to an eternity of homelessness for refusing to comfort Christ on the way to the Cross and a fictitious Sibyl who falls in love with a mortal. Several parts in the play were double- and triple-cast, with Sharon Bakker playing the Old Sibyl and Swedish actress Anna Retz playing the Young Sibyl. Layne Coleman, Dennis Gingrich, and Alex McPike all played the Wandering Jew at various stages of his life. Other members of the cast were Ken McEvoy, Eric Braun, Eileen Mackenzie, Mike Brannen, and Jan Kostyna. The production was directed by Hausvater himself — who had seemed to characterize Saskatoon as a cultural backwater in an interview given as he was in rehearsals for the play — and had a two-evening run at the Globe Theatre in Regina and a five-evening run at Castle Theatre (in Aden Bowman High School) in Saskatoon. In a long press release, 25th Street Theatre suggested that the play would be enacted in the style of total theatre, with a heavy reliance "on physicalizations, projections of parts of the body, non-verbal utterances, and strangely different perspectives." The company was attempting to remake itself not as a grassroots theatre, relevant to the common man and woman, but as an avant-garde company in the Artaudian style.

While they left it up to individual spectators to determine whether they liked the play or not, reviewers praised the production for its intensity, its attention to physical detail, and its experimentalism. After the Regina performances, the CBC Radio reviewer said, "Regardless of positive or negative feeling upon leaving the theatre, each of the 75 or so members of the audience had to agree upon one thing: you were never, never bored."[44] In Saskatoon, *Sheaf* reviewer Julianne Labreche praised the production's experimentalism: "For those who had never seen experimental theatre, the 25th Street House production of *The Sibyl* offered the rare opportunity to see the traditional stage conventions shattered and replaced with an atmosphere more typical of the combination of ritual festival and holy temple than of a theatre."[45] Under the headline "Sibyl — it can't be ignored," *Star-Phoenix* reviewer

Jean Macpherson enjoyed the leisurely pace of the non-verbal scenes, writing:

> *The Sibyl* is a play one member of an audience might love, another hate; but nobody in the audience could ignore its impact. Perhaps it was the director; perhaps the 25th Street people, so busy in so many areas, and so dedicated to improving their skills, have come this far in artistic improvement. *The Sibyl* will be hard to equal for dramatic experience.[46]

Perhaps no review captures the range of reaction to *The Sibyl* better than the 25th Street Theatre press release, issued on March 11: "Reaction to the performance ranged from such phrases as 'convention-shattering', 'captivating', 'irresistible involvement', 'distinguished, if not exactly inspired', all the way to 'boring', and 'too much avant, not enough garde'."[47]

Despite eliciting positive reviews, 25th Street Theatre had departed from its stated mandate in 1973–74, producing a piece of British absurd theatre and the adaptation of a European novel. Company members also got involved with a children's television show on local station CFQC, which scattered their attention even further from the company's theatrical focal point. The program was called *The Bashful Boris Show* and was broadcast on a weekly basis. It featured Sharon Bakker, Eric Braun, and several other members of the company.

Buoyed by the positive critical reception its second season had received, the company was ready to launch a slightly more ambitious third season of three Canadian plays. It was shortly after the successful run of *The Sibyl*, on March 11, 1974, that 25th Street Theatre issued a press release in which it outlined its "never-ceasing" search for funding and for new productions. More significantly, the company announced that it was looking "for its first permanent home" after two years of moving between the YWCA, Greystone Theatre, St. James Hall, the Centennial Auditorium, and Castle Theatre.[48] For the next few seasons, the company would perform in a disused commercial space at the busy intersection of 8th Street and Clarence Avenue, a move which would have at least one reviewer complaining about street noise during a production.⁴⁹ The space would become affectionately known as the Red Barn, and its loss would be mourned in the spring of 1976 when the theatre had to vacate and when the Red Barn would be replaced by a single-level office building. Having receded from the playbills for a season, Andy Tahn was also ready to re-emerge with a new play. The 1974-75 season would consist of Arthur Murphy's *A Virus Called Clarence*, a remount of *Pilk's Madhouse*, and Tahn's play *The Ballad of Billy the Kid*.

For its first production of the new season, a play about cancer research in the groves of academe, the company fittingly hired university drama professors to play some of the lead roles. Walter Mills played the research head, and fellow professor Bruce Salvatore played the foundation director in Arthur Murphy's play, while Doug Melville-Ness, Christopher Covert, Sharon Hughes (Bakker), and Anthony Sheldon rounded out the cast. The company continued to bring in directors from out-of-province for several of their productions, and Larry Ewashen was flown in from Calgary to direct *A Virus Called Clarence*. Twenty-Fifth Street Theatre was beginning to adhere to a standard production schedule for alternate theatre in Canada; stepping away from the earlier practice of running a show for two or three nights, the company ran *A Virus Called Clarence* from November 28th until December 8th. While she found the set unacceptable and complained about encroaching road noise, the *Star-Phoenix's* Jean Macpherson commended the company for "their special brand of dogged intrepidity." She also admired Murphy's play, both as written and in production:

> The best thing about this fine play was the solid ending, from the standpoint both of writing and acting. With the suspense finished and the story-line complete, it was something of a feat for Twenty-Fifth Street House to achieve the highly dramatic anti-climax and make it an integral part of the story. With a little help from its competent friends, Twenty-Fifth Street House has made another giant leap towards its goal of good professional dramatic entertainment in Saskatoon.⁵⁰

Macpherson felt that the company was right on target, this time not with a West End hit but with a new Canadian play.

The company reprised *Pilk's Madhouse* for its February 1975 slot, this time with a new cast and director. Sharon Hughes (Bakker), Rose Marie McSherry, Layne Coleman, and Chris Covert acted under the direction of Anna Retz, who had debuted with 25th Street Theatre in *The Sibyl* the year before. Also in the cast was Bob Collins, who had been a high school biology teacher but who had given it up to pursue a career in acting. Collins, a very tall man who performed one scene from *Pilk's Madhouse* in tights, would later become part of the tightly knit 25th Street Theatre creative team. Calling the play "a happily insane mixture of pathos, passion, and porn," Jean Macpherson suggested that the company's ensemble acting saved the sometimes weak script. "The steadily-increasing rapport among the members of the company is a pleasure to witness," she wrote, "as exhilarating as their constant drive to challenge themselves with more and more difficult subjects."[51] In Macpherson's reviews, the company's growth through the 1974–75 season is chronicled quite clearly.

Tahn's *The Ballad of Billy the Kid* was an ambitious nod to the company's populist roots. After reading Michael Ondaatje's long poem "The Ballad of Billy the Kid," Tahn had been reticent to write a stage adaptation because he wanted to concentrate on Canadian stories. Others in the company urged him to consider adapting Ondaatje's poem, however, and Tahn soon became immersed in the subject matter. "It was written in a rooming house on Eighth Street," Tahn said. "I mostly lived in the theatre, and I wrote it between rehearsals and meetings of boards, trying to slap this thing together. But I was so energized — I'd never written anything with such passion."[52] Although Billy the Kid was an American outlaw, he was also a folk hero who transcended time and place, as popular a subject in Canada in 1975 as in the United States. Furthermore, the play was written as a populist ballad. In a program note, director Chris Covert outlined the ballad-form's popular appeal: "It seeks to tell a story, simply, in the music and words; not because the story is new but because it is an old, old story that continues to haunt us, and one way of exorcising the ghost is to utter it."[53] The production featured nineteen actors, including Erika Ritter as Sarah, Linda Griffiths as Angela Maxwell, Bob Collins as Pat Garrett, and Layne Coleman as Billy the Kid. The only Equity actor listed in the program was Judith Hilderman, a graduate of the National Theatre School who had just returned to Saskatchewan after recovering from injuries suffered in an automobile accident. Don Freed composed and performed the music in the production, which consisted of songs like "The End of the Ride," "I Don't Trust You, Man," and "When We Next Meet." The production ran April 10-22, 1975.

Jean Macpherson, of the *Star-Phoenix*, predicted a great future for the play. She praised the "exceptionally good portrayals" by the principal actors in the company, and wrote,

It is probably a safe prediction that Andy Tahn's new play *The Ballad of Billy the Kid* will receive acclaim in a far wider area than Saskatoon, where it is presently getting its first exposures at 25th Street House Theatre. Following the popular trend of looking thoughtfully back at North American history, the ballad has the qualities of compassion, understanding, and simplicity.[54]

Later in the review, she wrote that the company "is steadily rising in the esteem of drama lovers in Saskatoon and surrounds" and urged everybody to see the play "which is likely destined for an important place in Canadian dramatic literature." Macpherson was critical, however, of the occasional poetic soliloquies which interrupt the otherwise realistic prose of the script. Her criticism was well-founded; it must have been difficult, for example, for Layne Coleman to speak poetic lines like "My head is reeling/like a drunk but worse/A thousand tiny suns burning my eyeballs/Pressure on my skull" after the far more realistic dialogue of the scene which occurs immediately before his soliloquy.

Unfortunately, Tahn's play opened just a few months before Toronto Free Theatre produced another play about Billy the Kid, based on Michael Ondaatje's *The Collected Works of Billy the Kid*. The Free Theatre production was more closely associated with Ondaatje himself (Ondaatje's book of poems had won the Governor General's Award), and its cast, including R.J. Thomson, was strong. The Toronto production was a hit, and it inevitably received more press than Tahn's production in Saskatoon. As a result, Tahn's play suffered the fate of most Canadian plays — it did not see a second production.

Three:
"BAD REVIEWS, GREAT AUDIENCES" (1975-76)

1975 WAS ARGUABLY THE year in which 25th Street Theatre found its direction; what began in that year would define the theatre for much of its existence. Twenty-Fifth Street's major competitor in Saskatoon, Persephone Theatre (then in its second year), announced a season of predominantly international hits. Staging their productions at the university's Greystone Theatre, Persephone would begin their season with Joe Orton's *What The Butler Saw*. They would also produce Edward J. Moore's Off-Broadway hit *The Seahorse*, starring Janet Wright, Richard Nash's *Rainmaker*, and the commedia play *Scapino*. The only Canadian entre would be *American Modern/Canadian Gothic*, Joanna Glass' hit play which had been a success in New York. With that choice of season, Persephone's artistic directors signalled their intent to become a regional theatre in the style of Edmonton's Citadel, producing mostly international plays with a smattering of Canadian drama on the side. The field of exclusively Canadian drama was left wide-open, and Tahn did not hesitate to jump in with an enthusiastic program of all-Canadian plays.

It was during the autumn of 1975 that Paul Thompson and a company of actors from Toronto, who called themselves Theatre Passe Muraille, arrived in Saskatoon to rehearse *The West Show*. Thompson and Tahn had met a year earlier, when Tahn was visiting Toronto on a theatre junket. They had communicated frequently after that time, and Tahn had agreed to let Passe Muraille use 25th Street's theatre space on Eighth Street for their rehearsals. Thompson wanted to work in his usual way, to have his actors interview people from the West about issues of local interest and then to develop, through improvisation, a play based upon those interviews. He also wanted to involve Western Canadian writers in the process, and to that end he invited Rudy Wiebe to sit in on rehearsals as story consultant. *The West Show* opened in Rosthern on October 8 and was, according to one critic, "enthusiastically received."[55] It later toured to various towns and cities in Ontario. Part of the deal which entitled Passe Muraille to use the theatre on Eighth Street was that Thompson would teach his theatrical methods to the 25th Street actors and co-direct them, with Andy Tahn, in a production about current issues facing young Saskatchewanians. The title of this production was originally *Prairie Landscape* but was later changed to *If You're So Good, Why Are You In Saskatoon?* in order to reflect the prevailing attitudes of local citizens about their own culture and arts scene. Thompson rehearsed with the Saskatoon actors in his free time after rehearsing *The West Show* with his own troupe, alternating between the two productions. Theatre Passé Muraille had committed $3,000 of its own budget in order to pay for a transfer of *If You're So Good, Why Are You In Saskatoon?* to its own space in Toronto.

1975-76 was also the year in which 25th Street Theatre was able to land permanent funding from the Canada Council. Later, Tahn remembered driving out to the airport in his beaten-up Volkswagen van to pick up David Peacock, the Head of the Canada Council, during the run of *The Ballad of Billy the Kid*. "We thought, we're not putting on anything for him. He's going to see it like it is. I drove him in our old van, half full of equipment, and he stayed at the Sheraton, I believe." Peacock saw *The Ballad of Billy the Kid* and enjoyed it. "I went out for dinner with him afterwards," Tahn said later, "and I said, 'So, what do you think?' He was a British guy, very staid, very formal, not your typical theatre person. He said, 'I liked the action of this play. I think you've got a future, and I'm going to recommend that you be put on permanent funding.'"[56] The company was awarded $8,000 which, as Tahn suggested in an interview, represented about fourteen per cent of the company's total budget. Still, as Tahn maintained, the grant was a significant step in the development of the new professional theatre company.[57] It meant that the Canada Council recognized and sympathized with the aims of 25th Street Theatre.

Over the past three years, Tahn had learned the value of producing new Canadian drama, and his statements to the press about that issue are categorical. At the beginning of the season, Tahn emphasized in an interview his company's commitment to Canadian drama in general and to Western Canadian drama in particular. "People want to see Saskatchewan drama," he said. "We want material that is Western Canadian. The job of Twenty-Fifth Street House Theatre, as I see it, is to develop drama that is truly our own, truly a part of our soil and heritage. We need to touch the earth with our own drama and our own people."[58] A *Sheaf* interviewer, whose article was published in January after the company had received its Canada Council grant, quoted Tahn as follows:

> The theatres that are producing new Canadian drama are now in the thick of the entertainment industry's action and are beginning to healthily compete for the public's night-out dollar. The Twenty-Fifth Street House Theatre is not an alternate theatre or a second stage. Our aim is to be a major popular theatre (and popular is the key word here) presenting the dramas of our Canadian playwrights on the legitimate stage with full professional treatment which includes first-rate professional actors and directors.[59]

The *Star-Phoenix's* Ned Powers wrote that when a theatre company receives a Canada Council grant, "it's really a mark of respectability within the industry." He suggested that theatre companies which produce a quota of Canadian plays are "growing into healthy competitors."[60] There could no longer be any doubt about 25th Street's commitment to new Canadian drama; the days of producing foreign plays like *The Birthday Party* had come to an end.

The reception of a Canada Council grant also carried with it a responsibility to conduct the business of the theatre in a professional manner. The company joined the Professional Association of Canadian Theatres (PACT) and was suddenly on the same footing as more established companies like the Vancouver Playhouse and Edmonton's Citadel Theatre. A board of directors had been created earlier, with Bernard John (Ben) McKinnon as its secretary, and with Jay Buckwold, E.C. Partridge, Ron McDonald, Walter Mills, Mrs. G.C. Short, Zenon Belak, and Doug Melville-Ness as its members. Catalogued with the 25th Street Theatre Collection at the University of Saskatchewan is a Canada Council document entitled "Readings On The Governing Boards Of Arts Organizations," to which Tahn clearly had access. The writers of the document favoured a democratic approach to the composition of boards:

> . . . the traditional arts audience is an affluent one; at the present time representatives of this audience overwhelmingly dominate arts Boards. If audiences are to grow, tickets will have to be sold to those sectors of the population not presently buying. The first rule of the good salesman is Know Thy Customer. If a wider spectrum of the population is to be sold on the arts, this same wider spectrum will have to find representation on arts Boards.[61]

In order to comply with the spirit of the Canada Council document, Tahn would have had to create a board which reflected the diversity of his theatre's audience, but he did not entirely achieve that goal. It was necessary to have some members on the board who might help in the procurement of funding, and so Tahn brought together a university professor (Mills), a doctor of medicine (Belak), an actor (Melville-Ness), and the son of a senator (Buckwold). Mrs. Short was the only woman on the Board.

Receiving a Canada Council grant also meant that actors would have to be signed to Canadian Actors Equity contracts. Twenty-Fifth Street Theatre had represented itself as a professional theatre in its early years, but actors either worked for nothing or were paid a stipend well below minimum Equity rates. (Tahn had often coaxed his university friends to come out and act for the company without recompense.) As the program for *The Ballad of Billy The Kid* demonstrates, the company had in reality been operating with a dispensation from Equity to employ professional actors alongside a majority of non-professionals. Receiving a Canada Council grant meant that the majority of actors in any production would have to be professional and that only a small minority of non-Equity players could be hired. Subsequently, the cast-lists of 25th Street Theatre were about to undergo a change; local amateurs disappeared from the lists, for the most part, while out-of-town names began to feature more prominently. The company was now a professional theatre in every sense of the word.

Tahn had only fourteen per cent of his budget covered by the Canada Council. Where would he go for the other eighty-six per cent? Tahn had originally budgeted for expenses of $58,350 in 1975-76 and for revenue of $36,865. He had planned on corporate donations of $6,000 and individual donations of $2,000, and he thought that his productions might garner $15,015 at the box office. The University of Saskatchewan Students' Union had promised to kick in $3,500, while Theatre Passe Muraille would guarantee $3,000 for the tour of *If You're So Good, Why Are You In Saskatoon?* With a projected shortfall in revenue, Tahn and his general manager Gerry Stoll would have to make fundraising a priority. Fortunately, Tahn and Stoll were particularly effective fundraisers. By the end of the season, they had procured $3000 from the Saskatchewan Arts Board, $5,000 from the SaskSport Trust Fund, and $500 from the City of Saskatoon.

The 1975-76 season would be entirely Canadian. In his pre-season brochure, Tahn advertised five productions: *If You're So Good, Why Are You In Saskatoon?*; Don Francks' touring one-man show entitled *The Insanity Of One Man*; a bit of holiday fluff called *Christmas Candy*; Michael Dorn Wiss' futuristic drama *Hermit*; and Tahn's own play *Kasper Beck*, about a Russian homesteader in Saskatchewan. The actors in the productions would also have ties to Western Canada; they included Don Francks, who was living on a reserve near North

Battleford; local actors Bob Collins, Layne Coleman, and Karen Wiens; and British Columbia actor Michael Collins who was projected to play the title role in *Kasper Beck*. These hirings were not a matter of happenstance; as Tahn wrote in his brochure, "All the artists in the theatre for this coming season were chosen specifically because of their past involvement and contribution to this part of the country."[62]

The much-anticipated opening of *If You're So Good, Why Are You In Saskatoon?* was greeted with enthusiasm, especially from university-aged audiences, but also with scepticism from mainstream reviewers. While so much of Saskatchewan drama tended to concentrate on the hard lives of European pioneers, Paul Thompson's production wisely focused on the experience of teenagers leaving home in the Saskatchewan of 1975. "We'd had a couple of days' rehearsal," said Tahn later. "The way Paul works is he does a lot of listening and asking prodding questions. And he looked at us and said, 'We're going to do a play about young kids, and it's going to be about what you know best.' And he sent us off on a wild goose chase. And I learned how to do collective creations through that. What we did was we researched our own parts. So I picked on a character named Speedo. He was a high-energy kid." After rehearsals, Tahn would have the opportunity to direct questions at Thompson about the job of being artistic director of a theatre. "Paul was a Canadian theatre gentleman," reminisced Tahn. "He was never self-serving. He planted seeds [of creativity] right across Canada."[63]

The *Star-Phoenix's* Jean Macpherson found the play naive and superficial, and noted that it had played "to a discouragingly small audience" on its opening night. She argued that the kernel of a good story was at the centre of the play but that the play was hampered by uneven acting. "There is a solid story in Why Are You In Saskatoon, but it is difficult to follow because of the variegated performances which make up the loosely connected scenes," Macpherson wrote. "There is such variance in the quality of acting the story unfolds rather like a set of sketches which the audience has to string together as best it can." She singled out Layne Coleman for praise, writing, "Absolutely the highlight of the performance is the sketch about a player, which owes its humor to the buoyant performance by Layne Coleman and his good body language."[64] Unlike Macpherson, the *Sheaf's* Kim Johnson applauded the company's improvisational skill and its concentration upon youth, calling the production "a very worthwhile and enjoyable performance."[65] After a tepid opening night attended by seventeen patrons, university students arrived in droves to see the collective creation. The *Sheaf's* Craig Grant noted that, for the final four nights of the regular run, "the cozy, intimate atmosphere of the theatre had its rafters raised with enthusiastic, guffawing response from capacity audiences."[66] One hundred and twenty-three patrons were in attendance on November 1, and when the production was held over, one hundred and forty-seven spectators clamoured into the theatre on November 8. The production ran October 14-November 8 in Saskatoon before being transferred to the Manitoba Theatre Centre. In its cast were Karen Wiens, Layne Coleman, Linda Griffiths, Bob Collins, and Andy Tahn.

The production did not garner positive reviews in Winnipeg. Lee Rolfe, of the *Winnipeg Tribune*, wrote that there was nothing wrong with the play "that a good playwright, armed with an anvil and hammer, couldn't correct." He found that the performers displayed "a ferocious contempt" for their home city in which the main pastimes of the residents seemed to be drinking beer and smoking grass. "Beneath the soap opera banality," Rolfe wrote, "was the foundation of a tough-minded little drama about rural life."[67] Under the headline "If You're So Good fails to sparkle," the *Free Press'* Alice Poyser described the acting as "adequate" but criticized the banality of the script. "It was the material that fell short," she wrote. "Like a college review, it didn't stretch beyond the interests of its actor authors."[68] Poyser suggested that the play might please a university crowd, and she was correct. Despite the bad reviews, university students adopted the play as part of their own story, and the production eventually played to large audiences in Winnipeg — one hundred and eighteen spectators, mostly university students, attended the play on November 15. Tahn was unhappy with the critical reception his company had received but gave it a characteristically positive spin, arguing that the cutting reviews signalled a change in the typically patronizing attitude displayed by our own critics toward Canadian drama. "If a review had been written two years ago, it would have been patronizing," he said, in an interview with the *Free Press*. "Now, they're hitting us right between the eyes. Now, if we're not cutting the ice, we're not cutting the ice, and that's it."[69] The bad Winnipeg reviews did not go unnoticed back in Saskatoon, where an arts commentator for the *Saskatoon Star-Phoenix* suggested that the "pattern of 25th Street House Theatre's *If You're So Good* is something of a phenomenon: bad reviews, great audiences." Tahn returned to Saskatoon more optimistic than ever about his company's future, publicly suggesting that *If You're So Good* "would have done well for another week in Winnipeg, but we had to get back to work on our next production."[70]

The next production was Don Francks' *The Insanity of One Man* which, by all accounts, was a rambling ecological "happening" interspersed with songs, film, graffiti, and stories. Tahn was later candid about Francks' work on the production. "I remember the first meeting [between us]. He would not sit on a chair. He sat on the floor. And I said, 'Don, why don't you come back, and whatever you want to do, we'll do.' I should have been smarter. It was a happening. It was whatever he wanted to do on any particular night."[71] For the production, Francks resurrected an orange suit from his Broadway musical days which, according to Tahn, looked bizarre with his long ponytail hanging down the back of it.

On opening night, the audience was greeted in the lobby of 25th Street Theatre with members of the company who displayed placards reading "A Francks is only worth one-fifth of a dollar" and "Do you suppose they're foolin' around? Because if they aren't . . . Don Francks is a friend of mine." Audience members were encouraged throughout the show to write graffiti on a special board on an interior wall of the theatre. Francks appeared onstage in bare feet and wearing a Greenpeace T-shirt. He sang songs — pleasingly, according to reviewers — which included "Home Again," "Superstar Shoes," "Working Class Hero," and "Maggie." He told stories and showed films, including a cartoon and some home movies and stills of his home on the Red Pheasant Reserve. His daughter Cree Summer performed "Let There Be Peace," and his wife Lily braided his hair onstage. Two members of the 25th Street company produced a brief skit, at one point, and Francks seated himself in the audience to watch. Francks encouraged the audience to discuss ecological issues with him but, on opening night, the discussion focused on a lactating woman in the audience who informed the other patrons that she had produced one hundred and eighty gallons of milk over the past two years and that she was leaving to go home and feed her baby. Once again, there was a disconnect between the mainstream media and the local student newspaper. The *Star-Phoenix's* Jean Macpherson disliked the show intensely, writing,

> *The Insanity of One Man*, with Don Francks as the guest of 25th Street House Theatre, is quietly and irretrievably insane. Don Francks, who does so well in prepared sketches, shows little talent for ad lib glib repartee; in his philosophizing, which in last night's show seemed interminable, he is articulately inarticulate. On the whole, *The Insanity of One Man* is an aggregation of non sequiturs.[72]

In contrast, the *Sheaf's* Harry Mandrill enjoyed the improvisational quality of the evening; he maintained that Francks' performance was "an experience well worth watching." Mandrill liked the philosophical scope of the production, as well, writing, "Francks takes us into our lives and shows us where we are in relation to the lives we live and portions of our existences that interfere with the future of human survival."[73] *The Insanity of One Man* ran from November 20 until December 7.

The 25th Street company was rehearsing a Christmas show entitled *Christmas Candy: The Unicorn* while Francks was performing on the mainstage. Tahn adapted the play from a well-known fairy tale, and Don Rutley directed Linda Griffiths, Layne Coleman, Bob Collins, Karen Wiens, and Eric Braun in the production, which ran

December 16–January 3. The production was marvellously inventive and quirky, winning over audiences and critics alike. Claire Eamer, then a CBC reporter for *Saskatchewan Today*, seemed quite prepared to dislike the production but found it "a very good show" if a tad too long. She praised the performing talents of Eric Braun, Layne Coleman, Bob Collins, and Karen Wiens:

> My favourite bits were Eric Braun as a klutz of a magician who tried for miracles but mostly ended up pulling scarves from his sleeves; or Layne Coleman as a mopey young prince who falls in love and, much to his dismay, finds he's turning into a hero with a compulsive urge to slay dragons. Then there's Bob Collins as a sort of superannuated Robin Hood character called Captain Kelly who's reduced to one Merry Man and has to make up his own ballads. Karen Wiens plays Maid Marian, twenty years on, with no illusions and dish-pan hands.[74]

The *Star-Phoenix's* Jean Macpherson praised the play as "exquisite fantasy" but saved her best reviews for the actors:

> But the greatest charm of this first annual Christmas Candy production of Twenty-Fifth Street House is the actual performance. These young actors have their ups and downs in their selection of entertainments; this might be said to be the first presentation which truly expresses the full talents and aspirations of the group. It is entertainment without cynicism, without strain, yet sophisticated enough to be absorbing.[75]

Macpherson might have been misguided in suggesting that the theatre group's aspirations were best expressed in a Christmas pantomime, but she had made the company happy, for the first time in the season, with a positive review.

The final production of the season, and in the Red Barn theatre space, was a curious science-fiction play from the pen of Saskatoon playwright Michael Dorn Wiss entitled *Hermit*. Christopher Covert directed Karen Wiens, Bob Collins, Linda, Griffiths, Layne Coleman, and Eric Braun in the production, which ran February 6-21, 1976. The tiny cast-size was a major obstacle for the production, which was set in a future over-crowded universe where privacy is seemingly non-existent. The first scene of the play, set in a futuristic cafe or night-club, begins with the following exchange between Hellin and her former lover Tob:

HELLIN (with wistful satisfaction)
Well, Tob. Here we are again.

TOB
It . . . was interesting, Hellin; and very good.

HELLIN
I'm glad. I like this planet. It has the finest pleasures in this Sector. And it's good to be out of uniform, not to be stared at. Good to be able to hide from curious and inquisitive eyes.

TOB
Good to be alone with you, even in a crowd. Hellin, it's been fifteen years.

HELLIN
I know.[76]

The play is part *Barbarella* and part *Star Trek*. Wiss goes to great lengths to portray Hellin as a liberated pleasure-seeker who has had many lovers. The plot revolves around Hellin's discovery of an alien race, infinitely more intelligent than man. These aliens have seen their own planet turn into a barren rock and their sun turn into an ember; they are now in search of another planet on which to live. The play has a pronounced ecological message about looking after one's own planet. It ends with one of Hellin's fellow searchers, a man named Galen, pleading "How do I live without open space? HOW DO I LIVE WITHOUT THE STARS?"[77]

Most reviewers applauded the idea of bringing science fiction to the stage because the genre was under-represented on Canadian stages. Jean Macpherson, of the *Star-Phoenix*, wrote that the playwright had "concentrated on a well-co-ordinated [sic] plot, but his side issues were just as carefully thought out" and noted that 25th Street Theatre "seems to have established for itself a loyal audience in the 20-to-30-year age group (the same group that applauds the protocol-breaking activities of Margaret Trudeau)."[78] The *Sheaf's* Jim Thomson was heartened that somebody had "the guts" to produce sci-fi on the stage but found the first act too long.[79] Thirza Jones, reviewing for CBC's *Saskatchewan Today*, was not as sympathetic toward the production as Macpherson and Thomson had been. She found the play slow — especially the first act — and argued that Layne Coleman's was "the only good solid performance."[80]

The 1975-76 season nevertheless ended on a positive note, with the company getting good press from Ned Powers, the entertainment editor for the *Star-Phoenix*. In an article dated April 10, 1976, under the headline "25th Street House gains footing," Powers wrote about the artistic and popular success of the company's four-play season (the fifth production, *Kasper Beck*, had to be cancelled for financial reasons). He quoted Ben McKinnon, the secretary of 25th Street's board of directors, who said, "The theatre has done an excellent job of presenting and developing four new Saskatchewan plays, and although we did not want to cut the season short, we did not want to go into a deficit funding situation." Interestingly, *If You're So Good Why Are you In Saskatoon?*, which was slammed by reviewers during its initial run, was touted as a major success, having been "held over to sold out audiences." *If You're So Good* would be remounted at the beginning of the next season, and the Toronto Filmmakers' Co-operative would be making a video of the production.

Four:
"like so much tumbleweed" (1976-77)

Although the 1976-77 season found 25th Street Theatre in some turmoil, it would also contain one of the theatre's defining moments. Having lost its Red Barn theatre at the conclusion of the previous season, the company was forced to perform its first production of 1976-77, a remount of *If You're So Good*, at Aden Bowman High School's Castle Theatre. Over the summer, available performance spaces had melted away before the eyes of Saskatoon's two professional theatre companies. The university's Drama Department had mounted its own ambitious theatre season and could no longer provide space for the professional companies. The Mendel Art Gallery had commitments with several amateur theatre groups and with the visual arts community and would not be available to either 25th Street or Persephone. Most of the high school theatres in Saskatoon were monopolized by their own drama programs and could only be leased to other groups on a one-off basis. Twenty-Fifth Street's manager Gerry Stoll founded an organization called the Union of the Arts, which included members from both professional theatre groups and from the Saskatoon Symphony. The Union was pushing for the City to establish a Saskatoon Arts Board, which would consist of four Union members, four City Council appointees, and a chairman acceptable to all members. The mandate of the local Arts Board would be to hammer out a municipal arts policy and to study the feasibility of a new performing arts facility.

The *Star-Phoenix's* Ned Powers was vociferous in his support for such a plan:

> Saskatoon has come to the realization that there is a major problem at hand. There are constant cries that Saskatoon should try to keep artistic talent at home by providing players with the opportunities. Unless theatres can be found, how are the acting, directing, and writing talents to be encouraged to stay in Saskatoon? If Twenty-Fifth Street House and Persephone Theatre were just upstarts, people might be able to say they should pay their dues and plug along as best they can. But the two professional theatre companies have been doing that for more than two years. They have worked hard in a business sense and honed their skills artistically to a point where they deserve a platform for their talents.[81]

In January 1977, the financial officer of the Canada Council, Thomas Bodnansky, weighed in on the issue, suggesting that the two theatres stage a financial campaign of their own before approaching municipal and provincial governments. "The pity is that two companies stand to lose much of their own identity when they don't have a regular theatre," Bodnansky said in an interview with Ned Powers. "When you have to go into a rental place on short notice, you are taking the chance that the rental place isn't that well-known and you are also forced into spending more money on promoting the location."[82] Bodnansky suggested that 25th Street Theatre and Persephone might well co-exist in one 300-400 seat theatre space, providing the theatre space was named in such a way as to avoid confusion between the two companies. Gerry Stoll's Union had claimed that there were monies available for such a project from the Secretary of State's Office and from the provincial Department of Culture and Youth but that both organizations wanted to see initiative at the local level before committing these funds. It would be thirty-one years before Saskatoon got a purpose-built professional theatre space, and unfortunately 25th Street House would no longer be a major player in the Saskatoon theatre scene by that time, but 25th Street had been at the centre of the theatre space debate in 1976-77. In the meantime, both of Saskatoon's professional theatres would have to struggle with theatre space rentals, a struggle which would bring both companies to the brink of insolvency. Twenty-Fifth Street Theatre's production of *Paper Wheat* — arguably the most important production in the theatre's history — would be born in this unstable environment.

Despite their lack of a permanent theatre space, Tahn and Stoll mounted a fund-raising campaign that would dwarf previous seasons' campaigns. On July 8, the company received a grant of $12,000 from the Canada Council and a letter congratulating the theatre "on the growth that Twenty-Fifth Street House has demonstrated this year as a professional theatre company and also for the success of your fundraising efforts."[83] The Saskatchewan Arts Board had agreed to provide funding in the amount of $1,000 in order to cover actors' salaries during the filming of *If You're So Good*. The provincial Ministry of Culture and Youth, under Ed Tchorzewski, provided the theatre with a generous initial grant and, then, in December 1976, with a supplementary grant of $5,600 in order to off-set the effects of inflation and "the current economic situation."[84]

The first production of the season was a remount of *If You're So Good*, staged at Castle Theatre, which ran September 15-19. Two new cast members had been added, owing to the departure of Bob Collins, who had accepted an acting job with Citadel-On-Wheels, and Chris Covert, who had moved to Toronto. New in the production were actor Bembo Davies, who had come to Saskatoon from Newfoundland where he had worked with the Mummers' Theatre Company, and folk singer Connie Kaldor, from Regina. (I was a young English and Drama student at the University of Saskatchewan at the time, and the remount of *If You're So Good* was the first production of 25th Street Theatre that I was able to witness. I remember being spellbound when Kaldor began singing in that play.) By that time, local theatre critics were prepared to grant that *If You're So Good* had some redeeming qualities. Nancy Russell, reviewing for the *Star-Phoenix*, announced that the production, like the city, grows on you:

Saskatoon grows on you and that is what the production of *If You're So Good Why Are You In Saskatoon*[?] does. It grows on you and for the last half of the 90-minute drama you are laughing out loud in not very typical . . . Saskatoon fashion. You are thinking to yourself "Have I heard this before or did I dream it?" and you begin to agree with the Twenty-Fifth Street House cast as to why you are here.[85]

Leah Watson, of the *Sheaf*, was similarly complimentary but not extremely specific about what made the production a success. "It is difficult to say what makes this play such a hugely enjoyable experience," she wrote, "but it had the audience rolling around like so much tumbleweed on the prairie . . . "[86] Watson eventually settled on the notion that the play's success was in its ability to portray situations with which Saskatonians could identify. She singled out actress Linda Griffiths for particular praise in her performance of a pissed-off and disenchanted student who ends up writing for the *Sheaf*.

An atmosphere of disorganization hampered 25th Street's next production, which was entitled *Heartbreak Hotel*. Originally conceived by Layne Coleman as a one-man show about various forms of prairie heartbreak, the play was later revised to include monologues for four actors. This revision took place during rehearsals, and the result was that 25th Street was forced to delay the opening from its scheduled date of October 25 to October 29. In an article in the *Star-Phoenix*, the delayed opening was blamed on an increase in rehearsal time, owing to script revisions. Another issue was space. Twenty-Fifth Street had originally announced that *Heartbreak Hotel* would be performed at St. Thomas More Auditorium on the university campus. The change in performance dates meant that St. Thomas More Auditorium was no longer available, and the company issued a public appeal to anyone who might make a suitable theatre space available.[87] To complicate matters further, *Heartbreak Hotel* had been scheduled to run in tandem with a visiting production of *2 Miles Off* from Edmonton's Theatre Network. While both companies were eventually able to perform in the Nutana

Collegiate Auditorium, the confusion surrounding performance dates and locations led Theatre Network to cancel one of its performances.

Most of the critics were unhappy with the lack of a cohesive story in *Heartbreak Hotel*. In the *Star-Phoenix*, Jean Macpherson commented on the actors' powers of concentration in conveying a difficult script: "There is no story line to Heartbreak Hotel, but the continuity and sustained level of intensity is stronger than that of many stories. Both the actors and the audience maintained a high level of absorption throughout the two-hour performance."[88] Macpherson commended all of the actors in the production on their performances and singled out Coleman for his growth as an actor. "Coleman is developing a special flair for [g]etting a laugh," she wrote; "his ability is growing in adding humour to the most homespun line." On Saskatoon's CFQC Radio, Ted Barris suggested that the play was too long ("When you're being drained this thoroughly, the therapy should be in shorter doses") but also that the audience was "heavily involved."[89] The *Sheaf's* Leah Watson found little to praise in the production in a review entitled "Heartbreak Hotel — Posterial Ache." She had sat through both *2 Miles Off* and *Heartbreak Hotel* in one evening and began her review with the following pronouncement:

> If the play is really bad the audience becomes restive not because their sense of dramatic propriety is being outraged — but simply because they get an ache in their buttocks. Sometimes there's an uncomfortable awareness that the elastic in their drawers is too tight. Sometimes there's a burning desire to visit the bathroom. But more often than not it's the proverbial pain in the ass that accounts for it.[90]

CBC Radio's Thirza Jones was similarly unenthusiastic about the production. She began her review by suggesting that *Heartbreak Hotel* "could be renamed '4 characters in need of an author — desperately'." Jones disliked the acting intensely. "The actors have not bothered to understand the people they are acting," she wrote, "but are quite willing to show their sorrow."[91]

Twenty-Fifth Street Theatre returned to Castle Theatre for the second instalment of *Christmas Candy*, which ran from December 22 until January 2. Based on a working script by Andy Tahn, the production took shape through improvisations during the rehearsal period. By this time, the company was more comfortable than most Canadian companies at creating plays through improvisation. A note in the program for *Christmas Candy: The Sacred Mountain* details the company's methodology:

> The original script provided the basis for characters and the general plot. The actors and director then revised and rewrote the play working through improvisation and individual writing. The first two weeks of rehearsal became an arena in which each group wrote specific scenes and then read them to the rest of the group. Upon approval, the new scenes became part of the play and replaced the original script.[92]

Working in such a way created a strong sense of commitment and character-actor identification, but these methods were not without pitfalls. There was no one unifying playwright to control the outcome, as there had been with John McGrath's 7:84 company, and consequently 25th Street's audiences had learned to accept that artistic failure was at least as likely as success. *The Sacred Mountain* was deemed a success, largely owing to the talents of Don Rutley, as director, and his actors Connie Kaldor, Robert Clinton, Layne Coleman, Bembo Davies, Linda Griffiths, and Eric Braun.

After the success of *Christmas Candy: The Unicorn* in the previous season, critics were waiting for another instalment with hopeful antici-pation. CFQC Radio's Ted Barris was mostly complimentary towards the production. His only complaint was that "unless the soliloquies and symbolic messages, vital to the play, are tightened, the cast is libel to lose its child audiences."[93] Jean Macpherson, of the *Star-Phoenix*, lamented the disjointedness of some of the writing but admired the ability of the entertainment to work on two levels: "As with any good fairy tale, the entertainment was served on two levels: the one for the adults, with innuendo and a little satire, and the other for the children, with lots of action and shouting." Macpherson was particularly fond of Linda Griffiths' performance, writing that she "undoubtedly stole the show with her sultry portrayal of a gypsy woman of wile and strength."[94]

During the run of *The Sacred Mountain*, Andy Tahn commenced a cross-country tour of his own in order to see the work of other Canadian theatres and to connect with other artistic directors. He had received a short-term grant from the Canada Council, which paid for transportation and accommodation, and he traveled the breadth of the country, from Victoria to St. John's. "You can imagine a young man from the University of Saskatchewan," Tahn said later, "who was already doing his own theatre. He goes to the hotbed of Canadian theatre in Toronto and Montreal, with Theatre de Quatre Sous and Theatre Aujourde-hui that were just on the rise. All the big names in [French] Canadian theatre were just starting out then . . . and I'd see some incredible flipping theatre — all in French, of course. And then I'd end up at some party or a bar, and nobody would speak to me in English. Artists being artists, they were on the front line of the political spectrum, and everyone was, I think, a Pequist."[95] Tahn returned to Saskatoon before the New Year with a reinvigorated sense of purpose; having witnessed the struggles of other alternate theatres across the land, he was now keenly aware of the importance of 25th Street Theatre. He had not admired the commercial "sterility" of most of the Toronto productions he had seen, the obvious exception being the work of Theatre Passe Muraille. While he professed admiration for the productions of Shaw's and Coward's plays which he saw on the West Coast, Tahn came home with a message of decentralization. Toronto was not the Mecca everybody made it out to be, he said; we should look to our own regions for stories and characters. "My most general disappointment was that the majority of theatres do not reflect the region in which they earn their daily bread," Tahn said, in an interview in the *Star-Phoenix* after his return. "The handful of theatres that attempt this are on meagre budgets."[96]

The only remaining production of the 1976-77 season was an unknown commodity, a play based entirely upon improvisations about the founding of the Saskatchewan Co-operative Movement. Working in a way which was by then habitual, the company researched the movement by reading books and by interviewing pioneers and farmers. After six weeks of conducting interviews during the autumn of 1976, in places like Sintaluta and Eston, the company had enough material to begin rehearsing the play. Directed by Tahn, actors Linda Griffiths, Sharon Bakker, Bob Bainborough, Brenda Ledlay, Catherine Jaxon, and Michael Fahey fleshed out the story during rehearsals. The result was a play of brief, cinematic scenes and musical interludes which told the story of pioneer hardship in its first act and of the rise of the Co-operative Movement in its second act.

Part of the difficulty in discussing *Paper Wheat* as a cohesive text is that the play exists in three distinct versions: the first version, which was premiered by Tahn in March 1977; the second version, which was revised by Guy Sprung and the company in October 1977; and a third (published) version, which was again revised by Tahn before he submitted it to a publisher. According to Alan Filewod, in his book *Collective Encounters*, the earliest extant version was simplistic in its presentation of character and history and lacked coherence; the play had not yet found its proper form. "The tendency towards recurring representative characters," writes Filewod, "results in a hesitant performance style which wavers between the presentational technique of revue and the mimetic action of drama."[97] Filewod attributes much of the play's later national success to changes in the script that Sprung was able to make when he was rehearsing for the touring production of *Paper Wheat* later that autumn.

Like much of the company's previous work, the original production of *Paper Wheat* was created in an atmosphere of hurried confusion. The production was originally set to open in Regina, but Tahn decided late in the rehearsal process to open in Sintaluta instead. One of the play's major figures Ed Partridge had been born in Sintaluta and, as Filewod writes, the town was "a safe testing ground."[98] Filewod describes an "insurrection" of the cast, two days prior to opening, which was precipitated (according to Tahn) when "every actor had a scene that he created that he wanted in the show." According to Filewod, the cast "also shared serious misgivings about Tahn's artistic and administrative competence."[99] The backdrop for the play, which consisted of a prairie mural and the outline of a map of Canada, arrived in Sintaluta while the audience was outside, waiting to be admitted to the hall.

There is, unfortunately, no newspaper account of the Sintaluta presentation, but an anonymous newspaper reviewer in Eston, where the production was mounted a few days later, called the play "a fine dramatization" and wrote: "These young players exhibited great versatility by assuming various roles and dialects and appeared to have a genuine feeling of the actual situations. The play moved along with no dull moments."[100] It is possible that the production had undergone extensive revision by the time it played in Eston. As Filewod writes, "In the days following the premiere, the play was trimmed of its more awkward excesses, including a monologue, delivered by Linda Griffiths, which described the history of the world as a stirring process culminating in the birth of Ed Partridge."[101]

When the production opened at St. Thomas Wesley Hall in Saskatoon, there was little sense that *Paper Wheat* would become a Saskatchewan theatre phenomenon. The Hall, for one thing, was not much like a theatre and was located in a neglected part of Riversdale. In his eloquent review of the production in the *NeWest Review*, Don Kerr commented that he had previously attended political meetings at St. Thomas Wesley Hall. The hall boasted a scratched linoleum floor, folding tin chairs, and plain walls. "Nobody in charge of the world would meet here," Kerr wrote, "but it's a very serious place. The kind of hall early co-operators must have met in. But not the place for theatre, aesthetics, beauty. Holding a play here is like hanging an art show in a Saskatchewan Liquor Board Store."[102] The play opened at St. Thomas Wesley on March 18 to an audience of 132 spectators, and the *Star-Phoenix's* Jean Macpherson predicted capacity crowds for the rest of the run. She gave the show a rave review:

It's also a fairly safe prediction that every one of the 132 first-nighters will tell at least a couple of friends each that *Paper Wheat* by 25th Street House Theatre is a show that shouldn't be missed. *Paper Wheat* has every kind of appeal: it's homegrown, it's dramatic, it's funny and it's true. It is also a well-acted and well-produced performance.[103]

Ted Barris, of CFQC Radio, was similarly enthralled with the production. He maintained that *Paper Wheat* "succeeds like no other 25th Street work to date" and that the company had "honed their production into a finely tuned piece of drama and humour."[104] Don Kerr noted that the production had already been a great success by the time he witnessed it ("the audience applauds after every episode") but that it was not perfect. He criticized the production for having too much improvised dialogue. "Only about half the play is really polished," he wrote, adding that the historical analysis in Act Two was a trifle confusing. But he also noted that *Paper Wheat* was the first of 25th Street's plays to venture seriously into the community and into politics, and he commented that the production had attracted a new audience: "This isn't a theatre audience either. I can't see another intellectual in the crowd. In fact the people look a lot like the ones who came to the land bank meetings."[105]

Tahn was too busy to worry much about the critical reception *Paper Wheat* was receiving. In February, he and Gerry Stoll had filed an application for a Young Canada Works grant in order to create a summer troupe for theatre students. The troupe would be called the Oxcart Summer Players and would spend the summer of 1977 researching and performing a play about the diversity of religious faiths in Saskatchewan. "The play that the Oxcart Summer Players will create will be concerned with the migration of the various religious groups in Saskatchewan," Tahn wrote in his grant application, "the problems of early settlement and the co-operation with the other inhabitants."[106] Tahn and Stoll applied for a grant of $24,379 to cover production costs and the hiring of seven student-actors and musicians. His original suggestion was that Layne Coleman would be on hand to direct the troupe, but when Coleman proved unavailable, Tahn himself stepped in to direct the project.

On April 27, after the closing of *Paper Wheat*, Tahn issued a news release about his new project, requesting applications from theatre students "from the Saskatoon, Biggar, North Battleford, Prince Albert areas" who would be willing to tour the province.[107] From these applications, six actors were selected for the project: Beth Lischeron, Mark Bolton, Daryn DeWalt, Stan McGaffin (who was hired when the need for a more mature actor became apparent), Ruth Smillie (whose father, the Reverend Benjamin Smillie, had been a political activist), and Rachel O'Reilly. The actors performed their research through the spring of 1977 and then developed some two hundred scenes for the play, which was then entitled *Prairie Psalms*. These two hundred scenes were eventually scrutinized and many of them were discarded; the play, as it was eventually presented, consisted of forty-three brief scenes and was about seventy minutes in duration. It celebrated the diverse religious beliefs of many of Saskatchewan's early settlers — Lutherans, Catholics, Mennonites, Dukhobors, and so forth. The play has a scene in which John Lake founds Saskatoon as a temperance colony and another in which a man wearing a Cree mask tells a Wesakechak (trickster) story. It ends with the beautiful last words of Crowfoot: "What is life? It is the flash of a firefly in the night. It is the breath of the buffalo in the winter. It is the little shadow which runs across the grass and loses itself in sunset."[108] The production opened at the Western Development Museum during the Saskachimo Exhibition on July 15 and 16, and then, in July and August, toured to Battleford, Kuroki, Buffalo Pound, Moose Jaw, Foam Lake, Eston, Bengough, Cypress Hills, and several other towns and cities.

Both in Saskatoon and on tour, *Prairie Psalms* received fairly good reviews, most of them touching on the risky subject matter of a play which seeks to chronicle the history of many religious faiths without giving precedence to any one faith. For CFQC Radio, Ted Barris suggested that religious differences must be set aside while watching the play: "Whether one believes in God or not has really nothing to do with enjoying Prairie Psalms; whether one is interested in fun, sometimes fascinating summer stock theatre, will determine your attendance at the Oxcart Summer Players' final performance at the St. Thomas More Auditorium tonight."[109] The *Star-Phoenix's* Jean Macpherson commented that the production's main virtue was its air of religious tolerance: "Good-humored tolerance smooths every touchy area. Every sect is made to smart a little and smile a little under the lively wit of the Oxcart Players."[110] Macpherson particularly admired the work of Mark Bolton, writing that many "Saskatoon actors will benefit from watching him work." In the *Prairie Messenger Catholic Weekly*, Kateri Hellman wrote: "The play is not a profoundly moving religious experience. It is simply the story of Saskatchewan told from the viewpoint of religion. No varnish, no whitewash. And no deep probing either."[111]

Even without a permanent theatre in which to perform, 25th Street Theatre had a remarkable season in 1976-77. It had acquired government grants totalling $29,000, not counting the monies received for the Oxcart Summer tour. It had employed fifteen actors, six technical personnel, and five administrators, all with competitive professional salaries, during the regular season. It had produced four new Canadian plays during the winter and a fifth during the summer. It had completed two successful tours of the province. The future looked happy indeed for Tahn and his associates and, although he was entertaining the idea of relinquishing the duties of artistic director to someone else, he was also confidently predicting that his theatre's expenses and revenues for the 1977-78 season would be somewhere in the range of $136,000.[112] This was not bad news for a company which had begun, five years earlier, with little more than a $45,000 Local Initiatives grant.

In the summer of 1977, Tahn returned to Toronto and Montreal, cities he had visited during his Canada Council-sponsored tour six months earlier. While in Montreal, Tahn saw Guy Sprung's production of David Fennario's play *On The Job* at the Centaur Theatre in Montreal. Backstage at the Centaur after the performance, Tahn met with the company's artistic director Maurice Podbury, who gave Tahn Sprung's phone number. Tahn telephoned Sprung that night at 11:30 PM and introduced himself. "I've got this script [*Jacob Kepp*]," Tahn said, "and I want you to see it." Sprung urged Tahn to bring the script over that night. Three days later, Sprung telephoned Tahn and invited him to meet at Sprung's cabin at the Kawartha Lakes. "We became good friends," Tahn said later. "We spent some days out there, and we went over my play. 'Okay, it's a good play,' Sprung said, 'but these are the changes I want.' It was too long; it had to be brought down from six hours to two hours."[113] After some negotiations, Sprung agreed to come to Saskatoon to direct *Jacob Kepp* during the next season. His arrival in Saskatoon would herald a new era in the development of 25th Street Theatre.

Five:
"lucky saskatchewan!"
(the *paper wheat* tours)

The stress of running a professional theatre company was beginning to take its toll on Andy Tahn, who was not yet thirty years old when *Paper Wheat* began touring the province. His theatre company had grown large rather quickly, with an elaborate touring schedule and a summer stock student company. Although 25th Street Theatre was on the verge of having a national hit in *Paper Wheat*, there were rumours of "insurrection" against Tahn by his own company. According to Alan Filewod, Tahn was forced to hire another director for the second tour of *Paper Wheat* "when his cast refused to work with him again."[114] Tahn met with several of the cast members, back in Saskatoon, to discuss their concerns about his direction of the play. "The cast came to me. They said, 'Andy, we want another director. You're just not capable of doing what needs to be done.' And that hurt . . . I went for a long walk, I walked most of the night. And I thought, they're right. So forget the ego, forget the pride, you've got to let it go. It's not your baby. You took it as far as you can take it, now bring in somebody who can take it to the next level. And learn. So I came back and told the cast the next day, the group that met with me, 'All right, we'll bring in a new director.' Tahn would later say that the recollection of this event was his unhappiest memory of his time at 25th Street Theatre.

In a letter to David Peacock, Head of the Theatre Section of the Canada Council, Tahn mentioned Guy Sprung and John Gray as his possible successors in the artistic director's position. On July 15, 1977, he wrote:

> This season the Board of Directors will be searching for a possible replacement for myself for the position of Artistic Director. With this in mind I am bringing to Twenty-Fifth Street House Theatre two directors who have proven themselves admirably in the Canadian theatre. Guy Sprung will be directing my JACOB KEPP. John Gray will be directing THE QUEBEC SHOW. Both directors are coming to Saskatoon with the idea of taking this theatre's Artistic Director's position.[115]

This letter must have been exceedingly difficult for Tahn to write, especially since, as he also noted, his production of *Paper Wheat* had garnered fifteen standing ovations during its twenty-performance run in the previous season. Sprung would be called in to direct the remount of *Paper Wheat* (*Jacob Kepp* would have to wait until the 1979-80 season for its premiere), and there were indications that Sprung and Tahn did not see eye-to-eye on the subject of script revisions. Filewod maintains that Sprung "felt no obligation" to follow the original script; he had been hired on the condition that he would have control over both script and casting. Tahn's understanding was that there would be no major changes in the script.

While other good productions were mounted during the next three years, all were dwarfed by the huge national success of *Paper Wheat*. The company toured the show widely, to the Vancouver East Cultural Centre, to the National Theatre Centre in Ottawa, to the Centaur Theatre in Montreal. How much of the national success of *Paper Wheat* was owed to Tahn and how much to Sprung? Tahn had overseen the original research and storyline of the play, and his production, while not without its shortcomings, had been a success. While Sprung maintained the original two-act structure of the play in his revision, with the first act focusing anecdotally on the experience of the sodbusters and the second act on the founding and growth of the co-operative movement, he also, according to Filewod, composed an essentially different play.[116] Sprung began the research process all over again, this time with new actors, most of whom were not from Saskatchewan. (When he arrived in Saskatoon, Sprung decided to retain only Sharon Bakker and Michael Fahey from the original cast; he brought in David Francis, Skai Leja, and Lubomir Mykytiuk, all from Montreal, to play the remainder of the roles.) Sprung reduced the number of major characters in the first act from fourteen to five, so that each actor might concentrate on one character and so that the audience might more easily follow the trajectory of each character. He made use of the ethnic backgrounds of each of the actors, having Francis play an English immigrant named William Postelthwaite, having Mykytiuk play the Ukrainian Vasil Havryshyn, having Fahey play an Irishman named Sean Phalen, and so forth. Sprung tightened up the historical second act, as well, including six new scenes which were meant to show how the co-operative movement had changed over the years. Sprung was interested in setting up the second act as a political dialectical whereas Tahn had been more interested in presenting the human story of the homesteaders and of the founders of the co-operative movement.

It was also Sprung's idea to bring a fiddle player into the mix. At Sprung's insistence, Tahn went out in search of a fiddle player who could provide background music for the revival of *Paper Wheat*. "I eventually discovered Bill Prokopchuk in Springside, Saskatchewan," wrote Tahn later, "and Bill invited me to his home to listen to him and his friend Peter play the old time tunes they knew so well. They treated me to sausage and whisky and I knew that Bill, Ukrainian, farmer and Western Canadian fiddling champion was the right personality to fit into *Paper Wheat*. I had met and interviewed many violin and fiddle players. I wasn't looking merely for a fiddler. I was casting a character and I found that character in Bill."[117]

According to Tahn, Sprung injected a great deal of political disputation into the play which Tahn had not originally envisioned. "I didn't want to be a political theatre," Tahn said later. "*Paper Wheat* kind of tagged us. I remember Sid Buckwold coming out of [the first production of] *Paper Wheat* . . . I wanted Sid and his wife to come out because their son Jay was a big supporter of 25th. Sid was a former mayor of Saskatoon and a major innovator. And I was just dying to see what he'd think. Because I knew Sid. [On the evening of the performance], Sid came walking out and looked at me with steely eyes, and he wouldn't shake my hand. He just walked out. But, you see, I didn't see it as a socialist play . . . It wasn't intended to be a political statement by 25th Street Theatre. Sid took it as that, a total slam against free enterprise." While Tahn was initially blind to the socialist undertones of the collectively created play, Sprung emphasized those points in the play that made a Marxist interpretation possible. "He was very Marxist, very political," Tahn said later. "Guy and I just locked horns. We had a big falling out. And we haven't spoken since."[118]

The changes that Sprung made to the script eventually led to a blowout between Tahn and Sprung. "He added scenes without my approval," said Tahn in a 2009 interview, "and I wasn't able to see them until it was too late. So I called a meeting and I said, 'Guy, I don't want these scenes in there.' He said, 'I'm not cutting them.' I said, 'If you don't cut them, I will.' You've got to remember I was not acting out of total confidence. I was somewhat in fear. I didn't know as much as Guy. Guy had directed all over the world. He was very proficient. Very good. He was a very good director." Sprung still refused to make the cuts, and Tahn went to the cast for support. "When I went to the cast, of course the cast were working for Guy, and I thought, okay, I've got to back off." Tahn and Sprung did not have the opportunity to speak about the issue again until after the new version of the play had opened in Calgary. "We had a showdown in Calgary," Tahn said later. "It didn't go so good. And after that, we never did speak. There were a couple of letters, legal letters that had to go back and forth for copyright issues, but there was no more contact with Guy." To this day, Tahn remains philosophical about his artistic differences with Sprung and about Sprung's contributions to the play. He credits Sprung with taking "the little garden that we had [in *Paper Wheat*] and turning it into a whole farm." According to Tahn, Sprung was able to take "the seed of characters and develop them fully." Tahn also credits Sprung with taking the musical numbers and maturing them, making them into something that was fully theatrical. "For example, the 'Grain Exchange Rag', he took that and turned it into a vaudeville number."[119]

As Alan Filewod maintains, neither version of the play approaches documentary realism, which is odd considering that *Paper Wheat* is often held up as a glittering example of that genre. Both versions owe a greater debt to the genre of satirical revue, with its emphasis on representational characters, music, and humorous patter. In his revision of the play, Sprung added a juggling scene, performed admirably by Mykytiuk, and a tap-dancing scene which made use of Francis' skill-set in that area. Filewod argues that Sprung's version was about theatricality, that the telling of the story became more important than the actual details in his re-drafting of the play. Both versions were a celebration of a heroic movement, but Sprung had added the elements necessary to making the play a national success. "By clarifying the historical account, drawing out the dramatic fable and stressing the ensemble performance style," writes Filewod, "Sprung gave the play the context it needed to speak to audiences outside Saskatchewan."[120]

On September 29, 1977, Sprung's version of *Paper Wheat* opened at the Saskatoon Theatre Centre, a church hall at 808 20th Street West, before transferring to Toronto and then embarking on a tour of Saskatchewan. In her *Star-Phoenix* review, Jean Macpherson noted some changes in the script but attributed the further success of Sprung's production to changing attitudes and economic conditions: "Last year's version of *Paper Wheat* was good entertainment; this year, in view of altering attitudes due to altering economic conditions, it is even more relevant, and therefore even more entertaining." She was especially receptive to Mykytiuk's performance as Havryshyn:

> If any performance was outstanding in Thursday night's performance, it was that of newcomer Lubomir Mykytiuk, an actor who was born in the Ukraine and who studied acting in New York. His was the juggling act which demonstrated a useful

ability to concentrate on several things at once. He is funny yet sincere, capable and sensitive, an actor whose personality is flung like a net over the audience, capturing them into closeness with him and with each other.[121]

Lorraine Froelich was similarly complimentary in *Shadowfax*, the newspaper of the Students Arts and Science Society at the University of Saskatchewan. She commented on how the production transported her to an historical era: "No longer are we seated in an auditorium but rather a community hall. We seem to have become prairie farming settlers united for an important cause: to discover some means of controlling the selling of our grain."[122] The production ran until October 8 in Saskatoon before transferring to Café Soho in Toronto.

Nothing sells in Saskatchewan so well as success elsewhere, and 25th Street Theatre eventually got a boost from *Paper Wheat's* Toronto transfer. The *Toronto Star* review, which came out the day after the October 11 opening, was not particularly glowing. While praising the plain-spoken and down-to-earth production values, the *Star's* Brian Freeman was also cognizant of the production's meandering lack of pace. "It's just too slow!" he writes, adding, "Actors wander in and out of scenes as though out on a Sunday stroll. Nothing is ever really allowed to build a head of steam. Themes get sidetracked. Songs start raggedly and tend to trail off inconclusively. In its present state, *Paper Wheat* flows with all the speed and precision of a CPR passenger schedule."[123] Fortunately for 25th Street Theatre, Ted Johns published a much more favourable article in the *Toronto Theatre Review* in December. Johns gave the production high marks, suggesting that "[l]ucky Saskatchewan seems to be witnessing the birth of a new, muscular and influential young theatre." He commended the production equally for the actors' and musicians' performances and for the text. "[A]ny writer would be proud to claim authorship of this play," he wrote. "Were he or she foreign or classical, thoughtful and generous essays would follow as the night the day."[124]

As an added dimension to the tour of Saskatchewan which followed the Toronto opening of the play, the theatre was able to negotiate with the National Film Board to create a film documentary based on the provincial tour. Guy Sprung made the initial contact with Albert Kish, who eventually agreed to direct the documentary. "It was Guy's idea to film the tour and production and it was he who encouraged the filming," said Tahn later, "and once that contact had been made, I naturally continued the process. I did the negotiations with the corporate offices of the NFB and Albert Kish himself as well as the subsequent management arrangements including credits and copyright issues."[125] The NFB documentary displays the sometimes hilarious hardships of a touring production in Saskatchewan during an early winter. In one of the film's scenes, Tahn arrives in Swift Current before the troupe to distribute posters. After filling his rickety vehicle with gasoline at a local gas station, Tahn asks the cashier to put a poster on her wall and then proceeds to get his vehicle stuck in the snow and ice as he is pulling away from the gas pumps. Also remarkable in the film are the receptive attitudes of the mostly elderly audiences who viewed the play in rural Saskatchewan. The film manages to make palpable the sense of identification between these spectators and the characters and events created for them on stage. The presence of the NFB film crew added an extra level of excitement for rural audiences; there was a sense in the air that something momentous was taking place. Several newspaper accounts comment on the presence of the film crew during the show. "The Moosomin performance was the fifth one of the play to have film crews on hand from the National Film Board, who will film 'Paper Wheat' as a one hour documentary," wrote an anonymous journalist in the *Moosomin World-Spectator*. "The film crew had their cameras trained on the audience as much as on the cast, capturing audience reaction to a drama based on their own story."[126] The National Film Board's documentary was not the company's only foray into film and television; the CBC also created a television special on *Paper Wheat*, which was broadcast nationally.

The autumn 1977 tour played in thirty-seven communities across Saskatchewan, almost always to packed houses. Reviews in rural newspapers were glowing, most of them referring to the fact that rural

Saskatchewan audiences were finally getting to see their own stories on stage. The review in the *Moosomin World-Spectator* was prototypical:

> There's no denying "the play's the thing", but you can wait a lifetime and never have a play written just for you. For farmers and near-farmers "Paper Wheat" was their play. And when Saskatoon's 25th Street House Theatre presented the farmers' own story in the Elks Hall last Monday, the predominantly farm audience had no difficulty in identifying with the characters, or recognizing the plot.
>
> Murmurs of "that's how it was alright" and more audible shouts of "It hasn't changed any either" rang through the hall, as the play proceeded.[127]

Similar sentiments were expressed when the tour reached Strasbourg on November 10. "The show brought back to life stories you've all heard from elderly citizens of our own and others in the community," the anonymous reviewer for the *Nokomis Times* wrote of the Strasbourg performance. "It will play an important part in keeping our young people aware of those early years which were heart breaking and yet rewarding to our early pioneers."[128] At the Sintaluta Memorial Hall on November 18, the company played again to a full house. The reviewer for the *Indian Head-Wolseley News* found the quietude of the audience through the play curious. "It was interesting to note the stillness, at many times, of the packed house," the anonymous reviewer wrote. "When humour was uppermost in the tale, laughter broke forth and, at the conclusion, the players received a standing ovation."[129] John Millar, reviewing for the *Moose Jaw Times-Herald*, enjoyed the production, which was mounted at the Union Centre there, but found the script lacking in some areas. "The play lacks a lot of the rudiments of drama, such as plot, lead characters, continuity, and the like," he wrote. "Those things become amazingly unnecessary when the results are all in."[130] Millar also wondered about the left-wing politics of the play, musing that "the stage is not the place for politics." As far north as Meadow Lake, more than five-hundred spectators turned up at Carpenter High School Auditorium to see the play. The anonymous reviewer for the

Meadow Lake Progress, who had seen the play in its earlier manifestation, had some reservations about the newer version. The reviewer found that the acting was of "good calibre" but that it could have been better in a few scenes. The music was played at a volume too low for such a large auditorium, and the reviewer lamented the "unfortunate omission" of Michael Fahey's Norwegian character in Guy Sprung's version of the play.[131]

At the end of the provincial tour, Gerry Stoll submitted a balanced budget to the Canada Council. The production costs had been $76,683.45, about half of that having been paid out as actors' salaries. The total revenue had been $79,170.81, with $43,085.67 coming from box office alone. The Canada Council Touring Office had provided $10,000, the Province of Saskatchewan had ponied up $9,000, and the National Film Board had contributed $1,400. Corporate sponsorship equalled $14,000, contributed by Credit Union Central, Federated Co-operatives, and the Co-operators. (At least one commentator found this corporate generosity to be misguided at a time when wheat farmers were suffering from lack of rain as wheat prices continued to spiral downwards. In an editorial in the *Free Press* "Report On Farming", he wondered what the executive offices of the grain industry would think of next. Thespians performing in elevators on abandoned branch lines? Eugene Whelan playing a starring role in *The Ten Commandments*, supported by a cast of thousands from Agriculture Canada? "Nonsense? Of course," he wrote. "But, no more nonsensical than responsible co-operatives financially supporting irresponsible drivel."[132]) On January 3, 1978, Stoll was extremely optimistic about the coming season, writing that 25th Street Theatre was already committed to a national tour of *Paper Wheat* and that a permanent theatre facility and a school touring company were in the works.[133]

It was the Guy Sprung production of *Paper Wheat* which toured to Montreal's Centaur Theatre in the autumn of 1978. The eastern critics were fonder, perhaps, of the performances than of the script. Writing for the *Ottawa Review*, Michael Carroll was especially complimentary about the acting ensemble: "As a chronicle telling of the advent of diverse immigrants to Canada at the turn of the century, and a witty documentation of the rise of the cooperative movement in Saskatchewan, *Paper Wheat* has everything going for it. The cast of the production, as good an ensemble company as I've ever seen, comes across with a uniformly splendid piece of work — not one weak link." Carroll particularly admired the intersection of theatre and reality in Bill Prokopchuk's musical performance; he found the poignant ending of the play remarkable, with Prokopchuk playing a two-step, intimating "that he too was a farmer once but now he makes his living with a fiddle."[134] Sandy Phoenix, writing in the Dawson College student newspaper *The Plant*, was similarly enthralled with the production as performance. "By itself, 'wheat' is not exciting," she wrote. "BUT, give it to Saskatoon's 25th Street House Theatre who collectively turn it into a play, add a brilliant and versatile cast, an ingenious director, and an inventive production staff; and then stand back and watch the damn stuff come to life!"[135] In the *Montreal Gazette*, Maureen Peterson complimented Prokopchuk and his musical collaborator Michael Fahey, along with the rest of the actors, on their performances. She also found something to admire in the script. "For those of you who have seen *The Farm Show*, *The West Show*, or even *Ten Lost Years*, the style will be somewhat familiar," she wrote. "But *Paper Wheat* surpasses what I have seen of collectively-created theatre for continuity and consistency, and achieves a delicateness of detail that in no way damages its rugged and hearty spirit."[136]

It was also Guy Sprung's production, with Peter Meuse replacing an unavailable Michael Fahey in the cast, which began touring nationally in the spring of 1979. From the initial opening of the first production of *Paper Wheat* in Sintaluta, Andy Tahn had learned the value of finding a sympathetic audience early in the production run. The national tour of *Paper Wheat* was meticulously planned to provide the production with sympathetic audiences, and to garner good reviews, early on. The tour kicked off in Calgary, where critics could be relied upon to understand and identify with agricultural themes and characters, on June 5, 1979. This stratagem almost backfired when the *Herald's* Eric Dawson panned the production whole-heartedly. "The traveling production of Paper Wheat being performed at Theatre Calgary is cabaret agriculture of no great merit," Dawson wrote. "It asks very little of an audience, feeds them a great deal of light humor and sentiment and neatly conforms to the rules of a quality dinner theatre presentation — to entertain and leave no memorable trace."[137] Fortunately, *The Albertan's* Louis B. Hobson liked the production as much as Dawson disliked it. Comparing *Paper Wheat* to Thornton Wilder's classic drama *Our Town*, Hobson was touched by the beguiling simplicity of the script and by its presentation of the heroic myth of the prairie sodbusters:

> At times, *Paper Wheat* looks like a Canadian version of Thornton Wilder's *Our Town*, a play that maintained and proved that there was great drama in the lives of ordinary people. The comparison is remarkable, especially in a scene when two isolated farm wives meet for the first time and share a cup of tea and struggle to tell one another how grateful they are for each other's company. Nothing could be more simple and yet more touching.[138]

After playing in Calgary and Edmonton, the production returned to Saskatchewan in early August for runs in Saskatoon and Regina. It then moved on to the National Arts Centre in Ottawa, where it garnered rave reviews. The production played in Vancouver in September and southern Ontario in October, finally opening at the Toronto Free Theatre in mid-November. Over the course of the national tour, the success of the production snowballed; reviews in the last half of the tour were almost always raves. Tahn suggested, in an interview with Lolly Kaiser in *Scene Changes*, that the production might even tour to New York. "But we sure as hell wouldn't open there," he said; "we'd open in some small town in Missouri."[139]

As Alan Filewod writes, national audiences did not fall in love with the play's razor-sharp analysis of the founding of co-operative movement: instead, they fell in love with the actors' retelling of the story, with the intersection of reality and artifice in the play, and with the play as "heroic myth." Reviewers of the national tour of *Paper Wheat* almost invariably refer to the production's acting virtuosity and usually commended the ensemble for capably employing mime, song, juggling, dance, and other theatrical elements in performance. Ray Conologue's review in the *Globe and Mail* refers repeatedly to these moments of virtuosity:

> Inventive and delightful moments come tumbling back in memory after seeing the show: a prairie couple who recount their first years of famine, drought, wind and frost by rolling and unrolling a blanket which symbolizes their beloved land; two tap dancers, each with only one shoe, who learn to make a complete melody by dancing together (a lesson in the virtues of prairie co-operatives); the exploitation of farmers by grain speculators wittily rendered as an old-fashioned radio thriller, complete with sound effects. And Lubomir Mykytiuk, demonstrating who gets the biggest chunks of a dollar spent on a loaf of bread, eats a roll while juggling it with two rubber balls. A ball lands on his neck, to show where the farmer gets it; the pitiful remnant crumb — the farmer's profit — is dismissed with a swift kick. It is dazzling.[140]

The *Calgary Herald's* Louis B. Hobson likewise emphasizes the acting company's virtuosity:

> The company for the national tour is, without exception, exceptional, and what is so important, it is a company that spotlights its performance but headlines no one. There may be favorite moments or characterizations, but it would be difficult to single anyone out as being superior to the others. This is a show that depends on the versatility of its performers to make the proper impact and Sharon Bakker, David Francis, Peter Meuse, Lubomir Mykytiuk and Skai Leja literally stun with their ability to dart in and out of numerous characterizations.[141]

As Filewod maintains, the virtuosic telling of the story of *Paper Wheat* was at least as important as the story itself.

Sprung's production was about the actors and musicians who played in it. Reviewers were quick to mention that Sharon Bakker had grown up on a farm in Saskatchewan (she was the only native Saskatchewanian in the national tour of the play) and that Lubomir Mykytiuk and Skai Leja were of Ukrainian and Latvian descent, respectively, like the characters they played. The intersection between reality and artifice, signified by the presence of these particular actors in this particular production, was highly seductive to audiences during the national tour. Arnold Edinborough did not hesitate to mention this intersection in his review of the production for the *Financial Post*:

> The company in the present 25th Street House cast are a remarkable bunch. Skai Leja, of Latvian origin, is striking to look at, delicious to listen to and has a variety of accents which, together with her acting ability, make her a remarkable personality on stage. Sharon Bakker, raised on a Saskatchewan farm, is equally good as a thieving elevator agent or a flustered, pregnant settler's wife. Lubomir Mykytiuk is a Ukrainian who starts the play off with a flood of Ukrainian talk, but after that dazzles both by his linguistic ability and, in one magnificent scene, his juggling.
>
> Bill Prokopchuk, also of Ukrainian origin, born and raised in Rhein, Sask., is a fiddler who left his farm for what the program calls "a very busy circuit of weddings, dances and parties with his band the Country Kings," joined the 25th Street House Theatre for the fall 1977 tour and has been with it ever since.[142]

In particular, fiddler Bill Prokopchuk's presence on stage seemed to provide the production with a degree of authenticity it otherwise would not have had. In the *Vancouver Sun*, Wayne Edmonstone was rapturous about Prokopchuk's performance:

> Bill Prokopchuk, himself a retired wheat farmer and the only member of the group old enough to have first hand knowledge of the period of the piece is — thank God — a genuine Canadian old time fiddler. Which is to say, his music is based on the folk fiddle tunes people actually used to play at square dances in

rural Canada, and not some imported bluegrass derivative. Like most things about this play, it's a treat.[143]

For several critics, Prokopchuk was living testimony of prairie hardship, cunning, and resilience.

At the heart of the critics' insistence upon relating the actor to the reality was the fact that the play, which celebrates collective initiatives, had been written collectively (or "co-operatively," as members of the company sometimes put it). Tahn himself shrewdly emphasized the production's beginnings as a co-operative effort. In the December 1979 issue of *Scene Changes*, Lolly Kaiser suggests that the success of *Paper Wheat* "lies with its roots as a cooperatively written production." She quotes Tahn as saying, "The biggest success of this play is that Mrs. Olive Well of Tuxford, Saskatchewan, is just as much a part of the show as we are."[144] In her review of the play in Kingston, Sherri Campbell refers to a sense of community which, she says, distinguishes Canadian theatre from its American counterpart:

> The sense of community in our theatre helps to distinguish Canadian culture from that of the United States. There is no character in the script who ranks as the protagonist, nor is there anyone who can remain independent of the others. Each actor may play up to ten roles, therefore the opportunity for any one of them to dominate the stage is diminished. In the creation of "Paper Wheat" all of the actors collaborated with the director to write the script and develop the characters.[145]

While celebrating the victory of the collective over the capitalistic model of individual enterprise, the production was itself an example of collective victory. In his review for the *Star-Phoenix*, Don Perkins attributed the production's success partly to "its unassailable sense of belonging to the people whose story it tells."[146]

In *Collective Encounters*, Filewod compares *Paper Wheat* to *No. 1 Hard*, which premiered at Regina's Globe Theatre in 1978, and to Barry Broadfoot's popular *Ten Lost Years*, arguing that *Paper Wheat* appeals "to a broader romantic sentiment" than *No. 1 Hard*. Of *Paper Wheat*, he writes, "In the body of Canadian documentary theatre, it is an anomaly: it is the least documentary of the plays in this study, but, along with *Ten Lost Years*, the most successful. Like *Ten Lost Years* it is a nostalgic hymn to the past, but in *Paper Wheat* fact and fiction flow into each other to define a heroic myth."[147] The reviews received during the 1979 national tour support Filewod's comments. Jacob Siskind, in the *Ottawa Journal*, offered a similar sentiment in his appraisal of the play. "It is a pleasant entertainment but it is also a tribute to those whose fortitude and patience gave this country the strength that made it distinctive," he wrote. "Years ago people used to say that Canada would be The country of the second half of this century. *Paper Wheat* gives you a feeling of why people should have said that would be so."[148] In the *Regina Leader-Post*, Denise Ball found the play to be "full of Prairie piety and sentimental gobbledygook, corny jokes and unabashed folksiness," but she also argued that the play works because of those faults. "[M]ost of all, it tells the people of the Prairies how wonderful they were and still can be," she wrote. "They struggled and endured, and Paper Wheat invites the audience to bask in their reflected glory. And no one can resist hearing that, particularly when it happens to be fun and entertaining as well." In *Saturday Night*, Martin Knelman suggested that *Paper Wheat* appealed to an audience that normally did not go to the theatre. "It milks its yokel gags about wives who are compared to tractors, it sentimentalizes the lives of people who grow up in tar shacks, and it flatters its own constituents by making them feel that their hardships have somehow made them superior to the rest of the human race," he opined. "It's the kind of theatre that appeals especially to people who normally don't go to the theatre."[149]

The phenomenon of *Paper Wheat* catapulted 25th Street Theatre into the national consciousness. Two years earlier, Tahn would not have imagined that any play of his theatre's making would be touring nationally. He would also have scoffed at the idea that any of his theatre's productions would be reviewed in the *National Post*, the *Globe and Mail*, *Saturday Night*, or the *Vancouver Province*. There was seemingly no end to the popularity of the production. There had been talk of a

New York opening for the play. Tahn himself proposed to keep the phenomenon alive by remounting *Paper Wheat* on a yearly basis after the national tour, and he did recreate the production in 1981 for a brief tour and again in 1982. Unfortunately, actors had to be replaced for these subsequent remounts and, as his been suggested, the success of the production hinged partly on the actors themselves. *Paper Wheat* was losing steam, and by 1983 Tahn had abandoned his idea of a yearly remount in the style of *Anne of Green Gables*. The company produced the play again in 1989, under a different artistic director, but without the fanfare of earlier productions. In 2001, Dancing Sky Theatre in Meacham, Saskatchewan, commissioned a sequel to *Paper Wheat* from Mansell Robinson. The resulting play was called *Street Wheat*, and it successfully toured the province (with Crooked Creek's Rocky Lakner providing songs and musical accompaniment) the following year. It was, however, a different beast than *Paper Wheat*, not collectively written and less concerned with meta-theatre than with the fictitious characters in Robinson's script.

Paper Wheat, with David Francis, 1982

Patrick Close

Paper Wheat, with Sharon Bakker and Michael Fahey, 1982

Paper Wheat, (l-r) Bill Prokopchuk, Peter Meuse, Skai Leja, David Francis, Sharon Bakker, 1982

Twenty-Fifth Street House Theatre & U.S.S.U.
proudly present

The Ballad of Billy the Kid

written by Andy Tahn
original music composed and performed by Don Freed
directed by Christopher Covert

April 10 - 20

Twenty-Fifth Street House Theatre: Clarence & 8th Street
Tickets: M.U.B. on Campus or 343-9966

Anonymous

Poster for *The Ballad of Billy The Kid*

Six:

"HANG IT ALL IF OUR GOVERNMENT CAN'T SEE BEYOND THEIR NOSES" (1977-80)

TWENTY-FIFTH STREET THEATRE PRODUCED other plays besides *Paper Wheat* in the period between 1977 and 1980, but these efforts did not get as much press coverage as *Paper Wheat*, owing to the fact that none of them had extensive national tours. For much of that period, 25th Street functioned as a purveyor of other companies' productions. After the huge success of *Paper Wheat*, the theatre's general manager Gerry Stoll was growing frustrated with a lack of provincial funding, especially since Persephone Theatre had been quite successful in accessing provincial funds. By 1977, 25th Street Theatre was in direct competition with Persephone Theatre which had mounted a prominent tour of its own with *Cruel Tears*. A crisis in finding a fulltime performance space was becoming a source of anxiety for both theatres, and this crisis found a temporary fix in 1980, when the Saskatoon Theatre Centre opened. The new Theatre Centre was, in fact, an abandoned church on 20th Street and Avenue H, in one of Saskatoon's poorest and most crime-ridden areas. (I performed there in 1981, in *Long Day's Journey Into Night* at Persephone Theatre, and I can remember coming out of a matinee to learn that the company's donation box, which had been left out in the foyer, had been stolen.)

Gerry Stoll was unhappy in his dealings with the provincial government and with the Saskatchewan Arts Board (SAB). He had noticed that Persephone Theatre, which got its start after the inception of his own company, was getting more SAB funding than 25th Street Theatre. He complained, in an August 11, 1977 letter to Ned Shillington, then Minister of Culture and Youth, that 25th Street's Arts Board Grant of $5,400, in 1976-77, had been a quarter of what Persephone received. He opined that "[t]he Saskatchewan Arts Board has become a totally ineffectual organization."[150] He noted wryly that Shillington's Special Minister's Fund had supported the Persephone tour of *Cruel Tears*, and he requested $10,000 for the provincial and Toronto tour of *Paper Wheat*. He complained that, while Shillington's department had donated almost two million dollars to the City of Saskatoon, in the form of a Recreation and Cultural Facilities Grant, 99% of that money had gone to recreation and less than half a percent had gone to culture. Stoll was extremely displeased with the way both the province and the city had dealt with the joint proposal for a new theatre centre on Broadway Avenue (which did not come to fruition). "To be honest," he wrote, "the Canada Council in Ottawa has a better idea of what is happening in Saskatoon than our provincial representatives." Stoll ended his letter to Shillington with three suggestions for the Minister: that he initiate a study of the Saskatchewan Arts Board, the Department of Culture and Youth, and SaskSport, to make them more responsive to the needs of artists; that there be greater liaison between the City of Saskatoon and Shillington's department; and that Shillington establish a Saskatchewan touring office.

Stoll was in no mood to let the matter rest. In November, when the editor of *Performing Arts in Canada* Arnold Edinborough offered to provide a national forum for artist reaction to recent cutbacks in provincial and federal funding, Stoll was only too happy to take him up on his offer. He was particularly vehement in his appraisal of the Saskatchewan Arts Board as a funding body, responding that the Board was the victim of its own archaic structure and "has now become a weak-kneed extension of the Saskatchewan Government." He argued that the Board distributed funds indiscriminately, without any real criteria; it simply passed on whatever monies the Government gave it and was too weak to be an effective lobbyist for the betterment of Saskatchewan artists. On November 8, 1977, he wrote in reply to Edinborough:

> The Saskatchewan Arts Board has no criteria for funding. A group is not judged by the size of its budget, its quality, the number of its performances, or its audience attendance. Frankly, I don't think there is any written policy or criteria for the Saskatchewan Arts Board other than to distribute the funds made available to it each year by the Government.
>
> The Saskatchewan Arts Board has no touring funds for professional companies. In other words, there is no money for groups to tour the province and no money for sponsors in Saskatoon and Regina. There is money made available to other provincial arts councils but they favor performers such as Maureen Forrester, the Festival Singers, or Jon Vickers. There is a tendency for these smaller arts councils to ignore their own provincial performers.[151]

Stoll closes his letter with the sentiment that he could not make anything but a sad case "for a province which takes pride in its unique culture."

Thirty-two years later, Tahn had not changed his opinion about the Arts Board's perceived lack of support for 25th Street Theatre. According to Tahn, the Canada Council was then in the business of encouraging the growth of a fledgling Canadian theatre whereas the Saskatchewan Arts Board did not seem to understand that mandate. Tahn maintained that the Arts Board was nervous about supporting the development of new plays that nobody had ever seen before. "If we were doing Shakespeare or some great American drama, they would have been more understanding," said Tahn. "For [the Arts Board] to see *If You're So Good, Why Are You In Saskatoon?*, well, what was that? You can't find that in the library. Who's gonna pay for that?" According to Tahn, the Arts Board didn't see, as quickly as the Canada Council saw, the emergence of a new Canadian theatre "where all you were doing was your own plays." Tahn later reiterated Stoll's earlier opinion of the Arts Board. "The Arts Board, in truth, was not supportive in the beginning. Absolutely not. They were critical. They were cautious. They were somewhat apprehensive about 25th Street Theatre."[152]

Other than its provincial/Toronto tour of *Paper Wheat*, 25th Street Theatre did not produce any plays in the autumn of 1977. After the New Year, the company hosted two touring shows and produced another collective piece called *Generation and ½*. The theatre had originally intended to produce Tahn's play *Jacob Kepp*, which was based on the true story of Allan-area farmer Kasper Beck, and also *The Quebec Show*, which would have been an expose of Quebecois separatism and its impact upon the rest of Canada. Both plays were announced but neither was produced in 1977-78, probably due to lack of money. Such a slim record of their own artistic creations would not serve 25th Street Theatre well in its bid for greater funding.

Ted Johns' one-man show *Naked on the North Shore* was nevertheless well-received in Saskatoon and during a brief provincial tour. Directed by Paul Thompson for Theatre Passe Muraille, the production was a furtherance of the mutually beneficial relationship between the two theatres. In years to come, Passe Muraille would view 25th Street Theatre as a safe venue for trying out new plays as well as a market for their own proven rural-based productions. They offered 25th Street, in turn, a Toronto venue for their own successful shows and a means to garner publicity at the centre of Canada's theatrical activity. Johns' play, which had been a hit in Toronto, ran at the Cuelenaere Library in Prince Albert on January 26 and 27, at the Globe Theatre in Regina on January 28 and 29, and at the Western Development Museum in Saskatoon February 1-5. Much of the performance hinged upon Johns' folksy manner and his acute observations of the people of Old Fort Bay, Labrador, where the play is set. Reviewing for the *Star-Phoenix*, Nancy Russell wrote, simply, "It will touch you."[153] In the *Sheaf*, m. d'entrement was more prolix in his praise for the play:

> For one man to create the atmosphere of an entire community is no simple feat and Johns' handling of this task is a marvel to be seen. He and his characters dominate the stage, and to borrow

an old cliché, they appear larger than life. He translates the feeling of the community for the audience by speaking to them informally and by making them feel as part of the community instead of making them spectators at events from which they are far removed.[154]

Johns' performance engaged Saskatchewan audiences as it had engaged Toronto audiences during its run at Passe Muraille.

In March, 25th Street Theatre produced *Generation and ½*, funded with a generous donation of $60,000 from the Cooperative Retailing System of Western Canada and from Federated Cooperatives. Although Guy Sprung's relationship with 25th Street Theatre had been bittersweet, Tahn asked him back to direct *Generation and ½* because of what Tahn perceived as Sprung's commitment to socialism and social justice. "Guy's work in East London [at the Half Moon Theatre] gave him the working class experience of socialist justice," Tahn wrote later. "I did not then nor do I now share that common socialist view. My interest is and always has been — people."[155]

The cast was filled with 25th Street stalwarts and veterans of *Paper Wheat*; it included Linda Griffiths, Connie Kaldor, Sharon Bakker, Bob Bainborough, Layne Coleman, David Francis, and Bill Prokopchuk. Sprung provided the actors and musicians with an original concept and allowed them to improvise around it. The frame story for the play was set in 2028, when all but a few die-hard Co-operators have abandoned Saskatchewan and headed East. Three of the few remaining Saskatchewanians set up a time machine, which transports various characters from 1978 to the play's present. These transported characters tell stories and sing songs of the way it was and warn of a future controlled by multi-nationals. Connie Kaldor wrote the music and lyrics, of which the following song entitled "Triple Threat" from near the end of the play is characteristic:

You've seen the big companies
And you know how they run.
They'll run you if given half a chance,
And the smaller you are,

The less they'll listen to you
And you're lost in that kind of song and dance
And they want to put a stop
To these grain co-ops
'Cause they can't merge and buy controlling shares
And they can't understand why the farmer with the land
Takes his wheat to the Pool.
You know it just isn't fair.

Triple . . . Triple . . . Triple . . . Threat!
Wheat Pool!
Credit Union!
Co-op Store!
The Triple Threat![156]

The production opened in Saskatoon at E.D. Feehan High School Auditorium on March 3, 1978, and proceeded on a tour of Western Canada in the following months. It played in Brandon and Boissevain in early April and in twenty-nine locations in rural Saskatchewan and Alberta in April and May.

Generation and ½'s problem was that it was *Paper Wheat* but it was not *Paper Wheat*. In his review in the *NeWest Review,* Don Kerr dubbed the play "Son of Paper Wheat," noting that the new play retained *Paper Wheat*'s starry-eyed lyricism when it might better have dealt with the hard realities of co-operatives when they grow big and dwell in a capitalist neighbourhood. "Co-ops start with poetry but live in an enormous welter of prose," wrote Kerr. "The road to the new life is paved with minutes, and qualifying clauses. *Generation and a Half[sic]* leaves out the prose. That's why it's a bit wet at the end."[157] In an article in *Panorama,* the anonymous reviewer again compared *Generation and ½* to *Paper Wheat* but this time favourably. Writing that he enjoyed *Generation and ½* much more than the original *Paper Wheat,* the reviewer added, "I found the characters more fully developed, the actors more consistent in ability, the story as such more complete, the sequence of events more logical and the philosophy more clearly communicated."[158]

The play's ideological stance, coupled with the notion that Big Business was using a publicly funded theatre company as part of its publicity machine, was noted by the critics. "There has been much said about the play's obvious political orientation and its financial relationships with Federated Co-operatives," wrote the *Panorama* reviewer. "The perception of the prairie experience as presented in the play, however, includes more than a few messages for Federated Co-op itself. Through humour and exaggeration it is encouraged not to forget its members its principles and its original goals in an effort to compete with big business."[159] In the *Star-Phoenix*, Nancy Russell suggested that the basic message of the play was "Dividends equal hope" and that the ideological message did not hamper the production. "But messages aside," she wrote, "the main dividend for Saskatoon audiences is more than two hours of energetic acting from a cast whose names are synonymous with Twenty Fifth Street."[160] Even the reviewer for the *Co-operative Consumer* gently poked fun at the production's relationship with Federated Co-operatives Limited (FCL). "A large portion of the premiere night audience rose to its feet to salute the players at the end of the performance," wrote Beckie Garber-Conrad. "Most of those at the premiere were delegates to FCL's annual meeting and their guests, and FCL employees and their guests." There were nevertheless some criticisms of the production, even from FCL employees:

> Despite numerous comments that the play was rather long and could use some "smoothing out" in places, the audience response was generally favorable. One couple said there was scene after scene which "really hit home." Several people said that many of the jokes and statements were things any rural audience could identify with, even though it zeros in on co-operatives.[161]

Most reviewers found, like Garber-Conrad, that despite the co-operative propaganda the play succeeded in entertaining audiences.

The mainstage season ended not with a production of Tahn's play *Jacob Kepp* (which Sprung was no longer directing as a result of his creative differences with Tahn during rehearsals for *Paper Wheat*) or of *The Quebec Show*, but with a presentation of the Mummers' Theatre of Newfoundland touring show *They Club Seals, Don't They?* The Mummers' show was performed at the Western Development Museum and ran April 11-15. The play had been created collectively by the cast, which included Pierre Beaupre, Rhonda Payne, Terry Rielly, Glenn Tilley, Donna Butt, Jeff Pitcher, and David Ross, under the direction of Chris Brookes. Its subject matter was the provocative seal hunt on Canada's east coast. The Mummers' Troupe came out in support of the sealers, even going so far as to trivialize the protestors' cries by naming their play after a movie that was popular at the time, *They Shoot Horses, Don't They?* In an advance interview in the *Star-Phoenix*, director Chris Brookes said that public opinion against the seal hunt was changing despite the appearance of movie stars among the ranks of the protestors.[162] While Nancy Russell did not take sides on the issue in her review of the play, she was careful to say that the troupe presented the pro-sealing argument well. "After watching the troupe's production of *They Club Seals, Don't They?* at the Western Development Museum," she wrote, "one can conclude the rest of Canada and the world has a great deal to learn about the Newfoundland people and baby seals."[163] In his review in *Briarpatch*, Gary Robins noted that the Canadian embassy in Washington had received over 14,000 letters in protest of the seal hunt during the winter of 1977-78 and argued that, while the Mummers' play was strong and convincing, it was not self-critical. "Although the hunt is important to the sealers' livelihood," he wrote, "clubbing seals to death so that someone can sport a luxurious fur coat is a hell of a way to make a living."[164]

In August of 1977, the Oxcart Summer Players incorporated under the Societies Act, listing Andy Tahn, Gerry Stoll, Dennis Friesen, and Sharon Bakker as its board of directors. In May 1978, 25th Street Theatre announced that it had been awarded a Young Canada Works project grant of $15,151 in order to create a summer touring show tentatively entitled *The Northern Legend Show*. According to Tahn, the aims of the Oxcart Summer Players' project were to conduct research on Saskatchewan's North and the people who live there, to rehearse a play based on that research, and to tour that play throughout Saskatchewan. Tahn applied for an additional $3800 from the Secretary of State and included with his application a letter of support from Chief David Ahenakew on behalf of the Federation of Saskatchewan Indians. "Despite the handicaps of having very little time to prepare their script and having only one Indian person in the cast," Chief Ahenakew wrote, "my information indicates their early research efforts have been characterized by receptive and respectful attitudes, a willingness to respect information, rituals, and ceremonies that are not for public display, and an overall professional attitude towards their work."[165] On June 20, 1978, Tahn announced that he had hired poet Andrew Suknaski to collaborate with the actors and director in order to create the play. The actors in the 1978 Oxcart company were theatre students from across Canada: Ruth Smillie, John Dibben, and John Agius of Ryerson Polytechnical Institute; Sharon Stearns of Simon Fraser University; Joe Charles of La Ronge; and Lisa Reitapple of York University. The resulting production, which came to be known as *Don'tcha Know — The North Wind and You in My Hair*, was researched and rehearsed for eight weeks in the early summer and was performed twenty-six times to over three thousand people.

Reviews for the production were mixed in the smaller touring stops and negative in the larger cities. In the *Prince Albert Herald*, Joy Murray opined that the production offered an accurate depiction of Northern life: "*Don'tcha Know — The North Wind and You In My Hair* depicts the warp and weft of northern life deftly and for anyone wanting to step into a different lifestyle or remember a familiar one it is a play to see."[166] In the *Meadow Lake Progress*, Doug Bird wrote that the play was "raw in the sense of jagged nerves and harsh feelings" but that it was also "an absorbing, fine crafted presentation of the hopes and frustrations of Indian and Metis people living in northern Saskatchewan."[167] Donna Pinay, in *New Breed*, noted a few shortcomings in the play — she argued that the role of Aboriginal organizations in modern Northern life and the changes that have taken place in recent years might have been included in the production — but found the play to be "quite representative of what is happening to Native people in Saskatchewan and throughout Canada."[168] Others were unhappy with the play. In an editorial printed in the *La Ronge Northerner*, La Ronge women Marg Beament, Linda Goulet, and Anne Dorion deplored the stereotyping of Aboriginal characters in the play:

> Stereotyping of characters is evident in many segments. The minimal inclusion of self-humour, spontaneity of community, and the progressive actions taken by people to change circum- stances of life in the North does not receive the exposure necessary to show the other side of the coin. It carries the theme that the North is a tragic world with insurmountable problems, personal or otherwise.[169]

The above quotation was also reprinted in New Breed, the flagship magazine of Métis politics, culture, and history in Saskatchewan.[170.] When the production was mounted in Regina on August 17, it received a chilly response from the *Leader-Post's* Denise Ball. While she admired some of the individual performances, Ball wrote, "The play as a whole is disappointing, mostly because of the inconsistency in the acting and a general lack of cohesiveness and thematic focus."[171] Similarly, after an August 29 opening at the Mendel Gallery auditorium in Saskatoon, the *Star-Phoenix's* Nancy Russell suggested that the production "didn't quite work." The core of the problem, Russell declared, had to do with the play's casting; a group of young (and mostly White) actors from across Canada "could never become a group of Metis and Indians from northern Saskatchewan."[172]

The University of Saskatchewan's Department of Audio Visual Services videotaped *Don'tcha Know* at various locations in Saskatoon, with hopes of turning the play into an educational media tool. The videotaping of *Don'tcha Know* took place over five days in September. Film director Danielle Fortosky had decided to shoot footage at the Mendel Art Gallery, at a house on Avenue S South, and at the Albany Hotel on 20th Street. Some of the Albany's regular patrons were hired as extras in the film, which featured several newly added Aboriginal actors. Andy Tahn had hopes that the film would be picked up as a teaching tool by the Saskatoon Public Board of Education and reported that there was "a great deal of interest from Saskatoon educators."[173] In the summer following, Tahn would mount a province-wide school tour of the play.

At the beginning of the 1978-79 season, 25th Street Theatre was still wrangling with the provincial and federal governments over funding for their theatre. Twenty-Fifth Street was not being singled out in the money crunch; an era of draconian funding cutbacks for the arts was upon us, and Toronto companies felt the financial crisis as keenly as did regional theatres. In the October 14, 1978 *Globe and Mail*, Ray Conologue wrote wistfully of large-cast and star-studded productions which were likely to be stricken from the Toronto season due to lack of funding. These includes a production of Aristophanes' *The Birds* at Toronto Arts Productions, of Brecht's *Mahogonny* at Toronto Workshop Productions, of Cone's *Herringbone* (starring Eric Peterson) at the Open Circle, and of *The Ecstasy of Rita Joe* at Passe Muraille. For their part, Gerry Stoll and Andy Tahn were befuddled with provincial and federal policy towards the arts, and especially, given the recent successes of 25th Street, towards their theatre. Tahn had asked for a large funding increase from the Canada Council but received only $25,000 and a warning that the theatre must maximize the resources at hand. The Head of the Council's Theatre Section, Walter Learning, wrote in a June 27, 1978 letter to Tahn:

> In such a climate, it is especially important that each company makes a careful reassessment of its operation and ensure[s] that it is maximizing the use of the resources at hand; that it examines the goals it has set for itself and whether they are still valid and how close the company is coming to realizing them and finally to ensure that everything possible is being done to generate box office income and to seriously pursue other areas of funding, private, corporate, governmental and special projects

as well as such cost-saving efforts as co-productions with other theatre companies.[174]

Learning also suggested that 25th Street Theatre look for shared accommodation with Persephone Theatre because the operating costs for two theatre buildings were excruciatingly high.

Learning's advice about approaching corporate funding agencies must have galled Tahn since he had been arguably at the forefront of this activity when he found funding for *Generation and ½* through the Federated Co-op. In fact, Federated Co-operatives' involvement with 25th Street Theatre was to earn them a Financial Post Award for Business in the Arts. Gerry Stoll attended the awards ceremony in Montreal in February 1979 on behalf of the theatre and heard how total "artistic freedom in the play — a time-machine look at the co-op movement from the past into the future — was given to the theatre."[175] Tahn later argued that reliance upon non-Arts Board funding was not healthy for professional theatre in Canada, referring to the pro-co-operative propaganda that his theatre had brought to the stage in *Generation and ½*. "Although we are grateful for the support received from the Department of Co-operation and Co-operative Development," he wrote in a letter to the Saskatchewan Arts Board, "I do not believe it is healthy for a professional theatre to receive support over a long period of time in this manner."[176]

In January 1979, Tahn "crossed swords" with John Roberts, Canadian Secretary of State, over a 9.6% increase in the budget of the National Arts Centre. As Tahn wrote, in a letter of January 18, 1979, his was a sword of "anger and mixed joy" at the fact that the Secretary of State was allocating money to an arts organization, albeit (in Tahn's opinion) the wrong one. He was appalled by the allocation because the National Arts Centre did little outside Ottawa, was a drain on the taxpayers' wallets, and persisted in producing non-Canadian plays. Tahn did not understate his case:

The Secretary of State is neanderthal [sic] in thinking it must support an enterprise for the sake of having a National Arts Centre centrally located in Ottawa. There is a life pounding in this country's arts, in English Canada as well as in French Canada; in Saskatchewan as in other regions. Hang it all if our government can't see beyond their noses not to support these creative aggressive forces in the regions. Unlike other countries, Canada does not have a centrally located national theatre, but a national theatre scattered throughout the land, nestled in the regions.[177]

Tahn maintained that the 9.6% increase was irresponsible and called on the federal government to turn the money over to the Canada Council rather than to the National Theatre. On March 28, the Secretary of State responded to Tahn's letter, stating that he hoped they did "not have to come to the point of crossing swords over the level of federal assistance to theatre in Canada because I think we are basically on the same side." While acknowledging that Canada's regional theatres were extremely vital, he cited the objects of the Arts Centre's Act: "to assist the Canada Council in the development of the performing arts elsewhere in Canada"; and "to encourage and assist in the development of performing arts companies resident at the Centre." He referred to recent tours by both the English- and French-language sections of the Centre's resident company as proof that it was encouraging development of the performing arts in the provinces.

If Tahn was frustrated with governmental support for regional theatre in Canada, his business manager Gerry Stoll was doubly unhappy. In March 1979, Stoll announced that he was leaving 25th Street Theatre temporarily in order to promote and coordinate Theatre Passe Muraille's upcoming tour to Great Britain. Stoll wrote, in a news release, that he had mixed feelings about leaving Saskatchewan. "It is pretty hot in the drama kitchen right now and I hate to be leaving — especially at such a historically important time in the development of Saskatoon's professional theatres — but this tour of Great Britain will add to my knowledge and my professional growth."[178] On the same date as Stoll's press release (March 16), the theatre announced that Edmontonian David Robson had been hired to coordinate 25th Street's last offering of the season, a presentation of the Toronto mime company Theatre Beyond Words.

In April 1979, Tahn challenged the Saskatchewan Arts Board over funding issues. Writing on behalf of his theatre's board of directors, Tahn was at his best, impassioned and forceful, hearkening back to the young man who had helped found 25th Street Theatre in 1972. He referred to the measly grant of $15,000, which his theatre had received for the 1978-79 season, to assist with its operating budget of $207,000. He referred to the fact that his fund-raisers had been "scamming" money from every source in order to bring the work of Saskatchewan artists to the stage. He called into question the criteria upon which the Arts Board made its allocations:

> By what criteria does the Arts Board make its allocations? If it is by audience count, then last season we must have out-drawn every arts organization in Saskatchewan (33,000 paying audience). Is it by Revenue and Expenditures? Last season over $200,000.00 was earned and spent, and next season higher yet. (And I agree that bigger is not necessarily better.)
>
> Is the judgement based on community support — private and corporate? Again we must surely rank in the tops.
>
> Is it based on the quality of drama? Actors? Directors? Twenty-Fifth Street Theatre employs the highest caliber of professional Canadian actors and directors while also maintaining and nurturing the homegrown talent, the homegrown drama.
>
> Is it based upon roots in the community? The theatre was started here, turned professional here — through the natural struggle of living and breathing in its own environment — as any true indigenous art form in all nations develops.

Tahn asked what the Arts Board wanted to see happen in Saskatchewan. Did it want to provide "nourishment to our rugged works . . . that flower with our humour, tears and aches"? Or did it wish to "wire in from Florida or Paris the exotic roses and orchids of some more 'civilized' 'sophisticated' clime"? The seven-page letter about regionalism ends on a nationalistic note which could have been the clarion call of 25th Street Theatre in 1979:

> Every decent nation on earth has built up a respected body of artistic expression. The only nation that I know of that produced no noteworthy or valued drama is the most imperialistic and militaristic of them all — the Romans. The only thing they are known for in Art is stealing and bastardizing every and any work of art they could get their hands on. They had no time to create, to nurture, to consider — they were too busy building monuments to past glories and exploiting conquered nations. That is not the kind of Community I wish to be a part of.
>
> OK. So if you, the Arts Board want theatre that imports great works to revive them for the enjoyment of Saskatchewanites; if you want to have theatres show our people what others can do, that's fine. It is by no means a bad or unhealthy objective. It is a noble thing to want noble things. But then you don't have your own window, your own doors by which to enter into dialogue with your fellows around the world.[179]

It is unlikely that the Saskatchewan Arts Board was used to receiving letters which compared Saskatchewan's artistic policies with those of the early Romans. At any rate, no response to Tahn's letter is contained in the 25th Street Theatre Collection at the University of Saskatchewan. For his part, Tahn was writing with the indignation of an artistic director whose annual salary was a mere $7,600 — certainly less than the wage of a filing clerk at the SAB.

While bemoaning the meagre funding their theatre received, Tahn and Stoll were active in their pursuit of a permanent performance space for their company. Stoll had several ideas for a new theatre and was willing to try them all. In June 1978, he approached the provincial Minister of Culture and Youth Ned Shillington about procuring funding in order to create a permanent theatre space at the Western Development Museum in Saskatoon. Shillington replied that he had discussed the matter with Terrence Heath, Executive Director of the Museum, and that Heath had responded directly to

Andy Tahn.[180] When the museum theatre seemed unlikely, Stoll and his counterpart at Persephone Theatre, Ron MacDonald, wrote a letter to the Department of Culture and Youth extolling the virtues of the Capitol Theatre (an historic disused cinema) as a possible theatre space. "We consider that it would be indeed possible to retain the historical motif while renovating the interior so that it becomes [suitable for] performing and visual arts groups, touring companies, etc.," Stoll and MacDonald wrote in their letter of July 6. "We envision a theatre that is convertible from approximately 400 seats to one of 1200 seats. With careful planning, we could include an art gallery, studio space, workshop, and rehearsal space, adequate dressing rooms . . . "[181] As it turned out, the Capitol Theatre idea never came to fruition, although 25th Street Theatre made use of the unconverted space later that season. The historic, spacious, and beautiful cinema was demolished a few years later, contributing to the unhappiness of many in Saskatoon's arts community who had campaigned for it to be designated an official historic building and thereby saved from the wrecker's ball.

In September 1978, after Stoll's departure, 25th Street Theatre announced its inaugural Season Subscription Series, which would help regular patrons of the theatre "to obtain seats for the night they wished" and which would put the theatre "on a more consistent and solid financial footing."[182] The Subscription Series offered three alternatives: weekend seats at $20.80 per show instead of the regular price of $26; weekday seats at $17.60 per show instead of the regular price of $22; and preview and Sunday matinee seats at $13.60 instead of the regular price of $17. When the Subscription Series netted only three hundred patrons in its first season, the company brought in Danny Newman, the author of the 1977 theatre management bible *Subscribe Now!*, to provide advice about attracting larger audiences. While Tahn described the move towards a Subscription Series as necessary and as "a very dynamic step forward for 25th Street House," it did have its pitfalls.[183] The Series attracted a new kind of audience for 25th Street and one which was not as interested in theatrical innovation as Tahn might have hoped. The theatre also had to come to terms with its responsibility towards this new audience, particularly when a play had to be stricken from the season for one reason or another.

Twenty-Fifth Street Theatre was touring *Paper Wheat* in the autumn of 1978, and it presented various touring shows, produced by other theatres, in Saskatoon. The season began with *Hard Hats and Stolen Hearts*, which had been a co-production of two Edmonton theatres, Theatre Network and Theatre 3. Directed by Mark Manson, the production featured Dennis Robinson, Layne Coleman, Tanya Ryga, Jonathan C. Barker, Shay Garner, and Stephen Osler in its cast. In his director's note in the program, Manson suggested that the company had chosen to create a play "about Fort MacMurray as a community whose sudden changes reflect the explosive economic growth which has influenced Alberta."[184] It played in Saskatoon at Aden Bowman High School's Castle Theatre between September 18 and 22 and then moved out on a national tour. The *Star-Phoenix's* Nancy Russell had mixed feelings about the production in her review. "The production needs a quicker pace, especially during the first half, and more enthusiasm from the cast," she wrote. "Ryga is the only member of the cast with a decent singing voice, yet the songs create some of the liveliest moments of the play, even when Ryga is joined with the off-key sounds of other cast members."[185] Reviews of the production in other cities were not as sympathetic. In the *Edmonton Journal*, Keith Ashwell described the performance as "tentative."[186] Audrey M. Asley, writing for the *Ottawa Citizen*, described the play as a "muddle" during its National Arts Centre run. "*Hard Hats and Stolen Hearts* has the look of a play designed by a committee," she wrote. "And like most projects involving too many cooks, it lacks clarity of purpose."[187]

The theatre company presented nothing more in Saskatoon until early February 1979, when the NAC productions *Hamlet* and *William Schwenk and Arthur Who* came to town. In an odd publicity manoeuvre in November 1978, Tahn explained to the *Sheaf's* Terry Pugh that he actually wanted to prove to the federal government that their financial support for the newly created theatre company at the NAC was ill-founded and that one way of achieving this was by allowing audiences to compare NAC productions with local professional productions. "They spend a million dollars to create a brand new company to give us British and foreign productions in order to promote national unity — whatever that is — when there's 136 local theatre groups just starved for money, they're dying for lack of finances," Tahn told the *Sheaf.* "We want to show the government they've got their priorities wrong."[188] Reviews for the two NAC productions were mixed. Writing for the *Star-Phoenix*, Don Perkins argued that director John Wood's "faith in Hamlet as a play and in Neil Munro as Hamlet are well founded" but also that, perhaps because the NAC had been used to smaller houses than the Centennial Auditorium, "several speeches lost impact because the actors did not project into the larger space."[189] As a young theatre student sitting in the stalls at Centennial Auditorium on February 5, I can personally attest to the fact that many of the monologues were frustratingly difficult to hear. Perkins was less enthralled with *William Schwenk and Arthur Who*, a musical revue conceived by Alan Laing and based on the songs of Gilbert and Sullivan. "With little in the way of story line, the production soon bogs down in a contrived message-ridden procession of solos and song and dance routines," he wrote on February 8. "It is this lack of continuity and the heavy, tedious handling of material that wears the audience down."[190] After the NAC tour had finished its Saskatoon run, Tahn informed the Secretary of State, in a tirade, that the National Theatre was elite unto itself and did not have to compete with other theatres for funding. "I might add," he wrote, "they are elite not by *any* artistic standards, but by virtue of the fact they get direct funding."[191] In another letter to the Saskatchewan Arts Board, Tahn made a similar point about the NAC's artistic merits. "I recently made the sad mistake of bringing the National Arts Centre to Saskatoon with *Hamlet* and *William Schwenk and Arthur Who?*" he wrote on April 19, 1979. "The theatre sold only 800 tickets to *Hamlet* and only 200 to *Schwenk* out of a 2,000 seat auditorium. Naturally 4000 students were bused [*sic*] in to 'enjoy' *Hamlet*. They came only because it was on the curriculum. Yet these same students flocked to our own creations."[192] In the NAC,

Tahn had found his bête noire, the ugly beast against which rugged regionalism must eventually triumph.

Also in February 1979, Tahn announced that his large-cast play *Jacob Kepp* would once again be postponed and that its replacement would be a one-night run of Sneezy Waters' musical revue *Hank Williams: The Show He Never Gave*. In an apologetic press release, Tahn informed his new subscribers that they could simply use their *Jacob Kepp* tickets in order to see the other show. Most of us who were in the audience that night were aware that the Capitol Theatre, where the production took place, was in danger of demolition, and there was at least as much significance in that sad fact as there was in the play about Hank Williams' descent into alcoholism and death. Nevertheless, it was easy to like the production and Waters' obvious identification with the character. In the *Star-Phoenix*, Don Perkins wrote that the Saskatoon audience was overcome with grief at Williams' demise, in Waters' depiction:

> It is Waters who carries the burdens of Williams on his shoulders as he slides lower and lower down the scale of humanity and as he and the play move inexorably to that unknown moment when it will all end. As the emotion builds, pulled along by renditions of I'm So Lonesome I Could Cry and The Angel of Death, separated by a recitation of The Men With Broken Hearts, the house becomes very quiet. You almost want to yell "Don't go!" when his wasted shell weaves his way off, having announced, "only 27 minutes to go. Happy New Year's, everybody."[193]

The audience waited for an encore at the end of the show, but the band left the stage and did not return — Hank Williams was dead. For many of us in the audience that night, it was the first time we'd seen Waters perform and the last time we were given the opportunity to spend an evening in the spacious and rococo Capitol Theatre.

The company's next production was of a homegrown play, written by Layne Coleman and William Hominuke. Originally entitled *The RCMP Show*, the play was later called *The Queen's Cowboy* and was presented in Saskatoon March 1-18 at the Ukrainian Canadian Hall on Avenue G and 19th Street. Mark Manson had been contracted to direct the show, and the actors were Coleman, Bob Collins, and Maureen Mckeon. The budget for the production is indicative of what it cost 25th Street Theatre to stage plays in 1979. Each of the three actors was paid $175 per week for six weeks' work. The director was provided with an honorarium of $2,000, which included his travel expenses. Airfare for the three actors (and airfare was an issue for 25th Street House since it regularly flew in its lead actors, unlike theatres in Vancouver and Toronto) was $900. The Stage Manager was paid a wage of $1,260. Sets, props, and costumes were budgeted at $500, while promotion cost $800. Equity benefits for the actors were valued at $793, and miscellaneous costs were $1,500. The production was rehearsed for three-and-a-half weeks and then performed for two-and–a-half weeks. Local reviews for the play, about a love affair between Mountie William Parker (Coleman) and prim Mary Allman (Mckeon) who is married to an opportunistic politician named John Allman (Collins), were generally unfavourable. Linus Kelly, in the *Sheaf*, wrote that the play was too ambitious. "The main problem with *The Queen's Cowboy* is that it tries to do too much," wrote Kelly. "Slated as a 'Royal Northwest Mounted Police Saga,' the play fails to clearly tell the story of the RCMP, fails in its attempt to make insightful comments on a historical era, and only partially succeeds as a melodramatic love story."[194] In the *Star-Phoenix*, Don Perkins found fault with the play's structure, especially with John Allman's narrative bridges which held the story together:

It is these bridges which deny the work much of its potential, as they contain material which might better have been developed through dialogue, giving the characters that much more room to grow, along with the story. As it is, we see too much of Collins mixing history and continuity while seated off to the side of the main set, or, even worse, striding about the front of the stage, with no real reason for doing so, other than to break the monotony of staying in one spot.[195]

Perkins felt that, if the new playwrights Coleman and Hominuke continued to write plays in the future, they would "look back at *The Queen's Cowboy* and wince." Don Kerr was much more charitable when he suggested, in the *NeWest Review*, that *The Queen's Cowboy* was "a fine play." He maintained that the play was written "well enough never to be boring, and writers and director have chosen a style appropriate to it, where real life is played off against theatrical stereotypes."[196]

Southam News Services reviewer Jamie Portman liked the production more than most of the local critics, partly because of the intelligent direction, stage design, and acting. "It's a play that could be tauter, tighter and with the conflicts more specifically defined," he wrote in the *Edmonton Journal*. "But it has been directed with care and imagination by Edmonton's Mark Manson, beautifully designed by Richard Roberts, and convincingly acted by co-author Coleman himself in company with Maureen Mckeon and Bob Collins." Portman's review is an excellent example of how 25th Street Theatre was beginning to be perceived on a national level. The theatre had successfully branded itself as a grassroots company that had endured many hardships. Portman begins his review with the following statement:

> If you want to know what grassroots theatre is all about, you need look no further than Saskatoon's Twenty-Fifth Street House.
>
> Through the years it has hung on to life by its fingernails. It survives on a poverty budget of about $100,000 annually. It can't afford more than three full-time staff members. It doesn't even have a theatre building it can call its own.
>
> Yet, you never fear for its survival. Talk to Andy Tahn, the irrepressible artistic director of Twenty-Fifth Street House Theatre and you may detect a lot of frustration about money. But you also find yourself enveloped in solid visions of the future.
>
> The visions are those of a populist nature, of a theatre which reaches out to the ordinary people, tugging at their hearts and stirring their minds.

In brief, Tahn believes in a theatre which can relate uniquely
to the psychology of the particular community which it serves.[197]
Twenty-Fifth Street Theatre had begun to project itself, in the image of
Andy Tahn, as the little guy with his heart in the right place who could
achieve great things against all odds.

The company presented Theatre Beyond Words between March 29
and April 7 at the Mendel Art Gallery, with their forty-five minute
production of *Potato People* and then produced a school tour of
Don'tcha Know in April and May. Don Perkins wrote that *Potato
People* was bound to be a family favourite "for those with the luck and
foresight to catch them in action."[198] The new Oxcart production of
Don'tcha Know — The North Wind and You in My Hair was directed
by Richard Epp, a graduate of the University of Saskatchewan who was
by then teaching at the University of Lethbridge. Sharon Stearns was
the only actor from the original production who would be returning.
New to the play were Brad Carson, Tantoo Martin (Cardinal), Gordon
Tootoosis, and Fred Yayahkeekoot. Stearns played the lead Flora, with
Tootoosis, who had recently acted in the CBC production of *Little
Judge Big Mouth*, as Flora's lover George. Fred Yayahkeekoot, who
played the role of Mooshum in the television production the summer
before, also played that role in the revival of the play. Tantoo Martin,
in her professional stage debut, appeared as Flora's sister Maria.

The objectives of the *Don'tcha Know* school tour were three: "to
heighten the awareness of Saskatchewan students in their history
and lifestyle"; "to tour schools in Saskatchewan"; and "to work with
teachers in designing suitable shows to complement the schools'
programming."[199] The company performed between April 27 and
May 12, opening at an English teachers' convention at the University
of Saskatchewan and then touring to Saskatoon region schools.
Twenty-Fifth Street Theatre provided teachers with a Study Guide
which called for a personal level of response ("how did I feel when
I saw it?"), a literary level of response ("What would you say was the
central theme of the play?"), an artistic level of response ("Did the
music/songs support the production?"), and further discussions about

the social and historical issues brought up in the play.[200] Don Perkins reviewed the production on May 4 and did not find much in the script to commend it. "[B]efore the play goes anywhere," he wrote, "someone should sit down and write it."[201]

1979-80 was in many ways a disastrous season on the home front for 25th Street Theatre, despite the fact that its national tour of *Paper Wheat* was garnering great reviews and a national reputation. Tahn had moved his theatre into the regional Triple-A leagues, with a new subscription audience and with a budget of well over $200,000. Now, more was expected of each production. Negative reviews became more unpalatable as the theatre struggled to maintain its good reputation. Twenty-Fifth Street Theatre's subscription audience was less tolerant of artistic failure than earlier audiences had been, and when a theatre is devoted to new indigenous creations, artistic failure happens frequently. The company received terrible reviews for its production of Ernie Carefoot's verse drama *Matonabbee* in March 1980, to which Tahn responded by suggesting that a public debate about the merits of the play be organized, with Tahn and Carefoot on one side of the table and *Star-Phoenix* reviewer Don Perkins on the other side. Tahn was also insistent upon producing his own play *Jacob Kepp*, at last, and he mounted a campaign to attract nationally recognized actors to the cast. While the eventual production of *Jacob Kepp* was well- attended and positively reviewed, the cost of producing such a large-cast play meant that there would be little profit at the end of the season.

Perhaps because collective creation was such a risky business and because his theatre could ill afford to take risks, Tahn announced publicly that 25th Street Theatre was moving away from collective creation and towards the unified vision of a single playwright. "*JAKOB KEPP* is the beginning of a new phase for the 25th Street House Theatre and its Artistic Director, Andras Tahn," wrote Julianne Krause in a press release on October 24. "Andras Tahn hopes to produce a season of completely scripted dramas, shelving (for the time being) collective creations. Although it is collective creations that have put 25th Street House Theatre on the international map, especially with its recent national tour of *PAPER WHEAT*, Tahn wants to move the theatre to the [fine-tuned] single vision of the playwright." In retrospect, although Tahn was clearly trying to put his theatre on higher artistic ground, one might question his choice of producing only scripted dramas after 1979. The company had branded itself, by that time, as a purveyor of populist and collectively created plays, like Paul Thompson's Passe Muraille but from the Canadian home of genuine Tommy Douglas democratic socialism. To mess with that brand was to risk sacrificing a national reputation that had been hard-won. Secondly, because there was no such entity as a Saskatchewan Playwrights' Centre in 1979, there were few professional playwrights living in the province. Tahn's insistence upon producing scripted dramas would force him to contract playwrights from outside the province, moving him away from his original mandate of finding the pulse of his specific region in his productions. Many of the plays produced by the theatre after 1980 had as much to do with Vancouver or Toronto as they did with Saskatchewan.

The season began with a rather dire warning from Walter Learning, the Head of the Theatre Section at the Canada Council. It had not gone unnoticed by the Council that 25th Street Theatre had reneged on producing the promised number of new Canadian plays in 1978-79 and had instead mollified its audiences with presentations of touring shows from other theatres. In a letter of June 20, 1979 to Board chairman Ben McKinnon, Learning made reference to the fact that *The Queen's Cowboy* had been the only new play produced by 25th Street in 1978-79 and that it had played to fewer than a thousand audience members. While approving a renewal of the $25,000 Canada Council grant, he referred to the 1978-79 season as a disastrous one for the theatre. "The renewal of last year's grant is made more in the awareness of the potential of Twenty-fifth Street House Theatre, and the tremendous contribution it can make," Learning wrote, "than in response to the rather disastrous results of last season." To ensure that the theatre produced all of the five new plays it had promised, the Council had chosen to pay out the $25,000 in five instalments for each of the five productions planned for 1979-80. Learning also referred to the fact that Gerry Stoll had resigned as the theatre's administrator at the end of the 1979-80 season and emphasized the importance of hiring a skilled manager, again with a dire prediction for the future if such a person could not be found:

> The hiring of a skilled manager to replace Gerry Stoll is seen as a critical factor in 25th Street House's future. There is no question that the company is capable of producing wonderfully fresh and truly original productions. However, unless a strong manager is found, capable of harnessing the financial resources to provide firm support for the artistic impetus of the theatre, we fear the company will have neither a long nor a happy life.[202]

These were strong words, from one theatre artist to another, and they cannot have been greeted with expressions of tumultuous joy by 25th Street's administrative and artistic team. Gerry Stoll's replacement, Calgary businesswoman Julianne Krause, was hired in time for the company's first production of the 1979-80 season. Among her first acts as the theatre's new manager was to cancel the Season Subscription Series, allowing the company some freedom to close unsuccessful shows early.

While the theatre's relationship with the Canada Council had been jeopardized by some unwise decisions made during the 1978-79 season, its relationship with the Saskatchewan Arts Board also continued to be an unhappy one. The 1979-80 season began on an amicable note, with Joy Cohnstaedt, Executive Director of the Arts Board, writing Ben McKinnon with news that the Arts Board had just approved an operations grant of $15,000 for the theatre.[203] The theatre had also applied for special funding through Festival '80, an Arts Board celebration of Saskatchewan's seventy-fifth birthday, but problems arose when 25th Street Theatre's project synopses was at variance with their original submission for funding. The theatre had originally requested $32,400 through Festival '80, $10,000 to cover pre-production costs for a tour of *The Queen's Cowboy* and $22,400 to cover all costs for a tour of *The Estevan Coal Riot Play*, which was to be directed by Tahn. The Arts Board responded with a grant of $20,000, which forced Tahn and the theatre to change their plans significantly. On December 21, 1979, Tahn received an angry letter from John Griffiths, Acting Performing Arts Co-ordinator for the Arts Board, complaining that a member of Tahn's staff had been reporting to government departments that 25th Street was underfunded on its Festival '80 projects. Griffiths' letter delineates the history of the theatre's Festival '80 application and ends with a thinly veiled warning: "It seems to us that 25th's reports of underfunding made to other agencies about the Board and Celebrate Saskatchewan can only hurt the financial reputation of 25th Street House Theatre."[204] Tahn, who was by this time quite adroit in his dealings with the Arts Board, simply denied that anyone in his company had made represen-tations of underfunding to a government agency but added that it was quite clear to everyone living in the province "that 25th Street Theatre is seriously underfunded by the Saskatchewan Arts Board." He requested that Griffiths phone him the next time a "simple mix up" like this happens rather than devoting time to letter writing when they both clearly had more important matters to attend.[205] At any rate, the projected provincial tour of *The Queen's Cowboy* went ahead as planned in January 1980, but *The Estevan Coal Riot Play* was never produced.

The question of Arts Board underfunding was a perennial one. Tahn referred to it again on March 15, 1980, when he applied for increased funding for the next season. "After reviewing the level of funding provided to other theatres in this province," he wrote, "and after reviewing the nature of these theatres and their levels of activity and artistic accomplishments, I find it appalling that we are receiving a mere $15,000 . . . "[206] Tahn itemized, in the letter, the reasons for 25th Street Theatre's request for a rise in funding: the salary for General Manager had substantially increased with the hiring of Julianne Krause; they were hiring an interim Artistic Director in the coming year, while Tahn would be on leave, and there would be no possibility of employing someone for the pittance that Tahn himself accepted; the theatre was employing a full-time house technician; general costs, including airfare, telephone and postage, were higher than in previous years; there had been increases in Actors' Equity rates; the company needed additional office staff to help with audience development; touring costs had increased; and the company had decided to increase the number of performance days for its shows. On March 17, the new chairman of 25th Street's board, Lynden Hillier, added his voice to the call for increased funding, writing in a letter to Joy Cohnstaedt that "in the future, it will be impossible for us to produce the quality of plays we have in the past for $3,000 per play."[207]

After beginning inauspiciously with the presentation of a musical revue from Regina called *Left Turns* in August (Denise Ball saw much that was fresh and original in the play but "also a number of stale hackneyed routines"), the 1979-80 season got underway with the long-awaited production of Tahn's own play *Jakob Kepp*.[208] Tahn's play was a Saskatchewan epic, in many respects, with a cast of approximately fifteen characters, and it required production values of epic proportions. In early 1979, Tahn mounted a letter-writing campaign to some of Canada's foremost directors and performers, trying to attract them to the production. (Saskatchewan's own Frances Hyland was contacted repeatedly about her possible participation in the project, as were Toronto actors David Gardiner and Jan Rubes, but to no avail.) By the time rehearsals started, Tahn had amassed a cast which included some nationally known actors, and he had hired a British director. The director, Burton Lancaster, had been stage manager of the original West End production of the musical *Oliver!* and had come to Canada in the seventies, where he was founding Artistic Director of Magnus Theatre in Thunder Bay. Burton brought two Magnus Theatre alumni with him when he came to Saskatoon: Claude Rae was cast in the title role, and Patricia Carroll Brown played his wife. Wayne Best, a graduate of Ryerson Polytechnic Institute, was cast as Eric Kepp. Manitoba's Howard Storey played George Kepp, Nova Scotia's

Allan Merovitz was Norman Kepp, and Toronto's Mary Griffen played Norman's wife Theresa. Seanna McKenna, who had recently graduated from the National Theatre School in Montreal, was cast as Helen Kepp. Saskatchewanians Walter Mills, Cindy Dyck, Darcy Dunlop, and Bill Dow rounded out the cast, as well as several local children who were cast as Jakob Kepp's grandchildren.

Jakob Kepp was based on the real-life saga of a Russo-Canadian patriarch named Kasper Beck, who had homesteaded near Allan, Saskatchewan. While many around him had accepted government assistance through the Great Depression, Beck had refused to do so. Consequently, Beck objected when the Canadian government continued to enforce income tax legislation after the Second World War, and he refused to pay what he thought of as an unfair tax. Much of Beck's land was repossessed, and the saga ended tragically when Beck, who was by then an elderly man, committed suicide.

The production, which ran between November 14 and 24 at the new Saskatoon Theatre Centre on 20th Street, played to seventy-five percent houses and was greeted with mixed reviews. When he arrived in Saskatoon at the beginning of rehearsals, Burton Lancaster had declared that there was enough material in Tahn's script for three plays. The play was cut and rearranged during the rehearsal period but, according to reviewers, the alterations were only partially successful. Several of the reviewers also found fault with Tahn's elevated poetic dialogue at moments of high emotion in the script, which contrasted with his extremely colloquial dialogue elsewhere. The play's opening speech was reproduced in the program. Its final lines were as follows: "It is these good customs of our people that/ Like a good candle flickers through the centuries/ A tradition that distinguishes you as an individual/ In the tapestry of this vast country."[209] In the *Star-Phoenix*, Don Perkins suggested that the shuffle of scenes "had a curious effect on continuity." While he felt that the play had much to recommend it, he also saw Tahn's use of "an elevated, poetic mode of expression" as a problem.[210] Kim Dales (later Morrissey), in her CBC Radio review, argued that the production was good but not a runaway hit and cited

Tahn's poor use of poetic metaphor as a major problem. Of the play's opening speech, she wrote:

This sort of speech is disastrous, because it slows down the production, and makes the audience resentful — because it's poetry, and audiences feel they ought to like poetry. Unfortunately it's not good poetry: the image is too flabby, the metaphors aren't carefully worked out, the vocabulary is inappropriate — latinate words like 'distinguished', 'centuries', 'individual' are simply not used by German immigrants, or prairie women when addressing children.[211]

Writing for the *Sheaf*, Donald Campbell called the performance "powerful" but felt that the play needed more cutting, especially in its most poetic moments. "Although beautifully expressing the characters' emotions in mini-soliloquies," he wrote of Tahn's poetry, "it does sound a bit inconsistent with the mainly colloquial dialogue."[212]

In February and March of 1980, two of the company's most celebrated alumni returned triumphantly with plays they had themselves written. Layne Coleman had spent a year revising *The Queen's Cowboy*, with co-writer William Hominuke and with the assistance of Hrant Alianak, and the result was a more immediate telling of the tale of Willie Parker and Mary Allman. The play returned to the stage at the Saskatoon Theatre Centre on February 5, with James Rankin playing Parker and with Bob Collins and Maureen Mckeon as John and Mary Allman. The playwrights had gotten rid of most of the long narrations which Don Perkins had criticized a year earlier, and Perkins was able to write, in a second review, that the "exciting thing about theatre, 25th Street House Style, is the chance to watch new material grow."[213] Perkins also admired the three actors' performances without exception.

Linda Griffiths' one-woman show *Maggie and Pierre*, about the relationship between Canadian Prime Minister Pierre Trudeau and his wife Margaret, had been a hit at Toronto's Theatre Passe Muraille before touring across Canada and to 25th Street Theatre. Griffiths had played Pierre Trudeau in 1978 in a production of *Les Maudits Anglais*, prompting Paul Thompson to suggest that she write a play based on both Trudeaus. She then journeyed to Ottawa, where she met Trudeau (and danced with him) at the Governor General's Ball and where she took copious notes before writing the play. The 1980 Toronto production gleaned fantastic reviews. "The trouble with reviewing Maggie and Pierre," Ray Conologue wrote in the *Globe and Mail*, "is knowing where to start admiring it."[214] Also in the *Globe and Mail*, Rick Groen admired Griffiths' "chameleon quality," both in the play and during interviews.[215] In *Macleans'*, Mark Czarnecki also admired Griffiths the performer: "Sexy, talented and filled with enough energy to make Petrocan obsolete, she deserves packed houses now at Theatre Passe Muraille . . . "[216]

Maggie and Pierre ran in Saskatoon March 18-April 30. Like their colleagues in Toronto, newspaper critics in Saskatoon were enthused about the play. In the *Star-Phoenix*, Don Perkins praised the script and Griffiths' acting. "What *Billy Bishop Goes To War* was to last season, *Maggie and Pierre* is to this one, the play that puts all others in its shadow," Perkins wrote. "There are more than enough places to begin to praise. But no matter where you start, you find Linda Griffiths."[217] In the *Sheaf*, Earl Fogel also complimented Griffiths on her acting. "*Maggie and Pierre* would be worth seeing for the techniques displayed alone," he wrote. "The rapid costume and personality changes that Linda Griffiths undergoes as she changes from Henry (a reporter) to Pierre and Margaret are phenomenal, but there is much more to the play than that."[218] Griffiths continued to tour with the play after her Saskatoon dates and later recreated the performance for a national broadcast on CBC television.

In April, 25th Street Theatre opened Ernie Carefoot's epic drama *Matonabbee: The Classic Killer*, about the great Chipewyan leader who guided Samuel Hearne to the Arctic Ocean in the 1770s. The play is written in verse, which gives the characters a classical, elevated quality; in places where the language works well, *Matonabbee* has the feel of a Greek tragedy. At the climax of the play, for example, when Matonabbee has died and Norton's daughter Mary is left to mourn him, the poetry is plain and forceful: "Come out with me in the plain/ Come out and mark this man's passing./Come out with me/and name our many fears."

Carefoot had been an instructor at Kelsey Institute in Saskatoon and had telephoned Tahn, some months before, about his playscript. Tahn later narrated the eccentric telephone conversation that led to the production of *Matonabbee*:

CAREFOOT
Are you Andy Tahn?

TAHN
Yeah.

CAREFOOT
I have a play.

TAHN
Yeah?

CAREFOOT
And I want you to read it. You'll come to my house tomorrow afternoon at three o'clock, and you will read my play.

TAHN
Well, I don't know about three o'clock tomorrow.

CAREFOOT
Three o'clock tomorrow. Be there.

Tahn was intrigued by the phone call, and so he appeared at Carefoot's house at three the next afternoon. Carefoot promptly escorted Tahn up two flights of stairs, sat him down in a room, plopped a script on the table in front of him and said, "I'll be downstairs if you need anything."[219]

Tahn himself directed the production, which featured the acting talents of Beth Lischeron, Bill Dow, Lois Pendleton, Larry Ewashen, Roger Mckeen, and others. After the theatre had created some suspense by promising that a mysterious actor named Red Dog would be playing the title role, it was revealed on opening night that Red Dog was Carefoot himself. This casting of the playwright, coupled with the playwright's choice of having all his characters speak in verse, made the local critics see red. The play was almost universally panned and in a pronounced fashion. On CBC Arts National, Don Kerr called the language of the play "dead" and found fault with the casting of the play. "There was little attempt to make the Indians look like Indians," he maintained, "and indeed the seven wives look like a sorority, while Carefoot is a red-haired very pale-faced Indian, so that part of the play that is based on racial rivalries does not work."[220] After taking exception to the casting of Carefoot in the title role and to the play's language and symbolism, Kim Dales called the play "boring" in her provincial CBC Radio review. "*Matonabbee* does not explain, or illuminate, or instruct us about Indian and White relationships in the North — nor does it entertain," she said. "The worst that can be said about the play is that it's self-indulgent; the best that can be said is that it's boring. Either way, it's a forgettable moment in Canadian theatre."[221] On *CBC Stereo Morning*, Ron Marken liked the play better than other critics but had some qualms about the clarity of the acting and the cohesiveness of the script: "It needs, first, tough work with the actors: clarity, timing, too much walking and not enough movement. Second, it might be cut in places, or written down more often to the groundlings' level. Perhaps it needs what a friend calls a "feather duster" scene or two — the kind of scene where the maid and the butler explain plainly who is doing what to whom and why."[222]

The coup de grace, as far as the director Andy Tahn was concerned, was Don Perkins' review in the *Star-Phoenix*. Perkins called the production a "graceless procession of embarrassing nonsense," savaged the script and Carefoot's performance, and ended on a damning note: "As a workshop presentation of a new script in progress, Carefoot's Matonabee might be acceptable. As a finished product, ready for public consumption, it seriously mars an otherwise successful season for 25th Street House Theatre."[223] Perkins' review prompted Tahn to write a two-page letter to the editor of the *Saskatoon Star-Phoenix* on April 21, calling the review "unacceptable by any professional standards." Outraged that Perkins had failed to mention his direction or the contributions of many of the actors, Tahn argued that Perkins had ignored the concept put forth in the script:

> The reviewer missed the entire concept of the script MATONABBEE and the staging of it. This is very obvious from the things he chose to criticize. He criticized the lack of black wigs and real Indians to play Indians. MATONABBEE was not meant to be an Indian play. Nor is it a documentary as my production of PAPER WHEAT was. MATONABBEE is a style drama in the vein of the classical theatre of Sophocles, Shakespeare and Chekhov. It grapples with the inner and outer truths affecting Matonabbee — first a man then an Indian.[224]

Tahn ends his letter by referring to Carefoot as "a very significant new playwright."[225] Later on the same day, Tahn wrote directly to Perkins, challenging the reviewer to "justify" his review in a public debate after a performance of *Matonabbee*. In an April 22 letter, Perkins refused to enter into an in-person debate, writing to Tahn: "I believe the review explains itself. You know from past experience how and through whom to take issue with the editorial content of this, or any other newspaper. I also think little could or would be done in a public forum to change either of our relative positions."[226]

On May 7-18, the season ended with a presentation of the 25th Street Theatre-Necessary Angel co-production *Boom*. Conceived and directed by Richard Rose, and enacted by Joe Charles, Ian Black, Roger Mckeen, Agi Gallus, and Shelley Goldstein, *Boom* was a modernization of Buchner's revolutionary nineteenth-century drama *Woyzeck*. Rose's modernization dealt with the effects of the Uranium industry in Northern Saskatchewan upon a young Metis named Joe Speck (played by Charles). On *CBC Stereo Morning*, Ron Marken found much to applaud in the play but noted that Rose had created two plays, not one: " . . . BOOM is both Joe Speck's play and a play about nuclear development and in a sense that makes it two plays whereas the forerunner was only one play."[227] In the *Star-Phoenix*, Don Perkins argued for better pacing and compression of the play. "Boom is a one-act play, but the 'act' is over 90 minutes," he wrote on May 2. "There appears to be some intent to accelerate the action as the process of change sets in, but this is not consistent, and there are several scenes that drag as a result. If Boom is to remain a one-act piece, it will have to be compressed."[228] The production toured nationally, after its run in Saskatoon. In the *Globe and Mail*, Victor Paddy wrote that the play got off to a slow start but picked up momentum over the course of the evening. He admired the versatility of the acting — with six actors playing sixteen roles — and Rose's courage to experiment: "Boom displays a willingness to experiment and an understanding of how to create a believable environment with a spare, ever-changing set."[229]

May was a month of upheaval at 25th Street Theatre in 1980. Two press releases hinted at the pandemonium which must have been going on in the administrative offices of the theatre. The first, dated May 8, announced the resignation of Julianne Krause as general manager. Krause cited lack of financial support from federal and provincial funding agencies as the reason for her departure. She noted, in the press release, that 1979-80 had been the theatre's most successful season, with the theatre playing to 7,138 patrons in Saskatoon and to 53,004 outside the city, with the tours of *Paper Wheat* and *The Queen's Cowboy*. Only *Matonabbee* had drawn small audiences, and yet, Krause noted, the theatre would have a $25,000 deficit even after its major successes. Regular operational funding from the Arts Board had amounted to a mere $19,000, she said, and the Canada Council had provided only $25,000. Krause blamed the provincial funding agency, mostly, for the theatre's poor financial health because she felt that the Arts Board should have had a better understanding of the theatre taking place in its own province. "This is one of the most vital and popular theatres in Canada," she wrote, "and Saskatchewan should now stop paying lip service and start providing adequate funds to the 25th Street Theatre, the worst funded professional theatre in the province."[230] After accepting Krause's resignation, board chairman Lyndon Hillier announced that he would serve as Acting General Manager until a new general manager could be hired, with Sandra

Dibb in the Audience Development and Fundraising Office and with Paulette Hanson as Administrative Assistant.

Andy Tahn had decided to take a one-year leave of absence from the theatre and was subsequently recruited to serve as interim Artistic Director at Theatre Network in Edmonton. George Ryga's daughter Tanya had asked Tahn to replace Theatre Network's former Artistic Director Mark Manson, who had abruptly resigned. "That was a tough year," Tahn said later. "They had no building and no board. So we formed a board, and we found a building that they used for many, many years . . . My job was to doctor and fix the wounded animal . . . We took some huge risks, but the theatre survived. And went on."[231]

The second press release of the month, dated May 21, announced the appointment of Layne Coleman as interim Artistic Director. Coleman had based his career in Toronto for the previous two years, only intermittently returning to Saskatchewan to perform in *Generation and ½* and his own *The Queen's Cowboy*. In Toronto, he had amassed a number of CBC television credits, including roles in *Harvest, The Great Detective, The Phoenix Team*, and *The War Bride*. He had also toured the British Isles with Theatre Passé Muraille. He had been chosen for the position of Artistic Director from among fifteen applicants, most of whom were directors and actors from Toronto. The press release emphasized Coleman's knowledge of Western Canada as one of the reasons for his hiring. Coleman would oversee a season, however, that was by far the most controversial and cosmopolitan — with little that could be described as "regional" in it — in the theatre's history.[232]

SEVEN:
"WE'RE NOT HOKIES AND WE'RE NOT HAVE-NOTS"
(1980-81)

ANDY TAHN HAD BEEN gracious enough to allow Coleman the freedom to choose his own season (with the exception of the production of a play entitled *Sisters*, which had been commissioned for August 1980 by St. Angela's Convent at Prelate), and Coleman was adamant that the 1980-81 season would be a reflection of modern times in Saskatchewan and Canada. He was tired of the grassroots image of 25th Street Theatre; there would be no collectively written *Paper Wheat*s during his tenure, if all went well. "I want to get away from the 'grassroots' image of this theatre; the 'we're poor but we're good for you' idea," he told Don Perkins in an interview on August 26, 1980:

> Most specifically, I'm going to do very contemporary things because this is the world we live in. I don't see the need to romanticize the West. We're past the point where we're 'funny little Saskatchewan.'
>
> And we're not pioneers here anymore, we're not hokies and we're not have-nots, and it's time to stop pretending we are. We have no need to be afraid of success and only ourselves to blame for our failures.
>
> We've suffered intensely in the past, but we're rich now and we have certain freedoms that most of the world do not enjoy. We're not underdogs anymore.

But we live in very dangerous times, when you can't be sure about the next year. And the world is no longer as simple as Left — Centre — Right. I want the theatre to reflect that discomfort, so we'll be looking at things more the way they are, in a naturalistic, more documentary style, and look for modern-day heroes.[233]

The season Coleman announced in September would make good on his promise. It included Marc Diamond's punk rock play *The Ziggy Effect*, Elaine Williams' *Conversations With Girls in Private Rooms*, Jim Garrard's *Cold Comfort*, and Don Wise's *Rodeo*. As Don Perkins wrote at the end of the season, there wasn't a prairie farmer to be found anywhere and the one rural Saskatchewan adult to appear was Floyd in *Cold Comfort*, who "was a long way from anything in *Paper Wheat* or *Generation and a Half.*"[234] The plays also had more literary merit than most of the work seen on 25th Street Theatre's stages in previous seasons. In Garrard and Diamond particularly, Coleman had found two assured playwrights with distinct voices. Unfortunately, even productions of assured playwrights' plays can lead to problems, and *Cold Comfort* would later come under fire for what its critics referred to as lewdness.

Added to that were the difficulties of two theatre companies trying to co-exist and work around each other's schedules in the old church which had become the Saskatoon Theatre Centre. The difficulties began to surface early in the season, when Persephone Theatre's production of *On Golden Pond* had done poorly in the first weeks of its run but had started to fill the house by its last week. Persephone's new artistic director, Eric Schneider, wanted to hold over *On Golden Pond* but found, to his consternation, that a hold-over was impossible. It was vital that Persephone vacate the theatre space on the appointed day, October 12, since Coleman, who had been rehearsing *The Ziggy Effect* in the poorly heated Modern Press Building for the past three weeks, was set to open his production on October 17. Schneider was not amused with the situation when he was interviewed by Don Perkins on October 18; he saw his theatre being handcuffed, through lack of two separate stages for two distinct companies, into producing nothing but short-run plays. "The best advertising is word of mouth, but it is slow," he said. "Many people, certainly people who've never been, see going to the theatre as an act of courage, and short runs are an easy way out."[235] There were other problems associated with the Theatre Centre on 20th Street and Avenue H: its backstage area was woefully inadequate due to lack of space in the wings or behind the stage; it had no rehearsal space; it only accommodated two hundred spectators; and there was a problem with brand recognition, when audience members would sometimes show up for a play, not knowing whether it was produced by 25th Street Theatre or by Persephone. As Schneider and Coleman argued, however, the biggest problem was the tight schedule which necessitated short runs. Coleman added his voice to Schneider's, maintaining that "you just can't make it pay on a three-week run."[236]

Fortunately, there were members of the artistic community and a few city aldermen who recognized the problem and were trying to do something about it. A move was afoot to create a purpose-built theatre centre in Saskatoon. Alderman Pat Lorje chaired a special technical committee for the development of a theatre centre and argued that such a facility would be mainly for professional theatre companies. While her committee's report was criticized by other aldermen, particularly Owen Mann, Henry Dayday, and Morris Chernesky, for ignoring the needs of amateur theatre groups in the city, Lorje defended her committee's decision by arguing that Council should beware of trying to achieve too much with the new theatre centre. "If we try to build a multi-purpose facility," she said, "we'll end up building a no-purpose facility."[237] The artistic directors of Persephone and 25th Street were both in favour of a purpose-built theatre centre back in 1980, but they were bothered by the lack of clarity surrounding the project. "I'm firmly in favor of a new theatre," Schneider told the *StarPhoenix*, "but nobody has firmly stated who is to use it or how it is to be used." Coleman expressed the hope that any theatre centre would be built "specifically for the groups that exist, to accommodate their styles."[238]

Both seemed to agree that the new theatre centre should provide space in which two theatre companies could build their audiences and that such a facility would have at least two main stages.

As well as inheriting a less than satisfactory theatre space, Coleman would also inherit a $22,000 deficit. Twenty-Fifth Street Theatre had requested, as usual, a rise in funding from both provincial and federal funding agencies, and they did receive a small increase — total funding from the Canada Council equalled $35,000, coupled with $19,000 from the Arts Board. (The Arts Board's letter of confirmation about funding came with a reminder that "management/administrative counseling is available either on a one-time or on-going basis" to the company.[239]) The theatre company also applied for deficit reduction through the federal Department of Communications; under the Cultural Initiatives Program, the federal government would pay off a third of the deficit, the provincial government would pay off another third, and the theatre would pay off the final third.

Coleman was, nevertheless, enthusiastic about the coming season. New board members had been added; joining Lynden Hillier (President), Ben McKinnon, Garry Rathberger, Cam Partridge and Walter Mills, were Gerry Stoll, Zenon Belak and Richard Roberts. (By the end of the season, the board would have grown to thirteen persons with the inclusion of Betty Ann Heggie, Joan Frederickson, Ollie Cowan, Stuart Poole and Holly Ann Knott.) Sandra Dibb had agreed to step into the role of Business Manager. And, as Coleman wrote in an August 13, 1980 letter to the Canada Council's Cathy McKeehan (who later became General Manager of Persephone Theatre and, still later, of the Saskatoon Symphony Orchestra), there was no scarcity of new plays to be worked on. Coleman thanked McKeehan for the Council's increase in funding, which he interpreted as a personal vote of confidence, and expressed joy and fear at the coming season. "I am enjoying most of my new duties immensely," he wrote. "(We just painted the offices — that was somewhat less than enjoyable.) However, this year ahead seems to be coming at me like a Mac Truck with all its wheels smoking."[240] While some of the 1980-81 productions might be worthy of a tour at a future date, Coleman vowed in his letter that the theatre would "retrench, stay at home, and try and create some new things."

St. Angela's Convent had paid the theatre company $9,000, and box office receipts up to the cost of producing the drama, for its commissioned production of *Sisters*. Featured in the cast were Bill Dow, Eileen Mackenzie, Irene Blum, Sandy Tucker, Marjorie Beaucage, Shay Garner, and Jonathan Barker. The play, which was collectively written under the direction of Ruth Smillie, was to be a history of the Ursuline Nuns in Saskatchewan over the past seventy-five years. Its heartwarming scenes included one in which a young lady announces to her family that she intends to enter the convent and another in which a young novice gives up her box of chocolates to a hungry traveller. Traditional Saint Angela hymns were the basis for the background music.

The play ran August 15-18, 1980, and was attended by over 1500 patrons in the community of Prelate on the western edge of Saskatchewan. Because the production never toured beyond Prelate (a tour had been planned and was partially funded through Celebrate Saskatchewan but was cancelled when the requisite number of bookings were not achieved), reviews are scarce. An anonymous reviewer in the *Prairie Messenger Catholic Weekly* quoted Sister Philomena, who had approached Andy Tahn with the idea of the commission and who maintained that in *Sisters*, "the 25th Street Theatre Players brought back many memories and taught us something new about our past."[241]

Marc Diamond's new play *The Ziggy Effect* was Coleman's choice for kicking off the new season in Saskatoon. Diamond, a theatre professor at Simon Fraser University at the time, called his script a "New Wave Survival Play." In the script, Diamond focused on the generation gap, and struggle for territory, between a teenaged punker and his unhappily married parents. The first scene is between father and mother, who worry about young Ziggy's laziness and his penchant for composing and singing lewd songs. Ziggy's father Bill, an ex-hippy-turned-survivalist, is particularly outraged by the songs. "Have you heard them?" he asks his wife Sylvia. "Have you heard 'Panty Love'? It's panties that I love. It's panties that I love. Then he takes a pair of panties and shoves them in his mouth."[242] It is easy to see that *The Ziggy Effect* was a departure from almost anything 25th Street Theatre had produced in the past; it was not necessarily a play that more conservative audience members would like, but it was a good play all the same. The play ends with the marital breakup of Bill and Sylvia. Bill is left in the house with Ziggy and his friends Val and Moon, who relegate Bill to the basement. Roles have changed, as Ziggy signals when he orders Bill downstairs: "Now you go down those stairs and I don't want to see you in this part of the house again."[243] Ziggy's final song is a taunt delivered at the audience: "This is the future I hope you like it/This is the future I hope you like it."[244] Sandra Dibb was later to write that *The Ziggy Effect* "was more than just an electric way to open the 25th Street Mainstage Season — it was also an indication to our loyal Saskatoon and surrounding country audiences that 25th Street Theatre was embarking on a new voyage of theatrical discovery."[245] Diamond was paid royalties of $1500, or 10% of gross box office revenue (whichever was greater), for the production of his play.

The play opened on October 16 with Stuart Clow, James Dugan, Andrew McIlroy, Penelope Stella, and Karen Woolridge in the cast. (Unlike many other 25th Street Theatre plays, *The Ziggy Effect* had been performed earlier in Ottawa, under the direction of the playwright, and Diamond had insisted that many of the original cast be included in the 25th Street production.) The *Sheaf's* Rod Macpherson had praise for much of the production; he wrote that *The Ziggy Effect*

> is potentially as powerful as the first episode of *All in the Family* must have been in 1972 before we knew what it was, before we realized it was OK to laugh. *Ziggy* takes the same sort of risks — big risks — and wins most of them. It has the same sort of inspired casting, with players who *are* their characters as much as they act them. Most of all, it's *true*: the shock of recognition is the same even if you don't know punkers or

survivalists; you simply can't imagine them being other than as portrayed.[246]

The only criticism Macpherson levelled at the play was for its lack of plot; he wrote that the playwright simply seized on the old "I Love Lucy" gag of "Mom-leaves-the-house-to-junior," sinking the play into "situation comedy and implausibility." Although *CBC Arts National* reviewer Lynn Morris criticized the "low-keyed style of delivery" in the production (and especially "unnecessary pauses, slow entrances, and lengthy blackouts"), she also argued that *The Ziggy Effect* was a harbinger of good things to come. "In spite of the risks attendant on working with new material, the commitment opens the door to interesting possibilities, as 'The Ziggy Effect' proves," she said. "The programmed fare is inventive, experimental, and refreshing; and gives lively promise of an interesting season ahead at 25th Street Theatre."[247] In the *StarPhoenix*, Don Perkins noted that *The Ziggy Effect* was "a radical departure" for 25th Street Theatre. Perkins admired the play and many of the performances although he also noted that there was not much action for long stretches and that "it might be possible to cut a fair amount out of the second act."[248] In *Maclean's*, Mark Czarnecki was effusive about the production. "*Ziggy* is a classic example of how an original Canadian work can be collectively created," he wrote, "fine-tuned by a skilled playwright, produced by a small experimental theatre to international standards of acting skill and technical expertise *and* still be sponsored by a large corporation (Labatt's)."[249]

Under the pseudonym Elaine Williams, Coleman and Bill Hominuke wrote *Conversations With Girls In Private Rooms*, the second mainstage play of the season. The play examined a day in the life of six pleasure-seekers who, while sedating themselves with drugs and alcohol, occasionally dream of getting back to the mainstream — in the words of Sandra Dibb, "finding someone to love, becoming happily married, finding success."[250] In three main segments, Coleman and Hominuke depict the emptiness of these valueless young lives. Eventually, several of the characters pair off and wind up in bed together. It was all, according to critic Ron Marken, "glossy fantasy," the men alternately sexual athletes or innocents, the women all voracious and readily available.[251] As Coleman later wrote, the play was an attempt to reproduce "the banality of present day conversation." According to Coleman, the play's title "was based on a sign I once saw in a back alley behind Yonge Street. That sign read, 'Conversations with naked girls in private rooms.' A radio host for CBC recommended I take the 'naked' out of the title. So I did."[252]

Coleman himself directed *Conversations With Girls In Private Rooms*, with Karen Woolridge, Paula Schappert, Gina Healey, Stuart Clow, Andrew McIlroy, and Bill Dow in the cast. (If the casting looked eerily similar to the casting for *The Ziggy Effect*, it is because Coleman had committed himself to using many of the same actors from show to show, in order to save transportation costs. In fact, Woolridge and Clow would both perform in three or more shows at 25th Street Theatre in the 1980-81 season.) The casting would itself pose some challenges, especially as Coleman had offered one of the roles to Gina Healey, who had performed as a dancer in a high-end club in Toronto. Healey had led an interesting life. "She lived for three years with the drummer from the Police and various other rock stars," according to Coleman. "Gina was the inspiration for the film *Flashdance*. The writer for that feature based his story on Gina and the club she worked in. She came to Saskatoon and I had to get her out of a law problem . . . in Edmonton where she was the crown's witness for a big LSD bust. She was under police protection in Edmonton. She got to come to our opening and witness for only one day. She told the judge in Edmonton that she was an actress now. The defendant's attorney asked [her], 'How long have you been an actress, Miss Healey?' . . . Gina answered honestly, 'Three weeks.' The judge was amused and allowed her to make our opening."[253] The play ran between December 5 and 20 in the Saskatoon Theatre Centre.

Reviews were not glowing, most of them focusing on the poorly organized script. On *CBC Arts National*, Ron Marken was bemused by the lack of information about the playwright. "No information whatsoever is available about the author — except she's from Alberta, and it's her first play and she 'wants to keep a low profile' (with good cause)," Marken said. "Elaine Williams' script is simply appalling; a two-hour string of banalities and clichés."[254] The script aside, Marken was quick to compliment the director, cast, and designers on a "very visual spectacle":

> I have compliments for the director, Layne Coleman. After a few ragged transitions between scenes, the production moved very smoothly, with steady, full-blast concentration demanded of the actors every moment. He made the whole a very visual spectacle, and even exciting at times, using movement, light, costume, and music extravagantly. The set design, by George Fathers, amplified by light designer Dan Mooney, had just the right blend of trendiness and plastic sameness.

Don Perkins, reviewing for the *StarPhoenix* (which had recently dropped its hyphen), concurred with Marken that the script needed tightening. "Somehow it is just not enough to keep showing how pointless these lives are, and have it hold much interest," Perkins wrote. "We spend a lot of time watching nothing happen."[255] Perkins also commended the actors and the "imaginative, graphic direction" of Layne Coleman but found that they were all hamstrung by a script "that takes too long to overstate the obvious."

Just before Christmas, 25th Street Theatre created a collectively written fairy tale called *Magical Festive Fantasy*, "with minstrel music, clowning, and puppetry."[256] The production featured Mark Eriksson, Marie-Helene Bourret, Kim Bater, and Maureen Johnson in its cast. It toured to hospitals, orphanages, daycare centres, and nursing homes, offering some twenty-seven performances in eleven communities. The production was an attempt to recreate the excitement which had been attendant upon the earlier 25th Street *Christmas Candy* presentations.

If *The Ziggy Effect* and *Conversations With Girls In Private Rooms* had stretched Saskatoon audiences in interesting ways, the third production of the season *Cold Comfort* would have them stretched to the breaking point. Jim Garrard's play, which he described as a "story of love and bondage on the Canadian prairie," would eventually inspire the wrath of several 25th Street Theatre patrons. The play is set in a run-down service station near Gull Lake, Saskatchewan. In the opening scenes, we discover that garage owner Floyd has rescued Stephen on the highway during a blizzard and has decided to bring Stephen home as a possible mate for Floyd's daughter Dolores. "I hope he suits you," Floyd tells Dolores. "Happy birthday."[257] Garrard's script features some raw dialogue, as is evidenced by the following scene in which Stephen tries to clarify Dolores' expectations:

STEPHEN (Chooses his words)
Do you want me to fuck you?

DOLORES (Pause)
That's pretty direct.

STEPHEN
That's not an answer.

DOLORES
Well, to tell you the truth, I'd like to find out what it's like.[258]

The greatest potential for offending the audience was not this dialogue however, but was Dolores taking a bath in full view of the audience. The play ends with Floyd and Dolores driving off and leaving Stephen incapacitated in the abandoned gas station.

Directed by the playwright, *Cold Comfort* ran between January 29 and February 14 in the Saskatoon Theatre Centre, with Gary Reineke as Floyd, Karen Woolridge as Dolores, and Layne Coleman as Stephen. Reineke had just won a Best Actor Dora Award in Toronto, and it was a measure of 25th Street's reputation and success that the theatre was able to attract a top-flight Canadian actor to take part in a premiere of a new play. Critical reception of the play varied but tended to focus on bewildering aspects of the production and to emphasize how out of character this new edginess was in comparison with previous 25th Street offerings. "When members of a contemporary audience leave during the performance of a play," said Lynn Morris on *CBC Arts National*, "I want to know why. It's surely no longer a question of social propriety; but it may well be a gauge of aesthetic propriety."[259] Morris, who argued that the play came off as gratuitous in its emphasis on violence and sexuality because the characters' actions were unsubstantiated, and therefore unmotivated, in the script, described the production as a frustrating experience. "Here is an exciting playwright — who has simply not yet mastered his craft," she said. "If Garrard could extend to the dialogue and the action the conviction he brings to his settings perhaps the audience that did remain wouldn't have been stricken by the sense of having witnessed a near miss." In the *StarPhoenix*, Don Perkins maintained that Garrard's "bewildering, unsettling, fascinating" script and production was on the leading edge of 25th Street Theatre's declared desire to challenge Saskatoon theatre audiences. Unlike Morris, Perkins was fond of the play and the production; he wrote:

> Garrard as a playwright and director asks a lot from his audience, especially patience. He has directed to a slow, low-key level that leaves you wondering if things are going to start; if anything is ever going to happen. Then he sneaks things in on you so you are left saying "run that by me again." He cleverly insinuates a perplexing array of questions, then like a composer ending on an unresolved chord, he leaves the audience suspended, groping for answers.[260]

Roving Southam News reporter Jamie Portman also commented on how the production was a departure from traditional 25th Street fare. "Good grief!" he wrote in the *Calgary Herald*, "Are there no certainties left? Can it really be that the theatre which gave Canada the folksy and lovable *Paper Wheat* has shifted abruptly into a world of madness and sexual obsession?"[261] Like Perkins, however, Portman was convinced that the play was worthy:

> It would be tempting to dismiss all this as perverse, self-indulgent nonsense were it not for certain significant factors. One can't ignore the strength of the writing — the sardonic humor, the playwright's gift for razor-sharp dialogue, his uncanny ear for the vernacular, the atmosphere of heightened realism and above all his success in suggesting that, given a specific synthesis of

character, environment and circumstance, the most bizarre
situations can logically emerge.

Portman ended his column by referring to Garrard as "one of the most
interesting but disturbing talents on Canada's current playwriting
scene."

A few Saskatoon theatre-goers disagreed with Portman's
assessment. One patron, calling himself "a disappointed customer,"
wrote to the theatre expressing his horror at the language in the play.
"I have been to a lot of stage shows but this one beats all for filth,"
he wrote. "Maybe Gary Reineke is a good actor but the writer who
made up that must be sick and I mean sick!!!!"[262] Jerry and Brenda
Hilderman mounted a letter-writing campaign to the director, to
Credit Union Central (who supported the production financially) and
to City Council, complaining about vulgar language and nudity in
Garrard's play. All of the letters were dated February 3, 1981. In their
letter to the director, the Hildermans noted that there had not been
signs posted in the theatre informing potential audience members of
the rough language and nudity in the play. They thanked the theatre
for posting signs after the opening and also for refunding the costs
of their tickets, then criticized the script for its vulgar language and
for its bathing scene. "We regret that you do not, as evidenced by this
production, understand the beauty of sex, as God created it," they
wrote. "It is a shame it must be portrayed in such a manner."[263] In their
letter to City Council, the Hildermans requested that a censorship
committee be struck in order to deal with productions like *Cold
Comfort*. "We would appreciate a reply from the city council regarding
a censorship committee that could be assigned to this, if possible, and
future previewing and censors of the Theatre's presentations to warrant
support of such drama," they wrote. "We are also of the opinion that
ratings should be required of the theatre on their drama." Perhaps the
most damaging letter went to Eldon Anderson, Corporate Secretary
for Credit Union Central, because it suggested that the Credit Union,
and other corporations like it, should not offer financial support for
the morally degrading work of the theatre. "In *our* eyes," they wrote,

"this particular production has done nothing for your own and your company's image."

Others in the community rallied behind Garrard and the theatre company. In letters to the editor of the *StarPhoenix*, E.F. Dyck and Jan Johnson expressed their approval of the production. "I too saw 25th Street Theatre's production of *Cold Comfort*; I too was shocked by the language and by the circumstances surrounding the nude scene," wrote Dyck. "But to suggest that the play was 'morally degrading' and offered 'no respect to love or sex or the institution of the family' is simply to misinterpret this play in particular and to misunderstand the functions of drama in general."[264] Noting that the Hildermans had left the play before it ended, Dyck suggested that the function of shock, in drama generally, is to effect an Aristotelian purgation of emotions. "Of course," Dyck wrote, "those who leave a play early cannot experience either the 'pity' for the victim or the 'fear' for themselves which the drama has always effected." Johnson was even more whole-heartedly in support of the production. She and her husband had seen the play twice. Johnson wrote that the play's language was appropriate to its characters and that the bathing scene contained "no suggestive gestures, eroticism, or vulgarity."[265] In a February 7 letter sent not to the *StarPhoenix* but to Layne Coleman, Saskatoon actor John Wright offered his support to the embattled artistic director, expressing his gratitude to Coleman and the rest of the cast "for providing me with a rare occasion to honestly say I was thoroughly entertained by a live theatre performance."[266]

Jim Garrard had been no stranger to controversy in his long and varied career in Canadian theatre, and he knew the value of creating the kind of controversy which drew patrons into the theatre. In 1969, while teaching at Rochdale College in Toronto, he had directed Rochelle Owens' play *Futz*, which detailed the emotional and erotic attachment of a farmer and his pig and which had so infuriated civic authorities that police began issuing summonses to theatre personnel. "The cops came breaking in on us," Garrard told Richard Ouzounian of the *Toronto Star* about forty years later, "after a front-page story in the *Star* about how obscene we were. They issued 32 [summonses] a day, every day for a month, but they didn't shut the production down."[267] There is no response from Garrard, in the 25th Street Collection at the University of Saskatchewan, to the controversy surrounding the production of *Cold Comfort* in Saskatoon, but he was savvy enough to include most of the letters to the editor of the *StarPhoenix* in his promotion package when the play was produced at the Toronto Theatre Festival in May 1981. The controversy brought patrons into the theatre, and *Cold Comfort* became one of the most popular productions at the Festival.

When the discussion had not abated by late February, the *StarPhoenix's* Ned Powers provided a summation of the month's events, noting that 25th Street Theatre had garnered a great deal of publicity from the controversy surrounding *Cold Comfort*. "If theatre companies measure public relations success in terms of column inches, with little regard for the content, they have to be pleased," wrote Powers. "But if they read the messages clearly, noting the negative insinuations, parochial patronage and some strongly-attributed quotes, they have to feel less than satisfied."[268] Powers was particularly piqued by a recent interview with Coleman which had appeared in the *Regina Leader-Post*, in which the artistic director asserted that a certain kind of regional pride results from feelings of insecurity and inferiority. "For some reason, the people here feel hard done by, as if they're saints of some kind," Coleman had said in an interview with Denise Ball. "I was born here and grew up here. The truth is that there are a lot of creeps in rural Saskatchewan. That kind of regionalistic pride comes out of an inferiority complex."[269] Expressing his aggravation at Coleman's unbridled statements, Powers suggested that the theatre's board of directors should step into the fray. "Admittedly he has a valid point in trying to build new audiences and he can afford to gamble with 25th Street because its success doesn't really depend upon the reaction of subscribers," Powers wrote. "But the stark reality of some of the plays he has chosen and the stern comments he offered in the *Leader-Post* interview, if he admits to them, tend to put Coleman in a position where he should be answering to his board of directors."

Years later, Layne Coleman was philosophical about Powers' comments and the hoopla surrounding *Cold Comfort*, noting that he was subsequently interviewed by the *StarPhoenix*'s Don Perkins and that he praised "the Saskatchewan status quo on that occasion." *Cold Comfort* was the only production, during Coleman's tenure as sole Artistic Director of the company, which was sold out through the entire run. "I can assure you," he wrote me in an email, "that the few people who wrote letters were in the minority. I had never seen such laughter as during Gary Reineke's 'the fuckin' frog hockey team.' I was amazed at all the women in the audience poking their men in the ribs to say. 'That's just like you, you know.' I believe we had standing ovations for every show."[270]

The angry reaction to *Cold Comfort* was still a hot topic in the theatre community in late February 1981, when I arrived in Saskatoon to perform as Edmund in Persephone's production of *Long Day's Journey Into Night*. Persephone's cast and crew were profoundly aware of the situation, especially since one of our company, Graham McPherson, had also been contracted to perform in 25th Street's production of *Rodeo* in March. We at Persephone were performing in an American classic, and so we knew that we were unlikely to create the kind of fervour that *Cold Comfort* had attracted. (The closest we would come to having a patron walk out of the theatre was when a friend of mine, a university professor and a bit of a ladies' man, came down to the dressing rooms at the interval and announced that he loved the production and my performance in it but that he was off to another appointment and could not stay for the rest of the show. I imagined that his appointment was with a lady.) We rehearsed at the draughty Modern Press Building while *Cold Comfort* finished its run and discussed 25th Street's problems over beers at the Albany Hotel. McPherson was particularly troubled: he had received an under-written script called *The Buckle* and had little idea of what the final product might look like. There were also rumours of a financial crisis at 25th Street Theatre, and several of the cast of *Long Day's Journey Into Night* attended a rodeo dance fundraiser for the company which, like all good rodeo dances, featured a fist-fight when some real-life cowboys arrived.

Coleman must have suddenly thought that he was born under an unlucky star, for his production of *The Buckle* was beset by problems from the beginning. The problems began on March 1, when Don Wise's script had been due. Wise, a photographer and journalism teacher from Calgary, submitted to the theatre what could be best described as a work-in-progress, a partial script with several scenes alluded to but missing. The concept of a play glorifying the modern-day cowboy had been Coleman's, according to letters on file at the University of Saskatchewan's Special Collections Library. The agreement by which Wise came to write the play had been verbal. Coleman contended that the agreement had specified three conditions: that the complete script would be received in its final form by 25th Street Theatre no later than March 1; that the script would be suitable for professional staging; and that the script would glorify the professional western cowboy. In a letter of March 4, Coleman suggested that Wise had defaulted on all three counts; he wrote: "Unfortunately, the material forwarded by you to 25th Street Theatre: 1) is not in final form and is incomplete (with several total scenes missing); 2) is unsuitable for professional production; and 3) portrays the cowboys as being highly racist, with unsavoury attitudes towards women, and with few socially redeeming features."[271] Coleman informed Wise, in the strongly worded letter, that the company would be proceeding to write a collective script but that Wise would nevertheless be paid $500 "for your time, advice, and for the three photographs provided to use on promotion." He also offered to credit Wise in the program, as follows: "25th Street Theatre would like to thank Don Wise for his special insight into the inside world of rodeos and their characters." Wise's incisive response came in a telegram the next day: "CHOICE: EITHER PRODUCE MY STAGE PLAY, 'THE BUCKLE' AS WRITTEN, OR I WILL TAKE ACTION TO PROTECT MY PROPERTY. REPLY EXPECTED BY

8 PM TONIGHT — MARCH 5, 1981."[272] After speaking to Wise by telephone, Sandra Dibb was able to negotiate a middle ground: the theatre would pay Wise a thousand dollars, which had been the sum originally agreed upon when Wise had been contracted to write the play; Wise was offered twenty-five per cent of future royalties; and the theatre offered to credit his contribution as "written by Layne Coleman with Don Wise and the original cast."[273] When the play, which had been re-titled *Rodeo*, opened on Friday, March 20, the program contained the following credits: "Written by Don Wise with Layne Coleman, Graham McPherson, Karen Woolridge, Stuart Clow, Paul Whitney, Shay Garner and Stephen Shipper. Characters, background, and certain aspects of the story by Don Wise. Book by Layne Coleman and cast."[274]

The script was only the beginning of Coleman's problems. Rehearsals for the production were stormy, with the cast, the director, and Coleman under a great deal of pressure to produce a viable show in a short time. A few days before opening, the director Stephen Shipper quit the production, leaving Coleman to take on the directorial duties. Then, during dress rehearsal, Graham McPherson, who was cast in the key role of Hank, a washed up rodeo rider, twisted his knee and was unable to perform on opening night. Coleman was left with an unhappy choice: he could postpone the opening indefinitely (and no one knew how long McPherson would be incapacitated) or he could assume McPherson's role. He chose the latter, rehearsing steadily on the day of the opening and then turning in a performance which, according to Don Perkins, "grew better and better as the premier performance moved along."[275] Later, during the run of the play, actor Stuart Clow was stricken with mononucleosis and had to be replaced.

Rodeo opened March 20, with Shay Garner, Karen Woolridge, Paul Whitney, Stuart Clow, and Coleman in the cast. (McPherson returned to the production when his knee had healed and was able to perform in the final week of the run.) Although the *StarPhoenix* review was quite favourable, the production did not fill the seats at the Saskatoon Theatre Centre. Sandra Dibb attributed the poor audience turnout to the fact that 25th Street Theatre was competing with the university Drama Department, which was producing *The Elephant Man* during the same time period.[276] *Rodeo* received a standing ovation on opening night. According to Don Perkins, the directness and brevity of the script were its chief virtues. "That is not to say there are no problems with it," he wrote, "but there is enough to show it could develop into a strong piece of theatre. Just now, it isn't exactly clear whether we are watching a 'Last Hurrah' as Hank goes out in a blaze of glory, winning one last buckle against all odds, or whether this is the tragedy of a has-been who forgets to quit living his own image."[277]

Twenty-Fifth Street had originally planned to co-produce, with Edmonton's Theatre Network, Ernie Carefoot's play *Rumplestiltzkin Breaks Out* in April, but financial problems mitigated against a Saskatoon opening. Sandra Dibb explained the cancellation of the production to the Canada Council's Cathy McKeehan, attributing the cancellation to an unexpected financial blow to the theatre company. The provincial electrical inspector had arrived at the Theatre Centre in March and given notice "that a minimum of $26,419 in electrical renovations to the Saskatoon Theatre Centre is required by April 10."[278] Dibb hoped the Canada Council would not penalize 25th Street for the electrical woes of the theatre and worried that the Saskatoon Theatre Centre would have to be shut down until some time in the autumn while repairs were being completed. News of the cancellation and of the possibility that 25th Street Theatre would renege on its co-production deal with Theatre Network did not make Ernie Carefoot happy. He wrote, on March 30, to the board of directors at 25th Street Theatre, suggesting that he intended to put the matter in his lawyer's hands. "I intend to suggest to my lawyer a figure of fifteen thousand dollars as restitution for breach of contract," he wrote, "although when I outline the list of damages I have suffered I rather think he will adjust the figure upward."[279]

Coleman made amends by offering to direct the production in Edmonton at no cost to Theatre Network and by offering to cover costs of the production beyond the original ten-thousand dollars that

Theatre Network had promised to invest. Theatre Network, with Andy Tahn temporarily at its helm, graciously accepted Coleman's financial offer and Coleman went to Edmonton to direct. Brenda Doner, the General Manager at Theatre Network, wrote a kind letter to Sandra Dibb on April 15, ironing out the details of the new agreement and offering hope. "Anyway, rehearsals are going well," Doner wrote, "and everyone feels good about it."[280] The production ran in Edmonton, with Shawn Lawrence as Rumplestiltzkin and Sarah Torgov as the Virgin between May 5 and 16. In Carefoot's retelling of the fairytale, Rumplestiltzkin was a disk jockey who spins gold records. The setting was a recording studio. Despite its inventiveness, the production was not well received; Tahn later referred to it as "a bust."[281] As Coleman remembered, several years later, Carefoot was quite pleased with the eventual production. "Of course, it did not do well at the box office," Coleman admitted. "I knew it wouldn't. Ernie didn't have that kind of relationship with audiences. He was ahead of his time."[282]

For eight weeks during the season (November until February), 25th Street Theatre had also conducted school workshops in several communities in Saskatchewan, funded by a grant from SaskSport Trust. The reach of these workshops — they took place in schools in Saskatoon, Prince Albert, Hague, Spiritwood, Medstead, and Moose Jaw — demonstrated 25th Street's intent to be more than a local theatre company. The workshops were led by recent university drama graduate Beth Lischeron, who focused on verbal communication in the hour-and-a-half classes she taught to high school and elementary students. Lischeron was assisted, occasionally, by actors with the company and other theatre professionals. In the words of Sandra Dibb:

> We have been able to offer some of the best people in Canada as instructors to Saskatchewan students, including Gary Reineke (winner of the Dora Mavor Moore Award for best performance in a feature role, 1980), Layne Coleman (nominated by the Toronto Chapter of ACTRA for his role in CBC's WAR BRIDES), Karen Woolridge (a movement and voice coach); James Dugan (co-star of THE GREAT DETECTIVE and a former professor

at the University of Ottawa, with a PhD in drama), Andrew McIlroy (who designed a curriculum drama guideline for the Ontario Department of Education, which is used throughout the province), and Marion Mills (a casting director and makeup and costume artist).[283]

While Lischeron was occasionally frustrated with the workshops (in her final report, she wrote, "Unfortunately, I wonder if this drop in the '12 year school bucket' does much good"), Dibb termed the process "overwhelmingly successful."[284]

Although Coleman had promised that 25th Street Theatre would not tour any of its shows in 1980-81, he was seduced into co-producing *Cold Comfort* with Salon Theatre and *The Ziggy Effect* with Toronto Free Theatre at the Toronto International Theatre Festival. Taking two productions to the festival was a high-stakes proposition and one which, in retrospect, paid off handsomely for Coleman and for 25th Street Theatre. *Cold Comfort* opened first at the festival, with Garrard himself directing and with Gary Reineke replaced by Booth Savage in the role of Floyd. Coleman and Karen Woolridge played Stephen and Dolores respectively. Reviews in the Toronto newspapers were immediately favourable. In the *Globe and Mail*, Vicky Sanderson wrote that Garrard's play rose above many works about isolation on the prairies. "Although the theme of bondage, both literal and metaphorical, is so vividly expressed that the possibility of love existing between any of the characters seems questionable," Sanderson wrote, "*Cold Comfort* is a well-written, well-directed and well-acted play that rises above the banality of many works about the isolation of life in remote parts of the Canadian West."[285] While admiring Garrard's dialogue, Sanderson maintained that there was too much of it: "Unfortunately, there's too much dialogue — 15 minutes could have been easily cut from the hour-long first act." Writing under the headline "Superb horror story puts chill on laughs," *Toronto Star* reviewer Henry Mietkiewicz was whole-hearted in his support for the production. "Writer-director Jim Garrard uses humor to create a play of astonishing power," he wrote, "thoroughly entertaining in its farcical moments, and so delicately paced that it glides seamlessly from comedy to heart-stopping drama and back again."[286] On May 18, the *Star's* Sid Adilman suggested that the Stratford Festival was in negotiation to transfer *Cold Comfort*, as well as George F. Walker's *Theatre of the Film Noir*, to its third stage for a 16-20 week run. Adilman quoted Theatre Festival board chairman Garth Drabinsky, claiming he had spoken with Stratford's artistic director John Hirsch, who "called to say he's quite interested in having them."[287] *Cold Comfort* was nominated for the Chalmers Award for Best New Play in 1981.

Sandra Dibb had predicted a happier future for *The Ziggy Effect* than for *Cold Comfort* at the festival when she wrote to Cathy McKeehan: "Our run of THE ZIGGY EFFECT will be open-ended, and we feel the show has strong potential of being a very big hit in Toronto, being both modern and futuristic, with good music and special effects, and having both strong entertainment and intellectual value."[288] Unfortunately, Penelope Stella, who had been a key performer in the Saskatoon production, suffered a stroke only days before the Toronto opening. She had to be replaced by Terry Tweed, who bravely stepped in with only a few days of rehearsal. Reviews for *The Ziggy Effect* were varied when it opened at the festival later that May, with Coleman directing James Dugan, Terry Tweed, Stuart Clow, Andrew McIlroy, and Karen Woolridge. Before the play opened, the *Star's* Bob Crew composed a flattering article about Coleman and 25th Street Theatre under the headline "Prairie boy kicks up dust with impressive directing." Noting that the theatre company had "some impressive achievements to its name" in the ten years since its inception, Crew wrote: "Layne Coleman has swept into Toronto like a prairie storm. The artistic director of Saskatoon's 25th Street Theatre is not only starring in *Cold Comfort*, Jim Garrard's festival hit about sex and bondage on the prairies, he's also directing *The Ziggy Effect*, which opens tonight at Toronto Free Theatre."[289] After the production of *Ziggy* opened, Crew allowed that the play "rings horribly true" in an uncomfortable way. He noted some stagnant patches in the writing and some rough patches in the staging, but admired the performances: "the three punk kids are dynamite.

Newcomer Andrew McIlroy's Ziggy is a wonderfully bizarre character, coldly destructive yet searching for understanding. Stuart Clow is inscrutable and menacing as the walking lobotomy Moon while Karen Woolridge plays Val with panache and energy."[290]

Carole Corbeil, in the *Globe and Mail*, was less enthusiastic, finding the play to be a superficial view of punkers:

> *The Ziggy Effect*, in short, kept reminding me of those New Yorker hippie cartoons of the late sixties, where Mom and Dad sit in armchairs and look at their yahoo son as if he has just escaped from the museum of natural history. This time around it's the ex-hippies who sit around and look at their son as if he has just escaped from the local planetarium. When the play is a chuckle — and I must admit there are quite a few — the chuckles are on that level. There are those, I'm sure, who could enjoy that approach."[291]

Corbeil later became Coleman's wife, and he was fond of regaling fellow actors with the story of his dreadful first review in Toronto at the hands of his wife. In a recent interview, Coleman maintained that an unhappy series of circumstances — including Stella's ailment and the lack of a full and proper set — hampered the Toronto production. "We mounted *The Ziggy Effect* in Toronto Free Theatre with no set, a couch, and in a black environment. The play suffered for it and the cast was in deep grieving because of what had just happened to Penelope Stella (who they loved as you would a real mother). Carol Corbeil knew none of this. Nobody did aside from us in the production."[292] It was an unhappy way to begin in Toronto.

Don Perkins had also been dispatched to cover the festival on behalf of the *StarPhoenix*, and he wrote back to his Saskatchewan readers that Coleman had been the subject of a flattering article in the *Star* and that *Cold Comfort* had been a hit. After mentioning Corbeil's lukewarm review of *The Ziggy Effect*, he focused on the successes of 25th Street Theatre: "Needless to say, 25th Street House people in town for the festival are thrilled with the response to their work."[293] The Toronto reviews for *Cold Comfort* and *The Ziggy Effect* were beginning to change perceptions back in Saskatoon of what was good and bad theatre. They also buoyed Coleman's career; he served as joint artistic director of 25th Street Theatre for the next two years before moving to Toronto and eventually becoming artistic director of Theatre Passe Muraille.

Despite the glowing reviews from Toronto, 25th Street Theatre was facing some enormous challenges, the greatest of which were financial. Sandra Dibb had worked hard at raising funds for the theatre and had amassed, by her own calculations, $40,000 by March 20, 1981 when she wrote Cathy McKeehan to plead for increased funding from the Canada Council. There were several reasons why Dibb's fundraising had not been more lucrative, and Dibb outlined most of them in her letter. Fundraising was more difficult in Saskatchewan than it was in the eastern provinces, owing to the fact that most large companies had their head offices in eastern Canada and were unlikely to support prairie theatre companies. It was more difficult to get sponsorships for new work than for tried and tested classical plays, partly because new work was an "unknown quantity" and partly because some new work, like Jim Garrard's play, was so controversial as to make potential sponsors squeamish. Unlike other jurisdictions, Saskatchewan law did not allow casino nights in the theatre, at that time, or other forms of gambling that could be used for fundraising. And because of the relatively brief history of professional theatre in Saskatchewan, there was a "lack of cultural consciousness on the part of most business people and individuals in Saskatchewan."

Dibb had attempted to assuage the financial hemorrhaging by introducing the "25th Street Theatre 6 Pak," by which adult patrons could purchase six tickets for any show on any night for twenty-five dollars. In her March 20 letter, Dibb announced her intention to re-introduce a regular subscription series, in 1981-82, in addition to the 6 Pak.[294] Because the theatre was largely dependant upon single ticket sales rather than subscriptions, its first week of production had usually been greeted by low audience numbers. An audience survey taken during the run of *Rodeo* had indicated that 28% of surveyed patrons had heard about the production from a friend, while 24% had learned of it by means of a poster and 22% by means of one of the local newspapers. Furthermore, 46% of the audience members surveyed had been under the age of twenty-five and 43% had been students or self-employed — not the most affluent of theatre audiences.[295] Dibb ended her letter to McKeehan with a plea for more money; she wanted the Canada Council to provide 40%-50% of the theatre's budget as it did for several other theatres.

Layne Coleman had written Cathy McKeehan, as well, and his letter was like that of a "foot soldier under a long siege at the front, waiting, hoping for supplies, relief, and more ammunition from Moscow." He lamented the under-staffing of the theatre, noting that the company had mounted six shows with an office staff of two and a tech crew of one. Coleman himself had directed two shows, acted in two, and stage managed two in order to save money. He did not hesitate in calling this under-staffing situation "BURN OUT Theatre":

> I have found this kind of high energy crisis push breeds incompetence eventually in an overly crowded, under funded theatre. We have had our tech man assume the duties of stage management and tech director on most shows. I have directed, stage managed, chased down props, blah, blah. Our Business Manager has been a miracle in staying afloat somehow. . . . Our secretary has had to deal with the demands of all of us, plus act as an accountant with a command of computerized bookkeeping. It has been a seat of the pants season.[296]

Like Dibb, Coleman pleaded with McKeehan for a substantial increase in Canada Council funding. "As the reputation of the theatre grows along with the theatre artists that work here," he wrote, "so must our funding, or we will be stuck forever, 'a bunch of enthusiastic kids out in the middle of nowhere in that terrible winter.' We are adults now doing adult theatre."

Near the end of the theatre season, 25th Street Theatre was invited to submit a paper about provincial funding to the Saskatchewan Cultural Review Committee. Coleman had been less than enthusiastic, in his letter to Cathy McKeehan, about the role of the Saskatchewan Arts Board in funding 25th Street, writing, "Our Saskatchewan Arts Board seems to us to be uninformed, amateur, and prejudiced against our kind of work."[297] His company pulled no punches in its submission to the Cultural Review Committee, noting that the province's support for the theatre had been "abysmally low."[298] 25th Street Theatre called on the government to provide at least twenty-five per cent of the total budgets of cultural organizations in the province in recognition of the rising costs of producing art, and particularly theatre, in Saskatchewan. The company also advocated for a purpose-built theatre centre in Saskatoon, which would house both 25th Street and Persephone. It called on crown corporations to provide leadership in support of arts and cultural organizations in the province and suggested government incentives, such as matching funding, for fundraising in the private sector. It suggested that a touring office be set up, under the auspices of the Saskatchewan Arts Board, in order to accommodate provincial touring and advocated for additional funding to schools in order to hire Saskatchewan artists more regularly as resource people. The company supported the resolution to make the arts board accountable to the Minister of Culture and recommended a clarification of the Arts Board's responsibilities: "While we are not against the SAB having some or possibly all jurisdiction over the funding of amateur art, it should be clearly understood that we want the Saskatchewan Arts Board to be primarily responsible for the welfare of the professional arts, and that new or increased jurisdictions into amateur fields should be done only with great caution." Several of the theatre's recommendations were forward-looking — especially in the realm of crown corporations as leading supporters of the arts — and were eventually adopted by the committee.

EIGHT:
"SASKATCHEWAN'S FAVOURITE THEATRE"
(1981-82)

FUNDING AGENCIES HAD BEEN impressed with the high standard of theatrical entertainment at 25th Street in 1980-81 and were prepared to reward the theatre monetarily. The Saskatchewan Arts Board agreed to provide $28,500 to the theatre in operational funding for 1981-82 and a further $7,587 as a deficit reduction grant. In addition, the Arts Board agreed to provide 25th Street and Persephone Theatre with a shared grant of $6,500 in order to pay for an electrical wiring upgrade at the Saskatoon Theatre Centre.[299] Cam Partridge, chairman of 25th Street's board, wrote a warm letter on June 9, 1981, thanking Executive Director Joy Cohnstaedt for the increase in funding. "The increase and deficit reduction grant were seriously needed and come at a crucial stage for our theatre," he wrote. "In hopes of decreasing our deficit, our theatre has raised approximately $50,000 in sponsorships and donations this year, and still anticipates an increased deficit."[300] Partridge suggested to Cohnstaedt that the theatre would pay off its deficit over the coming season by means of a subscription campaign, strong fund-raising, and granting increases. On June 25, Walter Learning wrote Partridge with the happy news that the Canada Council would provide 25th Street Theatre with a $65,000 grant for the 1981-82 season, which was $10,000 short of what the theatre had asked for but still a substantial increase in funding. Learning remarked that Council members had been impressed by the artistic successes of the theatre over the past year. "It is our hope that by substantially increasing your grant," he wrote, "an equally high artistic result can be achieved without the tremendous strain on your financial resources and on your staff."[301] The future suddenly seemed bright for 25th Street Theatre.

In his final year as chair of 25th Street's board, Partridge created inestimable good will by writing the editor of the *StarPhoenix* to commend the newspaper on its coverage of theatrical activity in Saskatoon and at the Toronto International Theatre Festival. (The relationship between the newspaper and 25th Street Theatre had been strained two years earlier when reviewer Don Perkins panned *Matonabbee* and when Tahn was compelled to challenge Perkins to a public debate on the merits of the production.) Partridge praised the *StarPhoenix*, especially, for its foresight in sending Perkins to the festival and included a sentence about how the experience must have been educative for Perkins:

> Saskatonians were privileged and delighted to read comprehensive, first class coverage of the festival by Don Perkins, who wrote very interesting, informative articles, and was familiar with many of the festival participants from his experience as a theatre critic in Saskatoon. His articles helped bring the festival, and our theatre's participation, more "close to home". As well, the experience gained by Mr. Perkins at the festival was invaluable, in that he can now knowledgably compare the work of our local professional theatres to that of international quality.[302]

Partridge's letter did much to defuse the tension that was, at least in the perception of members of the theatre company, palpable between the company and the newspaper. The stage was set for Perkins and Tahn to end their feud, and 25th Street Theatre could now carry on with the business of creating new Canadian work without fear that the newspaper might be biased in its reviews.

In 1981-82, Andy Tahn returned to 25th Street Theatre as part of an artistic triumvirate with Layne Coleman and Linda Griffiths. Tahn later maintained that he was already preparing to leave 25th Street Theatre when he agreed to the idea of an artistic triumvirate. He had been on the verge of burnout for several years. "I was already unhappy with my own life and what I was going through," Tahn said. "I was working 24/7, doing everything from directing shows, writing plays, searching for new playwrights, auditioning people, raising money, running the board. I was involved in everything. It wasn't healthy. And I wasn't delegating enough."[303] He informed the board of directors that he would be resigning at the end of the season and offered to help find a new artistic director. Cam Partridge would hear none of it. "Partridge indicated to me in no uncertain terms that if I resigned the theatre would close," Tahn wrote later. "In his exact words, 'Andy, you *are* 25th Street Theatre.'"[304] Tahn had also agreed to provide the theatre with a new (untitled) script, which was to be performed in the spring of 1982. While agreeing to serve with Tahn as co-artistic directors, Coleman and Griffiths were not much in evidence in Saskatoon during the season; both of them were busy pursuing opportunities in Toronto, most significantly with Theatre Passe Muraille where Griffiths was putting the finishing touches on her new play *O.D. on Paradise*.

In the autumn of 1981, the University of Saskatchewan's Drama Department hosted the Canadian Theatre Today Conference as part of what was then called the Learned Societies' Conference, a national conference of academics and practitioners in the Humanities and Fine Arts. Twenty-Fifth Street Theatre was determined to be part of the conference, never letting the academic and artistic communities forget the recent successes of the company. Tahn, Coleman, and Griffiths decided to set up their own Off-Conference Stage, patterned after the Salon Stage at the International Theatre Festival in Toronto, in order to provide "performing spaces, technical, office, and publicity assistance to theatre groups and artists from Saskatoon and across Canada."[305] They secured the lobby, green room, and theatre area of the Saskatoon Theatre Centre in order to house the project. They hired actors

Paula Jardine, Ernie Carefoot, Victor Sutton, and Henry Van Rijke to perform readings of new Canadian plays on the Off-Conference Stage, and they brought in the Nakai Players, from the Yukon, and Vancouver's Gordon House Players to stage productions there. Don Freed provided musical entertainment.

There was little independent analysis of the success of the Off-Conference Stage, but Tahn wrote in a letter that it was considered by professional theatre practitioners and theatre critics "to be an exciting and positive theatre contribution" during the conference.[306] Tahn would later have to defend the company's decision to employ the Saskatoon Theatre Centre as a second stage for the conference, when Jay Buckwold, the chairman of Persephone's board, mentioned in a brief to the Cultural Facilities Hearings that he was "dismayed at the risks involved" in such a venture. In a letter to Buckwold, Tahn argued that Persephone had not made its objections known at the time of the event and that the Off-Conference Stage had been considered a popular and critical success.[307]

The issues that arose between academics and practitioners at the Canadian Theatre Today Conference were issues that were crucial to companies like 25th Street Theatre at the time. It was a noisy and sometimes cantankerous conference, featuring plenty of distrust between the academics and the theatre-makers. "In theatre, as elsewhere, the best slugfest is between the professionals and the academics, 'them that kin and them that teaches,'" wrote Ray Conologue in the *Globe and Mail*. "You could see it operating in the wary circling of the writers, directors and critics who showed up . . . The actors, on the other hand, ducked the problem by doing what they always do: sleeping and playing the day away and showing up only for performances and late drinks."[308] At the centre of much controversy was a lecture given by Queen's University drama professor Richard Plant, in which he argued that script development centres and theatre critics were guilty of coddling new playwrights, thereby setting them up for failure on the international stage. "Is the essence of being Canadian finding joy in second-rate drama?" he asked.[309] Plant followed that question with a scene-by-scene breakdown of *Maggie and Pierre*, *Waiting For The Parade*, and *Automatic Pilot* and, according to Ray Conologue, argued "(convincingly) that each was sloppily structured and (less convincingly) that their themes were trivial."[310] Plant's lecture enraged theatre practitioners and critics, but several of them also recognized the veracity of his arguments after witnessing the New Play Centre's (NPC) production of Betty Lambert's *Jennie's Story*. Lambert's play opened at the conference and, according to Mark Czarnecki, "only highlighted the need for a thorough rewrite of the second act."[311] Czarnecki saw the NPC production as symptomatic of a deeply rooted malaise in Canadian theatre: "the premature presentation of a potentially worthwhile play paralyses its natural evolution and discourages the playwright from reworking. Who is to blame? The playwright? The dramaturge (if one exists)? The director? The producer?"[312] Ray Conologue agreed with Czarnecki and Plant that playwrights did not benefit from being coddled; Conologue was extremely critical of the NPC's production of Lambert's play and of NPC director Pam Hawthorne, writing, "[C]onsiderable money and the talent of some rather brave actors was wasted on a doomed production. Why? Because Hawthorne, like Passe Muraille's Paul Thompson or Factory Lab's Bob White, is intent on promoting the writer's personal esthetic rather than teaching him what makes a play work."[313]

Plant's lecture was not the only opportunity for fireworks at the conference. Des MacAnuff, Associate Director of the New York Shakespeare Festival, took part in a panel discussion entitled "Where Do We Go From Here?" and highlighted the exodus of Canadian theatre artists to the United States in the early eighties. According to the *StarPhoenix*, MacAnuff's answer to the panel's central question was, "A lot of us have gone to New York." He explained that in Toronto, the major playhouses were closely guarded by their artistic directors and were beyond the reach of a young playwright. In another panel setting, Vancouver critic Roger Langford asked the audience to agree with him that his fellow panellists Erika Ritter and John Gray were "boring."

Ritter responded by quoting a sentence from one of Langford's reviews which contended, ungrammatically, that she was a bad writer. "I don't need to apologize for my writing to anybody who could pen that sentence," Ritter replied.[314] When Wayne Fipke, of Edmonton's lavish Citadel Theatre, spoke lengthily about his love for new Canadian plays, playwright Brian Swarbrick leapt to his feet and scrambled over chairs to the microphone. Swarbrick accused the Citadel of timing its call for new Canadian scripts to coincide with its application for a Canada Council grant and suggested that "not one of those plays will be produced."[315] The controversies of the conference — the lack of good producers for new Canadian plays, the exodus of theatrical talent, the crossed swords between media and playwrights — were exactly the concerns that 25th Street Theatre had been facing, in microcosm, in Saskatoon. Tahn, Coleman, and Griffiths might have been heartened by the final words of Ray Conologue on the subject of the conference as Conologue described his flight out of Saskatoon:

> Morose thoughts on the flight out of Saskatoon were moderately dissipated by a farmer's daughter in the seat beside me. 'It's funny how a place like Saskatoon has such good theatre,' she said, referring to the popular 25th Street House and Persephone Theatre. 'A few years ago we thought it was crazy to go to the theatre. Now the kids go there before they go to a movie.'[316]

That farmer's daughter was speaking for the legions of young people in Saskatoon who had become theatre fans in recent years.

Twenty-Fifth Street's production of Patricia Joudry's new play *A Very Modest Orgy* was produced during the conference and was the subject of local and national reviews. Originally from Spirit River, Alberta, Joudry had been one of Canada's most widely produced playwrights in the period between 1941 and the late sixties, when indigenous theatres began to cater to the development of playwrights across the country. Much of Joudry's success was in the creation of radio scripts, including the famed "Aldridge Family" series, but she also published novels and stage plays. Her 1956 stage play *Teach Me How To Cry* had been translated into several languages and produced in countries around the world. When she returned to western Canada in the early eighties, Tahn was quick to get in touch with her. Joudry had been working on a novel entitled *A Very Modest Orgy*, and she agreed to provide Tahn with a stage play based on the novel.

The play, which is still extant and in the Special Collections Library at the University of Saskatchewan, is about a farmwife and painter named Phoebe, who is in the midst of a sexual crisis. Phoebe's fifteen-year-old daughter Francine is oblivious to sex while Phoebe's husband Bertram, who is a professor at the local university, refuses to talk about it. In the first scene of the play, we learn that Francine is out in the barn helping a mare deliver her colt. While Francine is outside, Phoebe tells Bertram about Catherine the Great's penchant for having sex with horses, a narrative which he finds distasteful. Later in the play, Phoebe hires Rick, a theology student at the university, to pose in the nude for her. Rick is extremely liberated about his own sexuality, and during a posing session he asks Phoebe if she swings. The following conversation ensues:

PHOEBE
Oh yes. Naturally. Of course.

RICK
Count me in sometime.

PHOEBE (paints with the stick end. Pause)
When?

RICK (shrugs)
Whenever.

(She pokes end of brush through canvas.)[317]

Meanwhile, Bertram has developed a relationship with Ellie, one of his students. When this fact becomes known to Phoebe, she talks Bertram into inviting the two students over and setting up an evening of "swinging" in their home. The evening finally arrives, but Rick and Ellie hit it off (predictably) and retire to the bedroom together, leaving Bertram and Phoebe to their own devices.

Tahn directed the play, which ran between October 1 and 17, at the Saskatoon Theatre Centre. In the cast were Graham McPherson (as Bertram), Sharon Bakker (as Phoebe), Kim Coates (as Rick), Laurie Pearson (as Francine), JoAnn McIntyre (as Ellie), Michael Fahey (as Nigel), Jane Kalmakoff (as Martha), and Rob Roy (as Bartholomew). Reviews of the production focused on the old-fashioned quality of Joudry's script and on the clichéd characters and acting. Perhaps the most scathing review came from the pen of Rod Macpherson, who wrote in the *Sheaf* that the play was "a collection of clichés," including a thoroughly modern mom who paints nude models, a professor/dad who yearns for the glories of ancient Greece and one night of glory with a female student, a whole-earth daughter who lives without benefit of running water, and a bubble-headed sexpot. He noted that several of the actors were "victims" of the script, "a granola nightmare come true, mixed with a bit of sixties sex-farce and finishing with — what else — the reassertion of traditional family values." Macpherson compared the script, unfavourably, with a television sitcom. "I find this a bad play, almost an offensive one," he wrote. "If I came across it on TV as one of those giggle-and-jiggle sitcoms, which it so much resembles, I'd turn it off before the first commercial, and so, I think, would most of the people who guffawed through the premiere."[318] In the *NeWest Review*, M.A. Thompson blamed Joudry for a verbally flat play with no emotional centre. "Though many of the lines are funny in context, none of them are particularly memorable," he wrote. "Finally, though the play's intent is clear enough intellectually, emotionally it is hollow. It is difficult to believe that Patricia Joudry cares about any of these characters, and so it is correspondingly difficult to care about them oneself."[319] The *StarPhoenix's* Catherine Lawson found fault with the writing and the acting, particularly in the scenes involving Graham McPherson and JoAnn McIntyre. "McPherson, very good in other scenes, just looks downright embarrassed trading those awful, hackneyed double entendres," wrote Lawson. "And there's an unfortunate touch of hysteria behind McIntyre's giggle. She lacks the sunny naivete needed to play the classic dumb blonde."[320]

Out-of-town critics tended to be more lenient about the play than most of the local critics. The *Regina Leader-Post's* Denise Ball called the play's style "somewhat anachronistic," noting that it was based on British sex farce, but maintained that the production succeeded as a result of Joudry's craftsmanship. "The production, directed by Andras Tahn, suffers under a weight of cheap tricks, miscasting and a few unfortunate performances," Ball wrote. "But it succeeds in providing a funny, often hilarious evening of theatre, thanks to Joudry's skilful craftsmanship and excellent command of the form, outdated or not."[321] In the *Globe and Mail*, Herbert Whittaker noted that Joudry's play was old-fashioned but expressed admiration for it nevertheless. "Styles have changed since the Joudry heyday," he wrote, "but her cheerful sit-com tickled Saskatoon's audience with hints of sexual revolution, though I did feel the Bakker talents were rather wasted in John Hughes' cardboard setting."[322] Brian Brennan, of the *Calgary Herald*, liked Joudry's play wholeheartedly. He wrote that the play, though old-fashioned, was surprisingly fresh: "It's the most amusing, if not the most profound piece of theatre seen at the conference so far."[323]

With the Canadian Theatre Today conference safely out of the way, 25th Street Theatre proceeded to a production of Brad Fraser's play *Wolfboy*. Fraser, who would later go on to write the international hit play *Unidentified Human Remains and the True Nature of Love*, was only twenty-two when *Wolfboy* went into production. His sensational, sexually frank stage plays have, in latter years, caused him to be seen as a forerunner to the British in-yer-face playwrights, including Mark Ravenhill and Sarah Kane. A native of Edmonton, Fraser had won several Alberta Culture Playwriting Awards, but he had never been afforded a professional production until 25th Street took an interest in him. In an interview in 2009, Tahn remembered meeting Fraser in Edmonton and telling the young playwright that 25th Street Theatre was interested in producing his play. Fraser was surprised at the interest shown by the theatre, Tahn said, "because he was just a nobody" at the time. "He had sent me the play cold turkey just to review, and I liked the language in the play, but I didn't understand what *Wolfboy* was about."[324]

Wolfboy features a curiously old-fashioned three-act structure, which necessitated that it be produced with two intermissions for its premiere at 25th Street Theatre. It is the story of two young men who are thrown together in a home for disturbed adolescents and who, bereft of help from the world outside, assist each other. Bernie is the high school jock, popular and attractive, who has attempted suicide. He finds himself assigned to a room across from where David, a boy who insists that he is a werewolf, is strapped to his bed. Together, the two young men resist the unhappy, if sometimes well-meaning, influence of psychiatrists and parents. The play was subsequently produced in Toronto, with Keanu Reeves making his theatrical debut in that production.

Layne Coleman had agreed to direct the 25th Street production, with Stuart Clow (as Bernie), JoAnn McIntyre, Kat Mullay, Angelo Rizacos (as David), Victor Sutton, and Karen Woolridge in the cast. The production ran between November 5 and 21, 1981. Reviewers, some of whom had high praise for the actors, consistently found shortcomings in the script. Several commented upon the risqué nature of the play's subject matter and how the more conservative portion of 25th Street Theatre's audience reacted to it. Reviewing for CBC Radio Regina, Glen Cairns noted the play's shock value. "Like last season's *Ziggy Effect, Conversations With Girls In Private Rooms*, and *Cold Comfort*, this show is guaranteed to offend the more conservative segment of 25th Street's following," he said. "A price the company must be prepared to pay if it is to continue exploring new forms of Canadian Theatre." Cairns admired the acting, calling Angelo Rizacos "riveting" and Karen Woolridge "electrifying," but found the script to be long and rambling, especially in scenes involving subsidiary characters. "Some quick editing of these scenes would allow the play to be structured into two acts and would eliminate one of the two fifteen minute intermissions," said Cairns.[325] In the *NeWest Review*, Janice Dales panned the production. While allowing that Rizacos and Clow gave strong performances, Dales criticized the supporting players for awkward speech rhythms, overacting, and emotional flatness. Her most damning criticism was reserved for the script:

> Interesting theatrical devices do not make up for gratuitous violence and gratuitous pornography. Two people walked out at the flagellation scene the first night I was there, and at least three left at the second intermission. The second time I saw the show, the lights went out in Saskatoon before the third act, and the management offered the audience tickets to another night. "Could we have tickets to a different show?" someone asked. No one laughed.[326]

That particular passage from Dales' review of the production aroused the ire of Andy Tahn, and he responded with a letter to *NeWest's* editor. The *StarPhoenix's* Don Perkins also had little good to say about the production, arguing that the script was "anywhere from 35 to 50 percent too long." He disliked the character of Cynthia, the psychiatrist, as played by JoAnn McIntyre. "Most of her lines read and are delivered as a string of pop shrink clichés," wrote Perkins. "There is also a lecture on werewolf lore she delivers to Cherry, the nurse, that is too obviously there to explain things Fraser couldn't work into the script as a more natural part of the action." Perkins' most stirring criticism was reserved for the director Layne Coleman, who was accused of sapping the production with slow pacing:

> For Coleman it is a disappointing return to the director's chair. At times this is an awkward production, not helped by a set, designed by Robert Robishek, that doesn't quite fit the stage, and requires some clumsy blocking to get around. But mostly there is the slow pace; the deadening blackouts. It takes more than bizarre music to create a sense that things are beyond the natural, and not much more than bizarre music and occasional moody lighting is offered.[327]

Rod Macpherson, writing for the *Sheaf*, admired the script and the production more than most of his colleagues. He wrote:

The best things about this remarkable play are the author's understanding of his generation and their ugly world, his ear for their speech and his ability to translate their confusions into the allegory of the wolf. When he sticks to the two disturbed boys, Fraser knows whereof he writes.

The singular excellence of the Bernie-David scene is enhanced by tense, spare direction (with one or two lapses), by good lighting and a great set — institutional red brick gone modern and art deco bars on the windows — but mostly by the two actors. Stuart Clow manages both sides of the mercurial Bernie — the careless golden boy and the instinctive sadist — and Angelo Rizacos gives a frenetic high-tension performance that can curl hair at moments. [328]

Macpherson later conceded that the supporting characters were "just sticks wearing clothes," but argued that his objections to these characters were not fatal. He ended by recognizing Fraser as an up-and-coming talent: "He is only 22 and he may be the Wayne Gretzky of Canadian letters."

While producing a play about incarceration on its mainstage, 25th Street Theatre was also developing a workshop production in a psychiatric prison. The workshop began in late October when actors Rob Roy and JoAnn McIntyre oversaw classes in relaxation, concentration exercises, and improvisation at the Saskatoon Regional Psychiatric Centre. The classes evolved into a collectively created production called *The Grunt That Almost Stole Christmas*, loosely based on Dickens' *A Christmas Carol*. It is the story of a prison guard who refuses to let the prisoners stay up late on Christmas Eve. Three ghosts appear and haunt the guard, helping him to see the error of his ways. The production was directed by Rob Roy and was enacted by ten inmates and three staff members at the prison. It ran for one night, on December 19 at 7:00 PM, under tight security. Members of the media and other special guests were invited to view the performance.

A production in a psychiatric prison, combining the talents of a professional theatre company and of the inmates, was unique in

Saskatchewan at the time. The Recreation Therapy Department at the Centre had developed a drama program in the facility but had never before invited a professional theatre company to participate. The inmates were not quite sure how to respond to the professional actors at first, and the actors were similarly in foreign territory. "[The inmates] were under the impression that actors or writers were people unlike [themselves]," wrote Rob Roy in a press release distributed before the performance, "until they realized that they also had unique and important things to say." For his part, Roy felt that the experience caused him to alter, and sometimes throw away, preconceptions about the prisoners and their incarceration. "The stigma generated by society towards those paying the price is by far the biggest wall that separated them from any future re-integration," he wrote. There was no doubt that the inmates found the experience rewarding. Said Bob, an inmate playing the Ghost of the Present, "By working as a team and relying on each other we are learning to trust and relate with others . . . It is building confidence in men who in the past have had difficulty in expressing themselves or their self-worth." Steve Wormith, a psychologist at the Psychiatric Centre, also had good things to say about the production, noting that Christmas is a difficult time for inmates in correctional facilities. He wrote glowingly about the drama program, and its therapeutic effects, in the Centre's press release:

> You may note that we refer to the Drama Program. Technically there is no doubt that we could refer to it as therapy. The motivation instilled in the patients, the challenges presented, the opportunity to test different styles through role-playing, and the development of confidence and self-esteem can all be found in the program. The patients' enthusiasm and dedication to the activity is testimony to its impact.[329]

All of the participants viewed the workshop production as a resounding success.

Twenty-Fifth Street Theatre began the new year with a production of Alun Hibbert's *Playing the Fool*. Hibbert's play bears the influence of Harold Pinter and Joe Orton; it is an absurd family drama about Harry, a nearly senile veteran of the Spanish Civil War, and his estranged (twin) son and daughter, Ben and Sheila, on the occasion of their mother Rachel's funeral. At the beginning of the play, Harry's old friend John rings the doorbell at Harry's front door; John has come back into Harry's life after forty years in order to attend the funeral. When Harry takes too long to answer the bell, John proceeds around the house to the back door. Harry, meanwhile, has opened the front door and stepped out on to the porch, locking himself out of the house. John, who has entered through the back door, walks into the living room and then opens the front door, letting Harry back into his own house. After a moment of senility when Harry does not recognize John, the audience learns that John saved Harry's life in the War. We soon learn other things, including the fact that John abandoned Rachel when she was carrying his twin children and that she took up with Harry after that. Harry raised the children as his own, and it is not until the end of the play that the children learn the truth about their parentage. In adulthood, Ben has become a greedy industrialist, and Sheila has turned into a neurotic anarchist. Through the play, the children relive their old grievances against their father while John listens. The following conversation occurs near the end of the play:

BEN (almost weeping)
You never took me fishing once you bastard. And look at what you made out of her. God. It's no wonder she's been such a fruit loop all her life.

SHEILA
And he's been such a greedy grasping pig of an exploiter.

HARRY
I never claimed to be perfect.

JOHN
I'm sure you did your best Harry.

HARRY
I thought so John.[330]

As in Pinter's *The Homecoming* (which also revolves around an ancient infidelity), Hibbert's main characters function by ignoring what is really being said to them and by using language as a smokescreen to mask what they are thinking and feeling.

Gary Reineke returned to Saskatoon to direct 25th Street's production of *Playing The Fool*, in which Sean McCann played Harry and George R. Robertson played John. Both were Toronto actors and stars of CBC television programs. Michael Fahey played Ben, and Ruth Smillie played Sheila. The production, which ran January 7-23 at the Saskatoon Theatre Centre, was brief and tightly paced; its duration was only seventy-five minutes most nights.

The House Manager's Daily Statements for the show provide a unique look at how dependant upon its subscription base 25th Street had already become. On opening night, fifty-four patrons attended the play, all of them subscribers. By January 9, one hundred and eighty patrons were in attendance, one hundred and twenty-five of them being subscribers. On January 12, one hundred and fifty-one audience members watched the show, one hundred and fifteen of them subscribers. The slow opening night was also indicative of how important word-of-mouth and newspaper reviews were, at the time, in creating a buzz for a particular show.

Reviews of the production were universally glowing. Don Perkins wrote, in the *StarPhoenix*, that the production was "instant cold medicine — an evening to spend laughing so hard you'll forget all about the deep freeze outside." He credited Hibbert with a script that makes an easy transition from the amusing to the ridiculous and called McCann "a joy" to watch: "He appears to trust the script and the direction, and lets situations and Hibbert's genuinely funny dialogue do their work, without ever forcing or milking the material."[331] In the *Sheaf*, Ron Marken wrote that Hibbert comes close to being a Canadian Joe Orton. "The characters and setting are wildly improbable, but not implausible," wrote Marken, "the dialogue is swift and sure, and gave a grateful audience *scores* of laughs — real laughs, not chuckles."[332]

Janice Dales, in the *NeWest Review*, raved about the play, comparing it
to various international hits:

> *Playing the Fool* reaffirms that Canadian plays can be as witty
> and amusing about politics as plays on the London stage.
> Hibbert's farce has none of the passion of *Accidental Death of
> an Anarchist* nor the slapstick of *Dirty Linen*, its wit is more
> sophisticated, accessible, and relentless than *Anyone for Denis?*,
> a recent West End political satire. Hibbert has an unquenchable
> love of language at its most exuberant, an irreverent sense of the
> absurd, and a proper distaste of excessive sentimentality, which
> makes him one of the best new comic writers in Canada.[333]

Also admiring the acting of McCann and Robertson, Dales suggested
that the production was "a promising start to the new year for 25th
Street Theatre."

Twenty-Fifth Street spent much of the spring of 1982 introducing
touring shows to their Saskatoon audience. The next two productions
were the work of other companies. On February 4-9, Theatre Passé
Muraille's remount of *Maggie and Pierre*, this time starring Toronto
actress Patricia Oatman, played at Castle Theatre. Oatman suggested,
in an interview, that she was at first terrified by the play. "At that point
I had never done a one-person show, being on stage two hours all by
myself," she said. "I compare playing *Maggie & Pierre* to running
a marathon."[334] Columnist Peter Ladner had admired Oatman's
Vancouver performance in the role, suggesting that Oatman had
stepped into Linda Griffiths' shoes admirably and had sparked "the
same jolt of electricity."[335] The *StarPhoenix's* Don Perkins disagreed,
arguing that the play was "dated" since its premiere two years earlier
and criticizing Oatman for not using a lighter touch in her portrayals
of Maggie and Pierre:

> Things are not helped when the performer is pushing too hard,
> as Oatman was on this occasion. Much of the fun in this show
> is the chance we get to laugh at ourselves, at our national foibles
> which are thrown back at us in some potentially sparkling
> one-liners. When these are rushed or even mumbled, as was the

case too often, the audience is cheated out of a laugh at its own expense.

As well, Oatman had trouble with both Trudeaus. Pierre came off more as a caricature than a character, played with a snide undertone that made it difficult to find him admirable in any way. Maggie lacked a convincing wide-eyed innocence in her fight to come to terms with the world she never learns to distrust enough.[336]

On February 8, 25th Street Theatre presented Les Ballets Jazz de Montreal at the Centennial Auditorium, this time with a happier response from the *StarPhoenix* reviewer. Sheila Robertson wrote that the production, which consisted of various dance numbers, was "perfectly swell." She noted that the audience had given the company a warm welcome, and wrote: "It's no wonder. All the ingredients are there: lithe bodies, varied music and choreography, and energy to burn."[337]

On February 18, 25th Street opened its own production of *O.D. On Paradise*, written by Linda Griffiths and Patrick Brymer. The play, about a group of eight tourists who arrive in Jamaica on a package tour and re-evaluate their own lives as a result, was based on the playwrights' own experiences of such a tour. It was written over the course of the summer of 1981 and was subsequently workshopped at Theatre Passe Muraille. Brymer and Griffiths acted in the premiere of the play at 25th Street Theatre, as did Diane Douglass, Michael Fahey, Nicky Guadagni, Dennis Robinson, Wendell Smith, and Sharon Stearns. Clarke Rogers directed, and designer Ramsay King hauled in several hundred pounds of sand to create a Jamaican beach for the production.

Reviewers hinted at, and sometimes named outright, the basic flaw in the script: that it tried to develop all eight characters with equal emphasis, resulting in what one reviewer called "quite a bouilla-baisse."[338] Ron Marken hinted at this shortcoming in his CBC Radio review. "The play's first act moves very slowly," he suggested, "but that is not really a complaint, because, remember, we have eight sets of emotional muscles to unwind, eight psyches to expose — and there is a small *host* in interpersonal relationships to intertwine." Marken particularly admired the celebratory tone of the play and commended the director "who kept the eight vivid characters ebbing and flowing with never a moment of confusion — although I had a devil of a time keeping everyone's name straight!"[339] It was a mark of the significance attached to 25th Street Theatre that Ray Conologue, of the *Globe and Mail*, was flown into Saskatoon to review the opening of *O.D. on Paradise*. He didn't like the play, however, calling it "a bit of a cul-de-sac." The main flaw, he argued, was the playwrights' self-imposed democracy in dealing with the characters: "each character gets about equal time. It's like glimpsing a range of eight similar-sized mountains in the foggy distance. You'd like to get close enough to explore one or two of them, but no matter how hard you hike they remain just as far away."[340] Only the reviewer for the *StarPhoenix*, Catherine Lawson, seemed to like the production almost without reservation. While noting that Guadagni's icy portrayal of Karen made her a standout in the cast, Lawson argued that there was almost too much good writing in the play:

> Playwrights Linda Griffiths and Patrick Brymer resisted the temptation to take the easy route and present a group of stereotypes exchanging one-liners. The characters defy one-sentence summations. Even the loud fat lady in the bright yellow pants (played with gusto by Diane Douglass) is a believable person.
>
> It is a well-written play. A rueful soliloquy on the essential problem with winter boots is especially memorable. In fact, there is almost too much good writing. Clarke Rogers' direction is tight but the play is overly long and just like too many lazy days in the sun it begins to drag.[341]

Lawson suggested that *O.D. on Paradise*, with it beach setting, was "the kind of play that can convert a person to theatre-going."

Given the intricate association between the two theatres at the time, it was not implausible to conjecture that 25th Street Theatre might become Passe Muraille's road house and Saskatoon a kind of Poughkeepsie, where productions could be honed without the intense critical reception that a Toronto opening might elicit. Certainly, productions of *Wolfboy* and *Cold Comfort* had used Saskatoon as a springboard to the Toronto stage and, in the near future, Linda Griffiths and Maria Campbell would work the bugs out of *Jessica* in Saskatoon and then present a more finished product to Toronto audiences at Passe Muraille. (The migration was in the opposite direction on at least one occasion, when Paul Thompson and Griffiths developed *Maggie and Pierre* at Passé Muraille and then toured the play nationally and into Saskatchewan.) A revised version of *O.D. on Paradise* would have a run at Theatre Passe Muraille in January 1983, a year after its Saskatoon opening, and would meet with a much happier critical reception than the play's Saskatoon opening had received. By that time, Clarke Rogers had replaced Paul Thompson as artistic director of Theatre Passe Muraille after a prolonged power struggle. In an effort to improve production standards at the theatre, Rogers hired nationally acclaimed designer Jim Plaxton to design the sets for the 1982-83 season, which included *O.D. on Paradise*. Plaxton decided that Griffiths' and Brymers' play was best produced in the round, as opposed to the proscenium arch production at the Saskatoon Theatre Centre, and he transformed the Passe Muraille stage into a huge sandbox with twenty-two tonnes of sand. According to Mark Czarnecki, in *Maclean's*, the production illustrated "how Plaxton can illuminate a work by plumbing its essence and creating an organic interplay between text and setting."[342] In the *Globe and Mail*, Ray Conologue also conceded that the play was much improved. "An earlier version, disjointed and riddled with shallows, opened in Saskatoon last year; it was hard to be encouraging about," wrote Conologue. "But Linda Griffiths and Patrick Brymer believed in their idea, reworked it and the script has finally settled into place."[343] Conologue referred to the play as "an engagingly peculiar comedy" at its Toronto opening.

In March, Cam Partridge announced the postponement of Andy Tahn's as yet untitled new play, which had been promised for the 1981-82 season. Little explanation was given for the postponement, and Partridge went on to congratulate the theatre's artistic directors for overseeing a splendidly successful subscription campaign.[344] The next four productions to appear at 25th Street Theatre in the spring of 1982 were presentations of the work of outside companies. On April 12-17, Alan Aldred was featured in *The Cockroach That Ate Cincinnati*, originally a production of Britain's Hull Truck Theatre Limited. In his CBC radio review, Ron Marken wrote that Aldred promised to tear "the lid off western civilization" in the play. "I know that he doesn't succeed in that laudable endeavour," wrote Marken, " — who could? — but he comes closer than any four playwrights (put together) we have seen in Saskatchewan in the last five years."[345] On May 3-8, 25th Street hosted the Toronto Free Theatre's production of two plays by Ted Galay, *After Baba's Funeral* and *Sweet and Sour Pickles*, both of them directed by 25th Street alumnus Lubomir Mykytiuk. Mary Walsh's production of *Terras de Bacalhau* came to Third Avenue United Church basement in Saskatoon on May 10-15, having played at the Toronto International Theatre festival the previous spring. The *StarPhoenix's* Don Perkins admired the Newfoundland Resource Centre for the Arts' production, writing that the company gave "a lesson in how an energetic and entertaining piece of theatre can overcome most of the drawbacks of its playing space."[346] On May 12-13, Mime Omnibus appeared at E.D. Feehan High School Auditorium, presenting a commedia-inspired *Zizi and the Letter*, with Jean Asselin playing Arlequin. It was a busy spring for 25th Street Theatre, mostly presenting other companies' work.

In early June, 25th Street produced Barbara Sapergia's play Lokkinen at Festival '82 (a festival of Saskatchewan's female playwrights) in Regina. Twenty-Fifth Street had agreed to pay Sapergia $350 plus ten per cent of box office receipts for production rights to her play and, in turn, received a production fee of $13,000 from Festival '82 for a three-day run. Sapergia's play is a domestic drama about the mad delusions of a rather patriarchal Finnish-Canadian (Aino Lokkinen) who dwells in the city during his retirement but who remains locked in the past with his memories of farming in Northern Saskatchewan. He ignores his wife Inga, who runs a lodging house, and his teenaged daughter Lanni, who has begun to experiment with sex. The old man obsesses about one of the lodgers, a pre-Med student named Judith Wright, whom he comes to regard as the incarnation of the Norse goddess Freja. In the play's final pages, Inga makes Aino confront the reality of his past and the farm that broke him:

AINO (pleading)
I wanted beauty in my life.

INGA
You wanted beauty, but you destroyed it wherever you went.

AINO
I needed the land, the beautiful land.

INGA
We could have had a good life . . . but you were always jealous of other people . . . you couldn't stand to see their success.

AINO
No.

INGA
You wanted to take us away, so no one could compare you with them . . . [347]

With his mad, petty jealousies and churlish ways, Lokkinen is reminiscent of Caleb Gare, the emotionally distant farmer who is swallowed by his own land in Martha Ostenso's novel *Wild Geese*. Unlike Gare, though, Lokkinen has survived and moved into the city, where he doesn't belong. Inga's last line in the play ("*You* destroyed us") is a line that could have been uttered by Gare's unhappy children in Ostenso's novel.

Ruth Smillie, who was by then artistic director of Persephone's Youtheatre, directed the production, which featured Merril Barreca,

Denise Beamish, Kay Nouch, Joyce Seeley, and Blake Taylor in the cast. Dennis Robinson played Aino Lokkinen. In his *CBC Stereo Morning* review, Ron Marken suggested that the play's first act featured some wooden exposition and poor character development, particularly as it pertained to the character of Mrs. McBride (played by Kay Nouch), a senile lodger in Inga's lodging house:

> The characters defined themselves, it appeared, a bit too clearly and a bit too soon, and presented us with the dubious spectre of stereotype: long-suffering mother, explosive daughter, book-worm student, senile old woman. And there were other problems in the first act too: the old woman spent most of her time "having her nap", hustled into the action only when she was needed. It wasn't until Act Two that her senility became a useful foil to the larger madness of Lokkinen. And the tensions of that act were much stronger as, in what was clearly the author's intention, stereotype gave way to myth — through music, dance, ecstasies, and a stronger script — including two splendid contrapuntal soliloquys: the hardened shell of the wife and the blooming virgin, Judith.[348]

Marken viewed the production as a workshop-in-progress and suggested that once the script's flaws had been dealt with, "this could be a stunning play."

⁓⦁⦁⁓

It was apparent that 25th Street Theatre had established a legacy as trailblazers in developing new Canadian drama, and the company was determined to protect that legacy. By the end of the 1981-82 season, the theatre had published two historical documents, "An Introduction to Saskatoon's 25th Street Theatre" and "25th Street Theatre — A History". Both documents highlight the achievements of the theatre. In "An Introduction to Saskatoon's 25th Street Theatre," the production and transfer record of the theatre company is front and centre:

> In total, 25th Street Theatre has produced 46 plays, and sponsored or co-produced an additional 25 productions

(including 21 contemporary Canadian hits). Over the past decade, 38 World Premieres have been created or produced by 25th Street Theatre.

Many of these have been produced, or are scheduled for production by other professional theatres, or have been produced in other forms of media (film, radio, television, book, or album form). Among these 25th Street Theatre productions are *Queen's Cowboy, Paper Wheat, If You're So Good, Why Are You in Saskatoon!, Rodeo, O.D. on Paradise, A Very Modest Orgy, Cold Comfort, Rumplestiltskin Busts Out, Don'tcha Know — The North Wind and You in My Hair,* and *Playing the Fool.*

Among the theatres which have [produced] or are producing these plays are Centaur Theatre (Montreal), Theatre Network (Edmonton), Kawartha Theatre (Lindsay, Ont.), Chilliwack Theatre Festival (British Columbia), the National Arts Centre (Ottawa), Belfry Theatre (Victoria), the NDWT Theatre (Toronto), Theatre Passe Muraille (Toronto), Toronto Free Theatre, and the Manitoba Theatre Centre (Winnipeg).[349]

"25th Street Theatre — A History" brings the reader further up to date, listing the theatre's enviable statistics for the 1981-82 season. In that period, 25th Street Theatre produced seven shows and had a total audience of 16,913, including 940 subscribers.[350]

While securing the legacy in print, Andy Tahn was also extremely vocal when he perceived that others were slighting his theatre. In a January 22, 1982 letter to Don Kerr, editor of the *NeWest Review,* Tahn complained about what he viewed as demeaning journalism on the part of reviewer Janice Dales. Tahn took exception to Dales' published comments about *A Very Modest Orgy,* about the Off-Conference Stage, and especially about Layne Coleman's production of *Wolfboy.* He questioned Dales' motives in writing that at least two people had walked out of *Wolfboy* during the flagellation scene and at least three had left at intermission. "Ms. Dales can choose to be a partner in enhancing the value of the theatre or she [can] choose to demean its existence by the nature of her evaluations," he wrote. "The choice is hers."[351] A more significant rift materialized, also in January of 1982, between Tahn and Jay Buckwold, chairman of Persephone Theatre's board of directors. Tahn was scandalized by Buckwold's brief to the Cultural Facilities Hearing, which the former interpreted as implying that 25th Street's production values were lower than Persephone's. In his letter, Tahn did not hesitate to compare the two theatre's records:

> 25th Street Theatre is recognized across the country and, indeed, in the international theatre community as a seminal force in the production of Canadian drama. In Canada, 25th Street Theatre is considered one of the top three companies producing professional Canadian work. Such plaudits are not, and cannot be, attributed to the Persephone Theatre. The only reason that I am mentioning this in a letter to you is that your brief has particularly maligned the work of this theatre. [352]

Tahn accused other members of Persephone's board, and its artistic director Eric Schneider, of uttering demeaning comments about 25th Street Theatre in public and noted that 25th Street's subscription audience had "grown tremendously" in the past year while Persephone's had remained almost stagnant. "It goes without saying," he wrote, "that we are Saskatchewan's favorite theatre."

The large concern that 25th Street and Persephone shared was, of course, the Saskatoon Theatre Centre with all its limitations and timetabling difficulties. "The office space, workshop space, dressing-room space, rehearsal space, performing space that they share would appall any director or patron," said Ron Marken in his overview of the 1981-82 professional theatre season for CBC Radio. "That two professional companies of national status should be sardined into the nightmare timetable that these people manage is a municipal and provincial disgrace."[353] The prospect of a new theatre centre became linked to a concept called Culturescape in 1982, whereby a downtown structure would be built to house the YWCA, the Western Development Museum, Persephone Theatre, and 25th Street Theatre. The concept was meant to revitalize Saskatoon's downtown core. The chair of the Western Development Museum's board, Don Leier, argued that rejection of Culturescape would signal a significant step in the decentralization of the city and, in the paraphrase of *StarPhoenix* reporter Derek Ferguson, send it "along a path of central cultural sterility similar to that in other major Western Canadian cities, such as Calgary, where the downtown is being reduced to office and apartment buildings."[354] The original proposed site for the Culturescape project was on 25th Street, directly across from Kinsmen Park, near the Mendel Art Gallery. The consulting firm of L.J. D'Amore and Associates was contracted to provide a feasibility report on the Culturescape project. The firm set up a series of Cultural Facility Hearings at the public library and heard briefings from all interested parties, including 25th Street Theatre. Andy Tahn, Sandra Dibb, and designer John C. Hughes presented the 25th Street briefing, proposing that the Culturescape project include two mainstage auditoria under one roof which, as Ned Powers argued, would "have the advantage of shared facilities, including box office, lobby, construction workshop and storage, washrooms, lounge and parking among others, while maintaining distinct individual identities for each company."[355]

When it was submitted to City Council, the consultant's report garnered negative reviews. The consultants recommended a $27 million multi-purpose facility on private property across from the Centennial Auditorium, which would house three theatres of 800, 400, and 250 seats as well as a museum, boutiques, galleries, and meeting rooms. Mayor Cliff Wright dismissed the proposal as an impossibility, too sprawling and too costly. Don Leier viewed the proposal as unrealistic and suggested that the consultant's report would do more harm than good in improving the city's cultural facilities. In the words of *StarPhoenix* reporter Les MacPherson:

> The relative merits of housing the museum in a separate building or combining it with other cultural facilities was not discussed. No cost analysis of the museum's options was presented. Questions of operating and capital costs and management structure were not dealt with. No rationale for the site selection

is offered, nor is any reason given for not choosing a downtown site already owned by the city.[356]

Leier proposed that a committee with municipal and provincial representatives be struck to try and work out a viable alternative to the D'Amore proposal. Representatives of Saskatoon's two professional theatre companies began to lose hope that a new purpose-built theatre facility would be constructed in the near future. On March 24, Persephone's artistic director Eric Schneider resigned, asserting that "because of the severe limitations of space and inadequate funding, I do not believe my continued efforts here will lead to anything more for me, personally and artistically, than 'running on the spot'."[357] Tibor Feheregyhazi was hired to replace Schneider in the spring of 1982.

On May 7, Ron Marken contributed an overview of the 1981-82 professional theatre season in Saskatchewan for CBC Radio. He noted that, of the nineteen professional productions he attended in Regina and Saskatoon, almost half were Canadian premieres. He suggested that each of the province's three professional companies, Globe, Persephone and 25th Street, had maintained a clear identity, characterizing 25th Street as the brash youngster of the three despite the fact that it had been in existence longer than Persephone. Marken both praised and criticized 25th Street Theatre for its "charming recklessness":

They take chances, they are defiantly Canadian in content, and encourage as many new scripts as they can afford. They court disaster occasionally, and find it. The TV sitcom tone of A VERY MODEST ORGY was trite. WOLFBOY was a sprawling, juvenile disaster. On the other hand, Alun Hibbert's PLAYING THE FOOL and Griffiths' and Brymers' O.D. ON PARADISE were delightful and original. Although 25th St. promised 5 plays, they only mounted four — for the other three they relied on their entrepreneurial talents and hosted touring productions instead. Their theatre season actually changed from month to month. There is a kind of charming recklessness here, although

I earnestly wished that some of their scripts would be more carefully edited and reworked before they are produced.[358]
Marken's overview is indicative of how Saskatoon's theatre community, in general, viewed the work of 25th Street Theatre, a view that does not necessarily take into account the difficulties of working with new Canadian scripts at a time when there was no Saskatchewan Playwrights' Centre (as there is now). The charming recklessness that Marken spoke of, would in the following year — when it became apparent that the theatre company's deficit had deepened — lead to the resignation of Andy Tahn.

NINE:
"ONE MONTH'S SEVERANCE PAY" (1982-83)

IN A LETTER OF July 13, 1982, Saskatchewan Arts Board consultant Rita Shelton Deverell delivered a summation of 25th Street's 1981-82 season, calling it a season of "artistic and audience consolidation." She noted that it had been filled with artistic energy and had included four new Canadian plays, school and psychiatric hospital workshops, and the off-conference stage for the Canadian Theatre Today Conference. She applauded the theatre's "extremely dedicated management" and the quality and energy of its artistic work. She also wrote that the theatre "has a history of 'over extending' itself, with touring, workshops, grasping at new ideas, even when the money was not there." She noted the theatre's plans to tour again on a limited basis in 1982-83, with *The Laffin' Jack Rivers Show,* and to develop a second stage, which would be called Theatre Downstairs. She was concerned, however, by the fact that the theatre was running a deficit budget, which she attributed to low levels of external funding but also to a "lack of fiscal caution" on the part of the theatre.[359]

The theatre's biggest problem was its accumulated deficit of $81,043. In a June 23, 1982 letter to Cam Partridge, Joy Cohnstaedt wrote that the Saskatchewan Arts Board had adopted a new policy concerning companies with accumulated or operating deficits. "In view of the 1981-82 one time only deficit reduction program, and the present serious economic conditions," she wrote, "the Board advises operationally funded companies to end the 1982-83 season deficit free." The penalty for not doing so, she said, was that deficit-ridden companies would be transferred from operations grant status to project funding.[360] Cohnstaedt's letter set off all sorts of alarm bells at 25th Street Theatre which had never had an overly close relationship with the Arts Board, particularly because the theatre company had only planned to chip away at the deficit in the next season. An initial proposed budget, included in the 25th Street Collection at the University of Saskatchewan Library, predicted that the deficit would be reduced by only $15,612 by the end of the 1982-83 season.[361] When asked to clarify, Cohnstaedt was ominously clear. "Being considered for project funding means that the company no longer has 'first call' on the Board's funds," she wrote, "that it is in competition with all other projects before the Board at the time, and that funding is on a one-time project, instead of continuing operation grant basis."[362]

In a letter to Rita Shelton Deverell, Sandra Dibb attempted to explain how the debt had grown so high. Dibb conceded that the deficit for the 1981-82 season alone was $45,987 and that it had materialized after several anticipated revenues were not realized. In particular, Dibb wrote, the Toronto International Theatre Festival had not paid the company the final instalment ($2,750) on its grant to tour *Cold Comfort* and *The Ziggy Effect*. SaskTrust had placed an unanticipated ceiling on matching fundraising grants, resulting in a loss of $11,500 for the theatre. Twenty-Fifth Street Theatre had also anticipated royalties of $20,000 from the Manitoba Theatre Centre's production of *Paper Wheat*, which was postponed. And the company had projected royalties of $10,000 for the publication of *Paper Wheat: The Book*, which was postponed until May 1983. No royalties were received in the 1982-83 fiscal year.[363] Furthermore, fundraising, including program advertising, had totalled $41,142 in 1981-82 as opposed to $69,542 in the previous year. "An extremely heavy adminis-trative load last season," Dibb contended, "made it difficult for me to focus much energy on fund-raising throughout the year." In the past, fundraising had been the responsibility of the theatre's management team, Dibb wrote, while in the future, the new board of directors would take an active role in raising funds for the theatre. There were other contributing factors to the deficit, including poor ticket sales for the tour of *Maggie and Pierre* and a $10,000 donation from IBM which fell through at the last minute. Dibb's rationale implies that the company was in the habit of spending monies that it could not be sure of or that were based on inflated estimates. To suggest, for example, that the company had made expenditures against a hoped-for royalty of $10,000 on the *Paper Wheat* book is wildly unrealistic.[364] In a letter of August 5, 1983, in which she thanked the Arts Board for its support, Dibb wrote that the company would try to eliminate its total deficit in one year but that the effort would be Herculean:

> Our fund-raising goals are high this year — over $86,000, and will have to be reached through a diverse fund-raising campaign, encompassing corporate sponsorships, business and private fund drives, foundation grants, and several special events. It is our goal to eliminate this deficit within the coming season. We are concerned about the decision of the Saskatchewan Arts Board to remove any arts group from operational funding which has not totally eliminated its accumulated deficit by the end of the next season. Certainly, given our situation, our limits as imposed by the seating and scheduling of this theatre, our limited choice of plays given our mandate, and the economic climate, it is a difficult task, but not impossible.[365]

Such a statement could not have instilled much hope in Arts Board representatives that the deficit would indeed be eliminated by the end of the season. Dibb's letter, however, expressed a great deal of hope about the drawing power of the company's new season, which included Paul Quarrington's *The Second*, Linda Griffiths' and Maria Campbell's *Jessica*, a new play by Andy Tahn, and Ken Mitchell's and Michael Taylor's new country-and-western musical *The Laffin' Jack Rivers Show*.

Based on these assurances, funding agencies were able to provide large grants to the deficit-ridden theatre company. The Saskatchewan

Arts Board agreed to provide 25th Street with an operational grant of $50,000 for 1982-83 and with a further $38,000 for the touring of *The Laffin' Jack Rivers Show*. The Canada Council increased the theatre's grant to $75,000 and provided a communications grant of $491. Even the City of Saskatoon provided two grants, one for $5,400 and another for $5800. PACT contributed a conference travel grant of $550. In total, the theatre received over $175,241 in public grants for the 1982-83 season.

Trouble was brewing, nevertheless, and it was reported in the *StarPhoenix* before representatives of the Saskatchewan Arts Board knew about it. According to Dorothea Fisher, who had been chair of the Arts Board's Performing Arts Committee before joining 25th Street's board of directors, the entire board of 25th Street Theatre had resigned in August of 1982, stating that they "were giving the theatre back to the general manager and the artistic director." According to Andy Tahn, in a letter of March 15, 1983, disputes between the Partridge board members and the artistic directorship of the theatre arose "out of the board's unwillingness to raise funds for the theatre." Furthermore, the Partridge board had doubled in number during the 1981-82 season, and Tahn argued that disputes arose when new members of the board "wanted the theatre to become something the theatre should never become," a producer of plays that have already had successful runs in other theatres. These new board members, Tahn suggested, had also insisted that the artistic directors would be answerable on financial and artistic matters to the general manager of the theatre, a resolution that the artistic directors fought on the grounds that it curtailed their artistic freedom.[366] Whatever the provocation for the Partridge board's actions, Dorothea Fisher felt the resignation constituted a violation of board responsibility, as it made no provisions for the theatre's continuation and as funding agencies were not advised of the mass resignation. She suggested that poor financial management on the part of the (now resigned) board had led to the increased deficit 25th Street Theatre now faced.

In September, the theatre's management approached Bill Hominuke Dorothea Fisher, Sean Kenny, and Wayne Wilkens and asked them to act as a board.[367] On October 7, Ned Powers reported in the *StarPhoenix* that the former board had resigned, "objecting mainly to theatre management's heavy concentration on artistic developments at a time when restraint should have been preached . . . "[368] He mentioned that a new executive committee had been formed, with Dorothea Fisher as chair, William Hominuke as vice-chair, and Sean Kenny as secretary-treasurer and that a new board had been constituted, including Andy Tahn, Linda Griffiths, Layne Coleman, and other 25th Street alumni like Gerry Stoll, Bob Collins, and Hominuke. Powers suggested that the new board of directors looked "suspiciously like it has been filled by some artistic friends" and that what it really needed was "people who can steer the company in proper, and probably tight-fisted, economic conditions." On October 8, Pat Adams wrote to Dorothea Fisher, on behalf of the Saskatchewan Arts Board, complaining that the Arts Board had not been notified of the resignation of the former board of directors. Adams reminded Fisher that it was to the board of directors that the Arts Board granted funding. She noted a significant difference in the projected deficit of $35,056 that the Arts Board had received in submissions from the theatre in March 1982 and the actual deficit, which was acknowledged in August as $81,043. Adams maintained that these financial irregularities raised "serious questions about the fiscal responsibility of the management and trustees of any organization," and she requested an interim report from 25th Street Theatre, deliverable on December 1. Adams' tone was ominous. "We are advising," she wrote, "that our interim review of 25th will be thorough."[369]

When the en masse board resignation was publicized, and with proddings from the Arts Board, Hominuke, Fisher, Kenny and Wilkens went into action. They set up a special meeting for the election of board officials on October 30. Because the new board, officially elected on October 30, included none of the previous board members, it refused to take responsibility for the budget that had been submitted to funding agencies at the beginning of the 1982-83 season. On November 17, Dorothea Fisher wrote Linda Sword at the Canada Council, listing the actions the new board had taken to rectify the financial standing of the theatre. They froze all salaries at the theatre, replaced the publicity director and eliminated the position of assistant stage manager. All of the artistic directors were taken off salary, and Hominuke was asked to act as executive director and to deal with the "day-to-day management" of the theatre. In addition, the board had set up three new committees: an Executive Committee, which would assist Hominuke in his duties; a Finance Committee, to oversee the re-budgeting process; and a Fundraising Committee.[370] On November 28, Hominuke wrote the Arts Board, asking for an extension of fifteen days for the interim report because an internal audit of the theatre was underway which would "dictate to a large extent what path the new Board's plans must follow." Hominuke suggested that the theatre's cutbacks might include the possible cancellation of the third show of the theatre's season, the mystery play that Andy Tahn was working on. He intimated that the Board had met on November 27 and had made the decision to "remove the post and title of general manager from the administration of the theatre." As of December 1, Sandra Dibb would no longer be in the employ of the theatre although she would continue to act as a fundraiser on a straight commission basis. According to Hominuke, the Board was also in discussions with Andy Tahn "about the possibility of his remaining off salary as Artistic Director for the remainder of the season." On the upside, Hominuke noted, the theatre had sold 81% of its tickets for the run of *Jessica*, which amounted to total box office receipts of $14,391.[371]

Andy Tahn did not find the board's recommendations palatable, and he did not appreciate having an executive director working over him. According to Tahn, he was informed in early December that the board had decided to cancel his new play, which was now entitled *In Search of a Sin*, and to replace it with a touring production of Richard Greenblatt's *Soft Pedalling*. "Needless to say," wrote Tahn, "there is now a gigantic hole in the roof over the table where I exploded in the restaurant when the news was delivered to me."[372] He pushed the matter, told the board members that they were fired and was fired, in return, by the board on December 6. Fisher wrote him as follows: "As you know, the Board of Directors of the theatre decided to relieve you of your duties effective December 6, 1982. Please find enclosed one month's severance pay."[373] Tahn was, however, quickly reinstated as Artistic Director (without salary) for the remainder of the season. He offered his own version of the events surrounding his re-hiring in a letter to Rita Shelton Deverell on March 15, 1983:

> To make a nightmare short, the Fisher Board, after consultation with Linda Sword of the Canada Council, Linda Griffiths, and Garry Rathgeber, our accountant, voted "motion, that Andy's play be done for a budget of under $10,000 and Andy be reinstated." Motion by Bill Brown, seconded by Wayne Wilkins, carried unanimously.[374]

On December 13, Hominuke again wrote to the Arts Board, enclosing an interim report and a revised budget but making no mention of Tahn's firing and re-hiring. In the letter, Hominuke summarized the company's largest budget cuts, which included a reduction of $12,000 in the budget for *In Search of a Sin*, the elimination of the artistic director's salary and the general manager's wage, a reduction of around $21,000 from the touring budget for *The Laffin' Jack Rivers Show*, and a cut in the technical director's and box office attendant's salaries. The budget cuts would save the company a total of $56,355 over the season but would not retire the total deficit of $81,000. Hominuke suggested that the theatre would have "an accumulated deficit of under $70,000 as of May 31, 1983."[375] This was not the news that the Arts Board had been waiting to hear, especially as there was a danger — happily averted when Tahn and Fisher met with a local manager of the Canadian Imperial Bank of Commerce in January — that the bank would withdraw 25th Street's line of credit. After receiving 25th Street's interim report, the Arts Board was sympathetic about the new board's problems but refused to back down from its initial stance on companies with deficits. "As you are aware," wrote Executive Director Kathleen Keple on February 25, 1983, "the Arts Board has indicated that companies that ended 1981-82 with deficits, and also end the present season with deficits will be transferred from operational to project grant status."[376]

The struggle over the deficit, and over the artistic direction of the theatre, was taking its toll on management and board members alike. On January 21, Dorothea Fisher wrote Rita Deverell, intimating that five of the theatre's seven board members would resign on January 30 and that their reasons for resigning were not always clear but "had a lot to do with [the] artistic content" of the theatre. "Some members wanted our theatre to be more like Persephone, geared toward the masses," she wrote. "As our mandate is to do new works, sometimes controversial works, we had a difference of opinion with artistic direction."[377] A general member's meeting was held on February 2, followed by a press release on February 7, which listed the new board as Dorothea Fisher (Chair), Matthew Miazga, Roy Morrisey, Bob Mitchell, Judy Buckle, Jim McManamy, and Eric Cline. The press release also included the following optimistic statement from Andy Tahn: "The worst is over. Now, through consistent diligence and hard work (while providing the high artistic and entertaining theatre our audiences are used to) our aim is to wipe out the deficit completely by May 31, 1984."[378]

For a brief shining hour, it looked as though Tahn and his band of theatre mavericks would again be able to save the day. In February, Sandra Dibb returned to the theatre in a fundraising capacity and sent publicity materials to PACT in order to complete the theatre's self-nomination for the Vantage Award. She mentioned to PACT's Curtis Barlow that her fundraising had been going well and that she had received confirmation of $8000 in corporate donations in the past week.[379] In March, Andy Tahn wrote to Rita Shelton Deverell that the theatre's final production of the season was in rehearsal. "I can breath a sigh of relief (. . . sigh)," he wrote. "We are finally bringing the last ship home to port." He outlined, for Deverell, several possible titles for the upcoming season, which included *Lively Times* by Don Kerr and Geoffrey Ursell, *Heros* by Ontario's David Jacklin, *Downtown*

Rooms by Vancouver's Jessie Boydan, *Skinner* by Calgary's Doug Hinds, *Chakyak* by Ernie Carefoot, a new play by Tahn, and a new play by Ken Mitchell and Michael Taylor. Tahn informed Deverell that in the 1983-84 season, he would function once again as sole artistic director of the company, "with Linda and Layne acting in an 'aunt/uncle' capacity." He requested $60,000 from the Arts Board, "not only because the theatre needs it, but because the theatre has emerged successfully from an extremely painful and trying season." He did not mention the Arts Board's resolution to fund debt-ridden theatres on a project basis only.[380] He remained positive about the new board and the theatre's adherence to the artistic principles on which it had been founded. "A Board chaired by Dorothea Fisher and Matthew Miazga as co-Chairman (both retained from the Fisher Board) is now in place and all are committed to bringing in the season as planned," he wrote. "We have re-established the artistic principles upon which this theatre has been founded, and this new and permanent board [is] committed to the production of new drama." According to Tahn, Miazga was chairing a committee whose mandate was to locate a theatre facility for use by the company in the 1983-84 season. Tahn's letter followed a press release from Dorothea Fisher, calling for applications for the position of general manager at the theatre.[381]

The theatre did what it could to avoid letting its financial woes get in the way of its artistic growth or of its mandate to produce new Canadian plays during the 1982-83 season. At the beginning of the season, the artistic directorship announced a Second Stage program, whose mandate would be to workshop new scripts in preparation for the mainstage, to give aspiring directors the opportunity to direct, to assist playwrights in the development of their scripts, and to introduce "new blood" into the theatre. While a location for the Second Stage had not been confirmed in time for the August 6, 1982 press release, some possible locations were the St. Tropez Bistro, the Shoestring Gallery, and the lobby of the Saskatoon Theatre Centre. Among the plays under consideration for the Second Stage were Gregory Nixon's *Firewalker*, Ernie Carefoot's *Chakyak*, Roy Morrissey's *Phonographic Revolution*, Janice Dales' *Victoria Court*, Brad Fraser's *Plastic Dreams and Platinum Blondes*, and Patricia Joudrey's *The Conjurer*. A selection of these plays would be presented free of charge for theatre subscribers and at a nominal fee for the general public.[382] Unfortunately, financial difficulties led to the cancellation of the Second Stage before it could make an impact.

Twenty-Fifth Street Theatre had planned to open the mainstage season with a collective creation called *The Saskatoon Show*, but when grants from Century Saskatoon and IBM did not materialize, the show was cancelled and replaced with Paul Quarrington's *The Second*. Quarrington had published several novels by this time, including *The Service* and *Home Game*, but *The Second* was his first play. It deals with seventy-year-old Jimmy Golightly, who has given up on life but does not have the courage to kill himself. He meets a gentle, dim-witted ex-con named Ernie Weeks in a bar and eventually offers Ernie $439 to put a bullet in his head. Ernie resists the temptation of the money because he is not sure that $439 is enough compensation to assuage the guilt he will feel afterwards. The play's suspense builds around the question of whether Ernie will eventually kill Jimmy. Because it was a two-hander, the play had the added virtue of being inexpensive to produce.

Randy Maertz, a former associate director at Edmonton's Citadel Theatre, directed the production, which featured Sean Mulcahy as Jimmy and Bob Collins as Ernie. The production ran from September 11 until October 9 at the Saskatoon Theatre Centre. Reviewers differed on the subject of the play's quality. In his CBC Radio review, Ron Marken called Quarrington's play "a weak script" which failed despite the actors' best efforts. "THE SECOND is, in other words, a discussion play — here is the problem, here are some variations on the problem, here are some alternate solutions to the problem," Marken said. "However, despite some heroic, but not always sustained, attempts by the actors to invest the script with life, it is finally unsuccessful."[383]

In the *StarPhoenix*, Don Perkins praised both the play and the actors. "Quarrington's dialogue, which comes on at first as tedious and lackluster, builds on itself," wrote Perkins. "The clichés, catchphrases and just plain clumsy repetitious attempts to fill the room with conversation, etch these characters with enviable precision." Perkins remarked on Mulcahy's "ability to give us a man terrified of what he might become" and suggested that Collins demonstrated with his range "why he is regularly praised for his talent all across the country."[384] At the end of the play's run, on October 9, the two actors remained in Saskatoon to present a benefit performance for the theatre of two brief plays, *African Chronicles* by Collins and *How To Succeed in Show Business Without Really Trying* by Mulcahy, with music by Don Freed.

Next up was a new play about a young Metis woman dealing with the ghosts of her past, written by Maria Campbell, Linda Griffiths, and Paul Thompson and entitled *Jessica*. The play had an unusually long and difficult developmental phase. It began when Paul Thompson and Maria Campbell met in 1976, while Thompson was touring *The West Show* through Saskatchewan. Campbell had published her autobiographical novel *Halfbreed* by that time, and she and Thompson met and discussed creating a project together. Thompson and Campbell met again in 1979 in Edmonton, where Thompson directed an improvisational workshop around some of Campbell's material. In 1980, at Thompson's behest, Campbell met with Linda Griffiths, who was on tour with *Maggie and Pierre*. Griffiths assembled a fairly detailed program of work, early on in the project's development, articulating the responsibilities of the participants. She wrote:

> The project is to evolve a play in conjunction with writer Maria Campbell (author of "Halfbreed" and writer in residence of the city of Regina) and director Paul Thompson (former artistic director of Theatre Passe Muraille). The play will tell the story of a Metis woman in today's society, who comes to a turning point in her life in terms of race, spirituality, and career and personal relationships. The project has evolved itself through discussions

with Ms. Campbell, and will be improvised and written with her into a dramatic form. It will concern itself with the growing involvement of native peoples with their original religion before European influence, as well as exploring the difficulties of remaining true to an Indian background while being successful in a white world. The difficulties of maintaining a male-female relationship in the midst of rebuilding a tattered culture will also be dealt with in the play.[385]

The script remained unformed until the summer of 1982, when Campbell and Griffiths embarked on a drive through Saskatchewan and Alberta in Campbell's old station wagon. During this research stage, Griffiths met Campbell's family, friends, and teachers, and she took part in dances and ceremonies. In August 1982, Griffiths, Campbell, and Thompson met in Toronto at Theatre Passé Muraille and began improvising the play based on the research materials they had gathered. They met again in Saskatoon a month later to piece together the script, which went into rehearsal in October.

Jessica was a difficult play for its white and Métis authors to put together because it included many scenes about Aboriginal spirituality and ritual. Maria Campbell summed up her own fears several years later in *The Book of Jessica: A Theatrical Transformation*. "This was not supposed to be a play about spiritual worlds," she wrote, "it was supposed to be a play about a woman struggling with two cultures, and how she got them balanced; because when she leaned into one, a part of her got lost, so she had to lean into the other one and try to understand and find a balance." She added that the "whole thing about 'spirits' and all this whooey-whooey stuff was enough to scare the pants off me," in part because there was pressure from her own community not to reveal spiritual details in a public forum.[386] In the same book, Griffiths described her own sense of uncertainty and uneasiness at one of those ceremonies:

The chanting rose up around me, something to concentrate on, something to follow with my senses. If I had been able to chant, if I hadn't been afraid of my uncertain voice mixed in with

the strange nasal call of the people around me, then it might
have been easier. But I felt myself to be still a watcher, as if the
comforts of the ceremony were not for me. The sounds pierced
through securities, realities, and the sweet grass smell was like
hands in my hair, fingers of smoke that changed the linear
attack of my thoughts. My brain clung to the way it usually
worked, but the smoke said, 'No, this channel also works.' Then
Bear came in . . . [387]

The rehearsal process was characterized by confusion, fear, and
anger as the actors waded into the characters and story. "I'd come
away from the rehearsals wasted, and go to Paul angry," Campbell
later wrote about the process. "I became even more fearful, not only
for [Griffiths], but also for myself, because if something happened I
wouldn't have anything left in me to give. That, coupled with the fear of
my community not understanding what I was doing and denouncing
the play . . . "[388] After the Saskatoon production closed, Griffiths
phoned Campbell to ask about the future of the project. According
to Griffiths, Campbell's response was "I never want to have anything
to do with you or Paul again. As far as I'm concerned, you can take
the play and do whatever you want with it."[389] Between 1982 and 1985,
there was no contact between Campbell and Thompson or Campbell
and Griffiths. Then, in 1985, Griffiths re-drafted the play and sent a
copy to Campbell. While Campbell was initially angry after receiving
the re-draft, she was eventually persuaded to contribute "suggestions
and comments" about the new script.[390] When the new version of the
play opened in Toronto at Theatre Passe Muraille in 1986, it received
the Dora Mavor Moore Award for Outstanding New Play and was a
runner-up for the Chalmers Award.

The 25th Street Theatre production of *Jessica* opened on November
5, 1982 at the Saskatoon Theatre Centre. Directed by Paul Thompson,
the production featured Linda Griffiths (as Jessica), Graham Greene (as
Bear Spirit, Sam, and William), Thomas Hauff (as Crow Spirit, Lawyer,
and GWG Salesman), and Tantoo Martin (as Vitaline-Grandmother,
Liz, and Coyote). Reviews of the original production were mixed, but

almost all of them contained criticisms of Griffiths' performance as the central Metis character in the play. In the *Sheaf*, Madeline McDonald admired several things about the production ("The play travels; it is rich and stimulating. The four actors cover ten roles and do it well.") but was of mixed opinion about Griffiths' performance. "Linda Griffiths is convincing as the big-city prostitute — she's sarcastic, defensive and tough," wrote McDonald. "In contrast, as a Métis woman in quest of her native consciousness, Griffiths seems a little pale."[391] In the *StarPhoenix*, Catherine Lawson called the play "harrowing" but felt that it was too long. She was also critical of the notion that a Caucasian woman could be convincing as Jessica, alongside other Aboriginal cast members. "Saskatoon audiences are familiar with the emotional intensity Linda Griffiths brings to each role," Lawson wrote. "Only one factor detracted from her portrayal of Jessica. Next to Martin and Greene, who are both native, it is too obvious that Griffiths is a white woman portraying an Indian [woman]."[392] Ron Marken, in his review for CBC Radio, raved about the play and the production. "Not only was the script exceptionally well-written, with vivid characters and telling dialogue," he said, "it was also produced in a way that made me happy to be in the theatre." Marken quibbled slightly about the play's "slow and quirky beginning" and also about the casting of the role of Jessica. "The four actors, Tantoo Martin, Graham Greene, Thomas Hauff, and Linda Griffiths, were magnificent," he maintained, "although I would have given anything to see Tantoo Martin, a fine Indian actress, in the lead role . . . "[393] The *Regina Leader Post's* Denise Ball was not so charitable about the play or the production. "The power of the play is found in its visceral exploration of native spirituality and political reality," wrote Ball. "The fundamental problem with Jessica, however, is the impenetrable mystical cloud surrounding the central character and the emotional fragments of her life spinning like a whirlwind out of control." Ball was also critical of Griffiths' performance, arguing that it did not translate into a centre around which the play could focus: "It's as if Griffiths is unable to find Jessica's voice — the core of her identity — which gives a basis for her search and her crisis."[394]

In *Maclean's*, Mark Czarnecki panned the production. "When Jessica operates in the white man's world, the writing and staging are trite and unconvincing," Czarnecki wrote. "Because her initial dilemma is not stated strongly enough, the first act recounts a familiar tale of native oppression without indicating why this story should be of special interest." Czarnecki also criticized Griffiths' performance, not so much because she was unable to make her audience forget that she was white but because she was unable to make them forget that she was the star of *Maggie and Pierre*. "Native audiences may not have heard of Linda Griffiths, but to white theatre audiences she is a star: the integrity of her interpretation is indisputable, but her performance is not sufficiently of a piece with its complex text to make them forget that fact."[395]

Tahn tried to drum up business for his next play, *In Search of a Sin*, by distributing a press release in which he took exception "to those who are going around town slandering me saying that I've written an inflammatory play about abortion." In the release, distributed a week before opening, he outlined the stormy background of the play which was, apparently, begun in 1979 after Burton Lancaster told Tahn that a play ought to be written about one of *Jakob Kepp*'s subplots. Tahn mentioned the fact that the play had been cancelled in 1981-82 and that the board had threatened to cancel it again in 1982-83. He offered a brief synopsis of the story, about Diana and Ted Fabian, a young married couple who live on Pinehouse Drive in Saskatoon. Diana is a graduate student in English, and Ted works temporarily at Canadian Tire in order to put Diana through university. A complication arises when Ted receives a letter informing him that he has been accepted into the Foreign Service Recruitment Program in Ottawa. "Diana is happy for Ted but is holding something back," Tahn writes in the press release. "She has a secret which she confides only to her best friend Susan who lives in the suite below them. Diana's secret could make a decisive difference in their marriage."[396]

The critic for the *StarPhoenix* saved her worst review of the season for *In Search Of A Sin*, which opened on February 10, 1983 with Denise

Beamish, Andorlie Hillstrom, Ian Black, and Heath Demers in the cast. The production was directed by Ernie Carefoot. In the *StarPhoenix*, Catherine Lawson argued that the play was indeed about abortion but with characters who are "no more than ciphers." She maintained that the dialogue was improbable. "A playwright is under no obligation to stick to gritty realism when he is writing dialogue," she wrote. "But when two women are having a heart-to-heart over white wine it's hard to swallow a line like: 'If it's a serious dishonesty it would seep into the relationship just like acid rain seeps into our land.'" Lawson had little to say about any of the actors, not even Denise Beamish, who played Diana, or Ian Black, who played Ted. "When a play has so little validity it is difficult to assess performances," she wrote. "Suffice it to say that Hillstrom, Denise Beamish, Ian Black, and young Heath Demers are talented and capable actors who could shine in another play."[397]

The final production of the season was of Ken Mitchell's and Michael Taylor's *The Laffin Jack Rivers Show*. There had been a good deal of conjecture that the play would do for 25th Street what *Cruel Tears* had done for Persephone Theatre. In fact, Brian Richmond, who had directed the premiere of *Cruel Tears*, wrote Tahn from Montreal to indicate his interest in directing the new Mitchell-Taylor project. "I am anxious to work with Michael and Ken together again," he wrote, "and am also anxious to work with 25th Street House with which I paradoxically find myself more in tune artistically than Persephone."[398] In return, Tahn offered to get in touch with Richmond after he had read the first draft of the play. "Persephone has never had the spark it had when you were at the helm," Tahn wrote.[399] The hope of hiring Richmond to direct the production apparently fell through some time later, and Janet Wright, who had played Flora in the original production of *Cruel Tears* was persuaded to come from Nelson, British Columbia, to direct the play. Twenty-Fifth Street had also hoped to produce the show for the Canadian Trucking Association's convention on June 16, 1982, for the sum of $7,875, but that deal fell through. When the production was about to open, a year later, Tahn invited Peter Gzowski to attend, writing that he believed "this will be a very popular show with national interest."⁴⁰⁰ After the tour of the play was completed, Tahn wrote Dolores MacFarlane at CBC television in Regina to discuss the possibility of a CBC broadcast of the show. He indicated to MacFarlane that the company was also contemplating a national tour of the play in 1983-84.⁴⁰¹

The realities of the production were stark in comparison to the hype surrounding the play. After the theatre's budget cuts of December 1982, the company was forced to scrimp on its wages for actors. Tahn pleaded with Christopher Marston, an Actors' Equity representative, to allow him to hire John LeClair and Colin Munn at apprentice rates.⁴⁰² When the company's insurer refused to insure the dilapidated Saskatoon Theatre Centre, 25th Street Theatre was forced to open the play in the basement of the Holiday Inn on 22nd Street. I can remember riding down the hotel elevator with my fellow actors, and Janet Wright, from our dressing room, a suite on an upper floor, for our first entrance on to the stage. Wright was a fan of Huddie Leadbetter songs, and she regaled us with her version of "See That My Grave Is Kept Clean" all the way to the basement.

Reviews of the Saskatoon opening were uniformly good. The *StarPhoenix's* Catherine Lawson admired the performances of Ian Black, as Laffin' Jack, and Denise Kennedy, as Eileen, and praised the script "in which neither the humor nor the pathos is contrived."⁴⁰³ Ron Marken wrote that the performers make or break a production such as *Laffin' Jack* because of its thin plot line and emphasis upon songs:

Jon Taylor is inebriatedly wonderful as a bombed and rude heckler. The opportunity his bit part gives for the play to be self-critical should have been more often used. And consider director Janet Wright's special task of finding a cast who could sing AND play instruments well AND act. Well, in John Leclair and Colin Munn she got them. Those boys are good on their instruments, and they can sing too — but not so well as Denise Kennedy, a woman with range, brass, and versatility.⁴⁰⁴

Writing for the *NeWest Review*, Caroline Heath found the play to be even better than *Cruel Tears*. "This time I think [Mitchell's and

Taylor's] collaboration was even more successful," wrote Heath. "The music and drama are inextricably bound, the characterizations and tensions more subtle."[405]

The tour of the show was not without its controversies (for a first-hand account of the tour, please see the appendix of this book). Probably the unhappiest letter Tahn received about the production was one from Mrs. Eleanor Lucky, who had viewed the play at a high school auditorium in Yorkton. Mrs. Lucky was the wife of Smilin' Johnnie and also a singer in his stage show. She had heard Andy Tahn interviewed on CBC Radio about *The Laffin' Jack Rivers Show* and was annoyed to hear Tahn say that the show was based on the life of "a fellow who's still in business in Saskatchewan, though he's on the skids, has been for years."[406] After seeing the show on April 19, she wrote to Tahn expressing her amazement "at the garbage you people produce on handouts from the Canada Council and others." Tahn responded, in a letter, that he felt awful about the comments he'd made on CBC Radio but that there had been a misunderstanding. "The information that I was given regarding the creation of THE LAFFIN' JACK RIVERS SHOW did include material based upon many bands that have either gone out of business or [are] in the process of folding," he wrote. "Although I am aware that Ken Mitchell and Michael Taylor may have received ideas from the Smilin' Johnnie Show, the show itself is a composite based upon several Saskatchewan bands."[407]

On March 30, Tahn announced, at a press conference on the set of *The Laffin' Jack Rivers Show* at the Holiday Inn, that he would resign as artistic director of 25th Street Theatre, effective May 30, 1983, in order to devote more time to his writing. He was asked if the poor critical reception of *In Search of a Sin* had anything to do with his resignation, and he defended his record as a writer. "I didn't fail as a writer," he said. "I consider the script in its final state and it will go to publishers that way. If anything, I failed as an artistic director because I didn't spot the weaknesses in selling the play and I didn't realize it was meant for a select audience."[408] The press release announcing Tahn's resignation was upbeat; there was little mention of the many issues that must have weighed on Tahn in the previous years — the chronic lack of funding, the struggle to find good new Canadian scripts, the promise of being moved to project grant status, the condemnation of the Saskatoon Theatre Centre. (In later years, Tahn maintained that he had "stayed on until under the Chair Dorothea Fisher circumstances were such that I could leave secure that the theatre would continue under strong artistic leadership."[409]) Tahn thanked the people who had helped the theatre to survive over the years and looked forward with confidence to 25th Street's future. "I will continue to convince the people of Saskatoon how much finer, more beautiful, and more attractive a place this will be to live in when we build [ourselves] a proper legitimate professional theatre facility," he wrote in the release. "I know we have the money. I know we have the energy. All we need is the will."[410]

It did not take long for applications to roll in from people wanting to fill Tahn's old job. One particular application, from Gordon McCall, Artistic Director at Winnipeg's Prairie Theatre Exchange, was mailed on April 8, after McCall had conversed with Tahn by phone. "I have had two very successful years at Prairie Theatre Exchange but am looking to move to a theatre with the mandate and tradition of 25th Street Theatre," McCall wrote, in his application to Dorothea Fisher. "Most particularly, I am looking to work for a theatre which has a structural setup as outlined to me by Andy today; i.e. a strong and supportive board of directors operating in conjunction with an Artistic Director and Administrative Director toward common goals."[411] McCall would eventually land the job.

Epilogue:
"THE THEATRE IS WITHOUT A HOME" (AFTER 1983)

GORDON MCCALL DID NOT inherit a theatre that was in eminent health. As promised, the Saskatchewan Arts Board took steps to demote the company to project status, albeit with a fairly large project grant of $45,000 for the 1983-84 season. The theatre's financial deficit, after proceeds from *The Laffin' Jack Rivers Show* were accounted for, was approximately $63,000. In August, just after Saskatoon City Council had agreed to provide Persephone Theatre with $180,000 in order to finance a new facility of their own, McCall and Dorothea Fisher went before Council to apply for a grant of $135,000. There was much debate and acrimony surrounding a motion, put forward by Alderman Marshall Hawthorne, to deny funding for 25th Street because of the theatre's deficit and also because it would be a "frivolous use of taxpayers' money" for council to support a second theatre company so soon after assisting Persephone. McCall warned that the theatre might disappear without city funding, and Fisher confronted Mayor Cliff Wright, who had supported Hawthorne's motion, arguing (according to the *StarPhoenix*) that "the mayor attends too few Saskatoon theatre productions to take a stance on the company's problems."[412]

There were also huge personnel changes, including the change in artistic directorship and the hiring of a new general manager. A look at the company list for McCall's first production, of Thelma Oliver's play *Diefenbaker*, reveals that changes had been made both behind and in front of the scenes. The two designers, Reginald Bronskill (set) and Larry Isacoff (lights), were new to 25th Street Theatre, as were the stage manager S. Tigger Jourard and the actors, Patricia Lenyre, Norma Edwards, and Terrence Slater. Pauline Russell had been hired as the new general manager. All of these people had to be brought up to speed with the theatre company and its goals.

McCall was determined to connect with 25th Street Theatre's past audiences and also to attract new patrons. To achieve both goals at once, he decided to depart from 25th Street's former mandate of producing only new Canadian plays. He promised to produce several Canadian premieres, including *Diefenbaker* and Ken Mitchell's *Gabriel Dumont*, but he would also include the national touring production of *The Women of Margaret Laurence* and the Vancouver hit *Last Call*. *StarPhoenix* writer Don Perkins viewed McCall's move to producing bona fide hits as a good one. "25th has had to replace the untempered enthusiastic idealism, which has been the operating principle for the past 10 years, with a more disciplined pragmatism," wrote Perkins. "Which is not to knock enthusiasm or idealism — they have taken 25th a long way, it's the 'untempered' that caused problems."[413]

Another pressing need, for McCall and his colleagues, was to find a new theatre space in which to perform. Back in March, Dorothea Fisher had written the Canada Council about the closure of the Saskatoon Theatre Centre. She was clear that the company's main goal was to eliminate its deficit. "Although we are looking for a new home," she wrote in a March 15 letter to Linda Sword, "we want to make it clear that a new facility is not a main concern of ours." Fisher suggested that the theatre's plans were "to lease a space for one or more years until a proper professional, legitimate stage is built in Saskatoon."[414] By September, 25th Street Theatre had changed its plans and went before City Council again, this time with an application for $75,000 with which to buy the former Christian Youth Centre on 601 Eastlake Avenue for the purpose of turning it into a theatre. Several home owners in the residential district surrounding 601 Eastlake complained that there would be insufficient off-street parking for such a facility and that noise would be created. Twenty-Fifth Street Theatre asked council to lift parking restrictions in the residential zone, but its application was held up in bureaucratic red tape. First, a discretionary use hearing was scheduled to hear 25th Street's application, and local opposition to it, and then, on the advice of city solicitor Marty Irwin, the hearing was cancelled. Irwin argued a discretionary use hearing might prejudice the provincial planning appeals board hearing, which had been scheduled for November 7. After the provincial planning board had reached its decision, there would also be a 30-day appeal period. And on it went. Twenty-Fifth Street was forced to open its first play of the 1983-84 season in the basement of the Holiday Inn. Eventually, the East Lake property deal fell through, and 25th Street Theatre was left, for the future, renting warehouses and church halls and doing its best to transform these venues into theatre spaces.

What made the debacle over a permanent theatre space particularly unpalatable for 25th Street supporters was that its sister theatre, Persephone, had gone out and secured a permanent theatre venue in short order. Armed with a $180,000 provincial facilities grant, Persephone's board members and its new artistic director Tibor Feheregyhazi had located a space at the end of Rusholme Road, the former Westgate Alliance Church. The church was, like 601 East Lake, located in a residential district, but city council nevertheless approved re-zoning of the area. The price tag for the abandoned church was $360,000. According to a *Leader Post* article, Persephone's board raised another $180,000 privately, and then the local Kinsmen Club kicked in $50,000. The building was purchased and Saskatoon architect Desmond Paine was given the job of drawing up plans for its remodelling. Feheregyhazi credited board chairman Bob Stromberg with doing the heavy work in fundraising. "I don't know how to raise money or suck up to politicians," he was reported as saying. "The board president really did it. He just bulldozed right through. There was tremendous positive energy from the board and administration."[415] When Persephone's "minor miracle" was reported in the *Regina Leader Post* on November 17, 1983, there was an article on the same page under the headline "25th Street's tortoise chases Persephone's hare." *Leader Post* reporter Denise Ball outlined the various difficulties 25th Street had had in locating a space but suggested that Gordon McCall and his theatre company were not about to give up on the race. "It may take awhile," McCall reportedly told her. "We have some building blocks in place. But the process is beginning to happen."

Without a permanent theatre space, and with tenuous financial backing, 25th Street Theatre was in trouble. General Manager Pauline Russell wrote a press release on December 17, declaring that 25th Street Theatre had to raise $25,000 within two weeks or else "cease operations entirely." She blamed poor box office figures for the first two shows of the season, *Diefenbaker* and *The Women of Margaret Laurence,* for the financial difficulties the theatre was experiencing. The theatre's bank had refused to extend any further credit, and preparation for the next show, Morris Panych's *Last Call*, were put on hold. In the dire press release, Russell wrote:

> Because of poor attendance at THE WOMEN OF MARGARET LAURENCE and less-than-projected box office revenue for DIEFENBAKER, the Theatre has experienced difficulty in maintaining its cash flow without short-term assistance from the bank. Although this policy of credit assistance has been in place with the bank for many years, it appears that the current situation coupled with the outstanding deficit has brought about the current decision of the bank.[416]

Although the theatre's financial problems were temporarily averted, and *Last Call* was produced, Gordon McCall's days at the theatre were numbered. He resigned from his post as 25th Street Theatre's artistic director less than a year later.

For Andy Tahn, the struggles of 25th Street Theatre under a new artistic director must have been difficult to watch. Tahn busied himself with freelance writing in 1984, contributing several articles to the *StarPhoenix* despite his run-ins with the paper's theatre reviewer a few years earlier. His articles were mostly celebrations of Saskatchewan artists, like painters Kevin Quinlan, Marguerite Smith, and John Kaufman. He also contributed an autobiographical article about crossing the Hungarian border as a five-year-old with his family after the 1956 uprising had failed and arriving in Austria. "Do not be afraid," an Austrian border guard reassured the family when they arrived in Austria, "You are on safe ground."[417] Tahn spent a few years in Saskatoon as a free-lance writer and then moved to Regina to work in the Department of Culture and Youth. As fervent in his religious faith as he was about the ideology of his theatre company, he also served for several years as Executive Director of the St. Therese Catholic College of Faith and Mission in Bruno, Saskatchewan.

I had the pleasure of attending Tahn's new production of *Paper Wheat*, in which he directed students and faculty members from St. Therese, on May 22, 2009. For the occasion, Tahn had rented the lavish new Persephone Theatre — a purpose-built theatre at last — on the banks of the South Saskatchewan River. It was heartening to see Tahn walk out on the stage before the performance began — an older Tahn than I had remembered, wearing an executive director's suit, his hair was grey but he still had the same passion. On that night, he was selling not tickets to his production but his marvellous new college in Bruno, which operated, Tahn said, under the kind benefaction of people just like us. There would be a draw, he said, at intermission, the winner of which would have his or her name entered into a second draw for a two-night stay at St. Therese College during Cherry Festival season. There were promises of cherry perogies, cherry sausage, cherry everything. And then the lights went down and the show began. Bill Prokopchuk wasn't playing fiddle; a female student was standing in his place and playing exquisitely. A flood of young actors entered the stage, mimicking the action of a train and singing "Roll Out!" with voices that were not reminiscent of Sharon Bakker and Lubomir Mykytiuk. But — what the heck! — the play showed few signs of aging. It presented the audience, for the most part, with a nostalgic look at their forefathers and foremothers. A few of the lines had been changed so that the internet generation could be included in the show. At the end of the evening, the audience (albeit a partisan bunch) leapt to its feet in genuine appreciation. The play had not lost its sparkle, the music still delivered a punch, and Andy was back on top.

There is still much left to write about 25th Street Theatre. The company did not die in 1985, when Gordon McCall resigned as artistic director. It experienced a resurgence, in fact, when Tom Bentley Fisher, originally from Biggar but trained in England, accepted the position of artistic director for the company. Under Bentley Fisher's direction, 25th Street Theatre was able to recover some of its old vigour. The theatre company never returned to its original mandate of producing only new, untested Canadian plays, but it did produce many premieres of works by a new generation of playwrights, including Don Kerr, Connie Gault, Anne Szumigalski, Mansel Robinson, Dianne Warren, and others. Bentley Fisher created a late-night one-act series and directed several workshop productions. For a period of nearly fourteen years, the company used a warehouse space on Duchess Avenue for a theatre and used it well.

In 1990, the old financial burdens began again to weigh on the theatre, and Bentley Fisher developed a new strategy for keeping the legacy of 25th Street alive. He would create a Saskatoon Fringe Theatre Festival, which would be part of the growing fringe movement across Canada. Proceeds from the Fringe would help the theatre stay afloat. Bentley-Fisher remained with 25th Street Theatre until 1997, when Glen Cairns became artistic director of the company. In 1999, which was 25th Street's final season as a producer of its own theatrical presentations, four plays were mounted: Robert Astle's *The Hats of Mr. Zenobe*, David Gow's *Bea's Niece*, Michel Tremblay's *Hosanna*, and Mansel Robinson's *Spitting Slag*. In later years, 25th Street alumnus Sharon Bakker served as an interim artistic director for the theatre and for the Fringe Festival. Soon it was discovered that the theatre did not really need an artistic director anymore, at least not so badly as it needed a general manager who could sign contracts with Fringe touring groups, locate theatre spaces in which to stage performances, and orchestrate ticket sales. Twenty-Fifth Street Theatre has survived, but it is presently little more than a presenter of the work of other companies.

Other theatres have sprung up, recently, to perform some of the work that Andy Tahn and his friends originally set out to do. Dancing Sky Theatre, in Meacham, caters to a rural audience, producing Canadian work (including a sequel to *Paper Wheat*, written by Mansel Robinson with music by Rocky Lakner and entitled *Street Wheat*) and collectively-written material. The Saskatchewan Native Theatre, located on 20th Street six blocks from the old Saskatoon Theatre Centre, has begun producing plays by and about Aboriginal people in Canada. The Station Arts Centre in Rosthern produces a Canadian play, usually with a rural theme, every summer. The Saskatchewan Playwrights' Centre, which came into being during Tom Bentley Fisher's final years as artistic director of 25th Street, has taken on responsibility for dramaturging and workshopping new Saskatchewan plays. These companies are part of the legacy of 25th Street Theatre, unimagined when Tahn and his friends applied for a Local Initiatives grant back in 1972.

Wherein did the "glory days" lie at 25th Street Theatre? The answers are threefold: the theatre company provided a much-needed forum for writers; it created a body of acting and directing talent that would have a resounding effect on Canadian theatre; and it provided a response to the mainstream theatre that had become entrenched in many Canadian cities.

Twenty-Fifth Street Theatre gave a voice to many new and seasoned writers who wanted to write about life in Canada and, more specifically, in the Canadian West. Many of these playwrights wrote about Saskatchewan in ways that solidified an identity or questioned long-held beliefs and opinions. By giving playwrights a voice, 25th

Street Theatre gave the population of Saskatchewan a voice — and not just the Saskatchewan of the literati or the intellectual elite but also the Saskatchewan of the farmer and the elevator agent and the truck driver and the mechanic. The theatre mirrored its audience.

As the theatre grew, so did a new body of actors who would figure significantly in the development of Canadian theatre in the latter part of the 20th Century. Layne Coleman, who later became Artistic Director of Toronto's Theatre Passe Muraille, is perhaps the most obvious example of this. As Artistic Director at that institution, he was able to showcase Canadian and collective theatre creations both in Toronto and also on tour across the country. Similarly, Linda Griffiths became a theatrical dynamo after moving to Toronto, writing (and acting in) major hit plays like *Maggie and Pierre*, *Jessica*, and *O.D. on Paradise*. Many of the actors who graced the stage at 25th Street Theatre in its early years were major players in Canadian and prairie theatre thereafter. The list of these actors is extensive, but certainly Lubomir Mykytiuk, Sharon Bakker, David Francis, Bob Baker, Don Francks, and Gary Reineke make an admirable roll call of 25th Street's alumni.

Twenty-Fifth Street Theatre was, above all, a theatre of which Saskatchewan and Canada could be proud. In its first ten years of existence, the theatre garnered an enviable national reputation. It was a theatre company with the foresight to realize that the mainstream theatre of the time was not particularly interested in giving the Canadian regions a voice. It was a theatre company which experimented with, and developed, a new model of theatrical creation (new at least in much of Canada) for which it became widely known. The specialization in collective creation was a risky business, but when it paid off (as with *Paper Wheat*) the dividends were huge. The fearless prospered in such instances, and that is the way theatre should be in an era where there is much competition from television and the cinema. At its best, 25th Street Theatre was a fearless place, sometimes risking its own financial health and sometimes risking its artistic reputation. And fearlessness has its rewards.

om, directed by Richard Rose, 1980   *Larry James Fillo*

Larry James Fillo

The Second, with Sean Mulcahy and Bob Collins, 1982

Larry James Fillo

In Search of a Sin, with Ian Black and Denise Beamish, 1983

Appendix

The following is an edited version of my first-hand article about the tour of *The Laffin' Jack Rivers Show*, published in the *NeWest Review* in Summer 1983.

Inside and out, theatre is a fragile affair. Its real currency is not money but lesser-prized thoughts and emotions. Actors, directors and playwrights must constantly toy with their own personalities, jeopardizing relationships in the process — and, of course, the monetary rewards are not great. For the spectators, less is at stake; they bind their dreams to their souls where mere actors are not likely to get at them. The properties of live theatre are such that the audience may be invited to participate in the spectacle, more so than in cinema or at home in front of the television. When this occurs, when the dreams of the spectator and actor and director and playwright are wed, when they are swept toward a common goal, then the theatre is more beautiful than the most beautiful woman under a moonlit sky.

I did not intend this article to become yet another treatise on the fragility of theatre, but my experience with *Laffin' Jack Rivers* has left me no choice. My journals of that period emphasize the fragile interaction of audience and actor and the efforts made to sustain that communion.

Laffin' Jack Rivers was produced at a time when stars were falling from the artistic firmament of 25th Street Theatre. The season before last, when it all began, had been an artistic success and a financial failure for the theatre. *Wolfboy* and *O.D. on Paradise* — both produced in 1981-82 — have since enjoyed national exposure. The following autumn, rumours of the theatre's eighty-four thousand dollar deficit were circulating. During the 1982-83 season, two boards of directors resigned. Artistic director Andras Tahn confided in me at the opening night party for *Laffin' Jack Rivers* that the next resignation would be his own. A few days later, after the public announcement of Tahn's resignation had been made, I was informed that board members had put liens against their houses so that we actors could be paid during the rehearsal period. *Laffin' Jack Rivers* was hopefully the deus ex machina that would reverse this downhill trend.

The administrative shake-up did not affect the writing of the play, which was commissioned from Ken Mitchell and Michael Taylor and workshopped last fall [1982]. Rehearsals were improvisational; the text delivered into the hands of the actors at first reading was polished but not sacrosanct. The actors were quick to suggest alterations, and in Mitchell's absence, Taylor and director Janet Wright freely cut and rewrote scenes. Wright, a teacher as well as an actor, established a workshop atmosphere in rehearsals, replete with Method exercises and lengthy discussions. The cast consisted of Ian Black, Denise Kennedy, Colin Munn, John Leclair, Jon Taylor and myself.

Early in the rehearsal period, Tahn, Wright, Taylor and Mitchell discussed the possibility of mounting *Laffin' Jack Rivers* in a local beer parlour. As it turned out, the insurance company made their decision for them, closing down the established theatrical venue, hitherto known as the Saskatoon Theatre Centre. A former nightclub in the basement of the Holiday Inn was finally settled upon. This move to a licensed room in the downtown core was in the best interests of the production, creating a parallel between the drinking audience and the play, which is set in a small-town beer parlour. The convenient elision from reality to fiction seduced the audience into actively participating in the play.

In my role as the hotel manager, I entered the stage fifteen minutes before the play began. The set, designed by Don Rutley and Stephen Wade, was so convincing and congruent with the former nightclub's ambiance that I was frequently accosted by patrons who would order a beer or a package of cigarettes; who would lean up against the bar, shooting the breeze with me until the house lights dimmed and they found themselves in the hard scrutiny of the theatrical lights, like tourists who had stumbled into Buckingham Palace in the middle of a coronation.

Partly because of the genuine barroom atmosphere, the audience often identified with the staged heckler, played by Jon Taylor. Spectators joined in with jibes aimed at Laffin' Jack and his Rhythm Ramblers. To our astonishment, their comments were frequently critical of political and social attitudes. As he gathered momentum for a long soliloquy, Laffin' Jack was interrupted one night by a man shouting, "Are you a musician or a politician?" Another night, as Eileen (played by Denise Kennedy) was confronted with the sexism of the other characters in the play, one patron stood up with his back to the stage and admonished the chuckling audience: "Every bourgeois in the place laughed."

Through the rehearsals and the Saskatoon run, there was a sense that we were training for a bigger challenge — the Saskatchewan tour. The least reliable factor in any theatre venture, but especially in touring shows, is the audience. Would they attend our show? Would they like it? How would audiences differ from city to city?

On 10 April, the day before we went on tour, Tahn accepted the resignation of John MacIntosh as publicity manager. This development, I suspected, was the result of poor ticket sales in the seven cities on our roster (although, as MacIntosh told me, the theatre's shoestring budget disallowed his visiting the communities personally).

The next day was clear and sunny. We arrived at the Circle S Country Palace in North Battleford at four o'clock — far too early since the show did not begin until eight. A local rodeo rider challenged me to a game of pool shortly after we arrived at the bar. I asked him if he was coming to the show. He wasn't too big on play-acting, he said. His remark turned out to be an omen; the show was poorly attended that night. Afterwards I met Nicole Doucet, grants person for the Canada Council, and it struck me that there are other motives for touring besides promoting a particular play: in Canada at least, arts councils view touring as a commendable function, worthy of more dollars when it's time to allot grants.

The next stop was Moose Jaw. It seemed fitting to perform *Laffin' Jack Rivers* at the Union Hall since unions and theatre collectives are both off-shoots of the kind of democratic socialism that grew up in southern Saskatchewan during the twenties and thirties. The charm of 25th Street Theatre is its collective spirit, similar to that of a barn-raising or a quilting bee, which Mark Czarnecki referred to as "benevolent anarchy" in a recent issue of Maclean's. The Union Hall has a stout, muscular character, men in their working clothes sitting around scratched wooden tables, drinking beer out of the bottle. Before the play began, the stages heckler, who was sprawled across a table as if in a drunken stupor, was asked to leave by one of the Hall's staff. In the middle of the performance, a Fire Inspector sauntered through the playing area and checked the exits. During the curtain call, a workman lofted his hardhat on to the stage — an act of spontaneous appreciation which the fictitious Laffin' Jack craves from "real people" (as he says).

The audiences in Swift Current and Weyburn were older and more sedate than we had previously experienced. Onstage, we found ourselves softening the sometimes coarse language of the play. We had no end of fun with our new-found righteousness for the rest of the tour, chastising offensive semi-truck drivers to "heck off" or exclaiming "gosh darn gee whiz" after burning our tongues on truck-stop borscht. In the process, several wayward vocabularies were domesticated.

Our three-day stint in Regina was transferred to the Seven Oaks Motel at the last minute because officials from the Fire Department and the university had condemned Darke Hall. What might have been perceived as a problem again turned out to be a blessing, allowing us to perform in the intimate atmosphere of a bar instead of an echoing, expensive theatre. The day after opening in Regina, Ian Black and Colin Munn (who played Jack Rivers and Guy Wolowidznyk respectively) and myself were interviewed by Kay Saddlemeyer of CBC Radio. He asked if there was a hex on the show, causing trouble with Fire Departments of various cities. "It's a hot show," Ian replied.

Also in Regina, we experienced our first disruptive spectator. The interesting fact is that he was ejected by one of the playwrights, Ken Mitchell. After the show, Mitchell came backstage, pointed at me and said, "From now on, you do it."

In Yorkton on 19 April, the cast was interviewed by a local newspaper reporter. She started with the traditional question: "Is acting a precarious business?" We did not have to tell her that we were sleeping five persons to a room in order to save money; she could see that. We answered with the usual dramatic examples but neglected to mention the expiration of our contracts at the end of the week. Oh, there were all sorts of talent agencies and production companies wanting to back our show and to send us on a national tour with lavish salaries and free accommodation; there were even more immediate offers of holding over in Saskatoon or Regina; and word was out that the CBC wanted to televise our production, making us millionaires several times over with Bugattis and mansions in Beverly Hills. But nobody had seen any contracts which would secure our future for another month. In the meantime, we deliberated how we would negotiate more severely this time so that we could each afford lifetime subscriptions to Modern Screen.

Prince Albert has a reputation for being Saskatchewan's frontier city. I had an idea that this last and northern-most stop on our tour would be a tough nut to crack, even with a show featuring country and western music. I was wrong. The audiences there were relatively large and most receptive — cause for hope even though Tahn announced on closing night that our contracts would not be renewed immediately.

Endnotes

[1] McGrath, John. *A Good Night Out: Popular Theatre: Audience, Class, and Form*. London: Eyre Methuen, 1981 4.

[2] McGrath 63.

[3] McGrath 19.

[4] McGrath 21-22.

[5] Rudakoff, Judith, ed. *Dangerous Traditions: A Passe Muraille Anthology*. Winnipeg: Blizzard Publishing, 1992 viii.

[6] McGrath 38.

[7] Tahn, Andrew. "Isn't it time for young voters?" *The Star-Phoenix* 18 April 1968: 21.

[8] Tahn interview, August 2009.

[9] Tahn interview, August 2009.

[10] Wright, Bunny. "Saskatoon play praised for direction." *The Star-Phoenix* 28 March 1969: 8.

[11] "State of Castle theatre flayed." *The Star-Phoenix* 10 April 1969: 5.

[12] Tahn, Andy. "Reflections on local theatre." *The Sheaf* 26 Sept. 1969: 8.

[13] Tahn 8.

[14] Clews, Hetty. "Reply to Mr. Tahn: Local theatre 'Good.'" *The Sheaf* 30 Sept. 1969: 11.

[15] Powers, Ned. "Theatre group striving to keep talent at home." *The Star-Phoenix* 17 Dec. 1971: 8.

[16] Tahn interview, August 2009.

[17] Elder, George. "Conception." *Targya* 1 (spring 1973) U of Alberta Rutherford Special Collection, Edmonton.

[18] 25th C, I.1. constitutional material.

[19] Tahn interview, August 2009.

[20] Tahn interview, August 2009.

[21] "Dramatic group find direction." *The Star-Phoenix* 27 June 1973: 27.

[22] Tahn interview, August 2009.

[23] 25th C, I.1. programs.

[24] "Saskatoon Underground." *The Sheaf* 10 Nov. 1972: 11.

[25] "A Grimm Evening." *The Sheaf* 14 Nov. 1972: 8.

[26] Tahn interview, August 2009.

[27] 25th C, I.1. press releases.

[28] "At the Mendel." *The Sheaf* 26 Jan. 1973: 10.

[29] Cardiff, Gayle. "Art for eyes and ears." *The Sheaf* 30 Jan. 1973: 16.

[30] There were several coffee shops in Saskatoon highlighting the work of emerging writers during the seventies. Tahn remembers performing at three or four locations in a single evening and making five dollars in each coffee shop. (Tahn interview, August 2009)

[31] "Twenty-Fifth Street House Premieres: 'Covent Garden.'" *The Sheaf* 20 March 1973: 19.

[32] Tahn interview, August 2009.

[33] Tahn interview, August 2009.

[34] Macpherson, Jean. "School play on too big stage." *The Star-Phoenix* 31 March 1973: 23.

[35] 25th C, I. reviews.

[36] Tahn interview, August 2009.

[37] *Targya* 1 (spring 1973) U of Alberta Rutherford Special Collection, Edmonton.

[38] *Targya* 2 (autumn 1973) U of Alberta Rutherford Special Collection, Edmonton.

[39] 25th C, I.1. press releases.

[40] "Dramatic" 27.

[41] Macpherson, Jean. "'Eyes' have it; new drama group shows improvement." *The Star-Phoenix* 14 Dec. 1973: 24.

[42] 25th C, I.2. reviews.

[43] Labreche, Julianne. "The Birthday Party in Review." *The Sheaf* 8 Jan. 1974: 8.

[44] 25th C, I.2. reviews.

[45] Labreche, Julianne. "The Sibyl." *The Sheaf* 29 Jan. 1974: 16.

[46] Macpherson, Jean. "Sibyl–it can't be ignored." *The Star-Phoenix* 24 Jan. 1974: 10.

[47] 25th C, I.2. press releases.

[48] 25th C, I.2. press releases.

[49] Macpherson, Jean. "A Virus Called Clarence." *The Star-Phoenix* 29 Nov. 1974: 10.

[50] Macpherson 10.

[51] Macpherson, Jean. "Pathos, passion, porn mingle in 25th St. Madhouse." *The Star-Phoenix* 14 Feb. 1975: 22.

[52] Tahn interview, August 2009.

[53] 25th C, III programs.

[54] Macpherson, Jean. "Ballad faces bright future." *The Star-Phoenix* 12 April 1975: 10.

[55] Macpherson, Jean. "Drama steps to forefront in Saskatoon: . . . four companies ready for new season." *The Star-Phoenix* 10 Oct. 1975: 19.

[56] Tahn interview, August 2009.

[57] "Saskatoon Theatres Present–Saskatchewan Drama." *The Sheaf* 7 Jan. 1976: 6-7.

[58] "Twenty-Fifth Street presents Five Shows." *The Sheaf* 23 Sept. 1975: 14.

[59] "Saskatoon" 6-7.

[60] Powers, Ned. "A deserving award." *The Star-Phoenix* 3 Jan. 1976: 15.

[61] 25th C, I.4. Canada Council.

[62] 25th C, I.4. publicity.

[63] Tahn interview, August 2009.

[64] Macpherson, Jean. "Play opens to small audience." *The Star-Phoenix* 17 Oct. 1975: 38.

[65] Johnson, Kim. "If You're So Good Why Are You Here?" *The Sheaf* 21 Oct. 1975: 8.

[66] Grant, Craig. "25th St. House Held Over." *The Sheaf* 7 Nov. 1975: 9.

[67] Rolfe, Lee. "Tough-minded little drama: Prairie landscape needed trimming." *The Winnipeg Tribune* 13 Nov. 1975: 65.

[68] Poyser, Alice. "If You're So Good fails to sparkle." *Winnipeg Free Press* 13 Nov. 1975: 38.

[69] Keys, Janice. "Canadiana feeds theatre group." *Winnipeg Free Press* 14 Nov. 1975: 7.

[70] "Play audiences grow despite poor reviews." *The Star-Phoenix* 18 Nov. 1975 10.

[71] Tahn interview, August 2009.

[72] Macpherson, Jean. "Francks show may improve in repetition." *The Star-Phoenix* 21 Nov. 1975: 17.

[73] Mandrill, Harry. "Review–Twenty-Fifth Street House: Reaching a Personal Understanding." *The Sheaf* 25 Nov. 1975: 9.

[74] 25th C, I.4. reviews.

[75] Macpherson, Jean. "Unicorn production adds to holiday season." *The Star-Phoenix* 20 Dec. 1975: 8.

[76] 25th C, I.4. playscripts 2.

[77] 25th C, I.4. playscripts 130.

[78] Macpherson, Jean. "Play carries audience into future." *The Star-Phoenix* 7 Feb. 1976: 18.

[79] Thomson, Jim. "25th Street House Theatre: Science Fiction ZAPS Saskatoon." *The Sheaf* 10 Feb. 1976: 12.

[80] 25th C, I.4. reviews.

[81] Powers, Ned. *The Star-Phoenix* 16 Nov. 1976: 9.

[82] Powers, Ned. *The Star-Phoenix* 19 Jan. 1977: 37.

[83] 25th C, I.5. correspondence.

[84] 25th C, I.5. correspondence.

[85] Russell, Nancy. "Play concerning Saskatoon starts slow, grows on you." *The Star-Phoenix* 17 Sept. 1976: 17.

[86] Watson, Leah. "We're so good we've come back to Saskatoon." *The Sheaf* 17 Sept. 1976: 10.

[87] "25th St. House delays opening." *The Star-Phoenix* 13 Oct. 1976: 41.

[88] Macpherson, Jean. "Concentration, continuity main feature of Heartbreak Hotel." *The Star-Phoenix* 30 Oct. 1976: 26.

[89] 25th C, I.5. reviews.

[90] Watson, Leah. "Heartbreak Hotel–posterial ache." 2 Nov. 1976: 10.

[91] 25th C, I.5. reviews.

[92] 25th C, I.5. programs.

[93] 25th C, I.5. reviews.

[94] Macpherson, Jean. "A Sacred Mountain." *The Star-Phoenix* 23 Dec. 1976: 13.

[95] Tahn interview, August 2009.

[96] Macpherson, Jean. "Quebec play highlight of national theatre tour." *The Star-Phoenix* 30 Dec. 1976: 11.

[97] Filewod, Alan D. *Collective Encounters: Documentary Theatre in English Canada.* Toronto: U of Toronto P, c. 1987 93.

[98] Filewod 91.

[99] Filewod 91-92.

[100] 25th C, I.6. reviews. *Eston Press* 30 March 1977.

[101] Filewod 92.

[102] Kerr, Don. "History As A Six Pack." *The NeWest Review* 2.9 (May 1977): 6.

[103] Macpherson, Jean. "Paper Wheat." *The Star-Phoenix* 30 March 1977: 58.

[104] 25th C, I.5. reviews.

[105] Kerr 6.

[106] 25th C, I.6. Oxcart Summer Players.

[107] 25th C, I.5. press releases.

[108] 25th C, I.6. playscripts.

[109] 25th C, I.6. reviews.

[110] Macpherson, Jean. "Prairie Psalms." *The Star-Phoenix* 18 July 1977: 23.

[111] Hellman, Kateri. "Prairie Psalms gives honest account: Play tells tale of pioneer faith." *Prairie Messenger* 21 Aug. 1977: 6.

[112] 25th C, I.6. Canada Council.

[113] Tahn interview, August 2009.

[114] Filewod 99.

[115] 25th C, I.6. correspondence.

[116] Filewod 92.

[117] email from Andy Tahn to Dwayne Brenna, 3 March 2010.

[118] Tahn interview, August 2009

[119] Tahn interview, August 2009.

[120] Filewod 110.

[121] Macpherson, Jean. "Paper Wheat." *The Star-Phoenix* 30 Sept. 1977: 15.

[122] 25th C, I.6. reviews. Froelich, Lorraine. *Shadowfax* 6 Oct. 1977.

[123] Freeman, Brian. "Saskatchewan story too slow in telling." *Toronto Star* 12 Oct. 1977: F1.

[124] 25th C, I.6 reviews. Johns, Ted. *Toronto Theatre Review* (Dec. 1977).

[125] email from Andy Tahn to Dwayne Brenna, 3 March 2010.

[126] 25th C, I.6. reviews. *The Moosomin World-Spectator* 23 Nov. 1977.

[127] 25th C, I.6. reviews. *The Moosomin World-Spectator* 23 Nov. 1977.

[128] 25th C, I.6. reviews. *Nokomis Times* 16 Nov. 1977.

[129] 25th C, I.6. reviews. *Indian Head-Wolseley News* 23 Nov. 1977.

[130] 25th C, I.6. reviews. Millar, John. *Moose Jaw Times-Herald* 28 Oct. 1977.

[131] 25th C, I.6 reviews. *Meadow Lake Progress* 9 Nov. 1977.

[132] 25th C, I.6. reviews. *Free Press Report on Farming* 11 May 1977.

[133] 25th C, I.6. Canada Council.

[134] Carroll, Michael. *Ottawa Review* 9-15 Nov. 1978.

[135] Phoenix, Sandy. *The Plant* 27 Oct. 1978: 11.

[136] Peterson, Maureen. "Prairie play comes east in real style." *Montreal Gazette* 13 Oct. 1978: 17.

[137] Dawson, Eric. "Theatre Calgary production: Actors lost in Paper Wheat chaff." *Calgary Herald* 6 June 1979: A17.

[138] Hobson, Louis B. *The Albertan* 7 June 1979.

[139] Kaiser, Lolly. *Scene Changes* (Dec. 1979): 28.

[140] Conologue, Ray. "Dazzling Paper Wheat inventive and delightful." *The Globe and Mail* 22 Nov. 1979: 19.

[141] Hobson, Louis B. *The Albertan* 7 June 1979.

[142] Edinborough, Arnold. "A fine stage harvest." *Financial Post* 15 Sept. 1979: 42.

[143] Edmonstone, Wayne. "Show has warmth and honest humour." *Vancouver Sun* 13 Sept. 1979: B5.

[144] Kaiser, Lolly. *Scene Changes* (Dec. 1979): 27.

[145] Campbell, Sherri. *Queen's Journal* 23 Oct. 1979: 17.

[146] Perkins, Don. "Paper Wheat at theatre centre." *The Star-Phoenix* 14 Aug. 1979: B3.

[147] Filewod 111.

[148] Siskind, Jacob. *Ottawa Journal* 21 Aug. 1979: 27.

[149] Knelman, Martin. "Moral uplift on the Prairies." *Saturday Night* (Dec. 1979): 62.

[150] 25th C, I.6. correspondence.

[151] 25th C, I.6. correspondence.

[152] Tahn interview, August 2009.

[153] Russell, Nancy. "Naked on the North Shore." *The Star-Phoenix* 2 Feb. 1978: 24.

[154] D'entrement, M. "Naked on the North Shore." *The Sheaf* 2 Feb. 1978: 24.

[155] email from Andy Tahn to Dwayne Brenna, 3 March 2010.

[156] 25th C, I.6. playscripts 101.

[157] Kerr, Don. "Son of Paper Wheat." *The NeWest Review* 3.8 (April 1978): 3.

[158] 25th C, I.6. reviews. *Panorama* 17 March 1978.

[159] 25th C, I.6. reviews. *Panorama* 17 March 1978.

[160] Russell, Nancy. "Generation and ½." *The Star-Phoenix* 4 March 1978: 22.

[161] 25th C, I.6. reviews. Garber-Conrad, Beckie. *Co-operative Consumer* 14 March 1978: 9.

[162] Russell, Nancy. "Mummer's play shows other side of seal hunt." *The Star-Phoenix* 11 April 1978: 16.

[163] Russell, Nancy. "The Club Seals, Don't They." *The Star-Phoenix* 12 April 1978: 45.

[164] 25th C, I.6. reviews. Robins, Gary. *Briarpatch* (May 1978): 33.

[165] 25th C, I.6. Oxcart Summer Players.

[166] 25th C, I.6. reviews. Murray, Joy. *The Prince Albert Herald* 12 Aug. 1978.

[167] 25th C, I.6. reviews. Bird, Doug. *Meadow Lake Progress* 23 Aug. 1978.

[168] 25th C, I.6. reviews. Pinay, Donna. *New Breed* 8 (Sept. 1978): 26.

[169] 25th C, I.6. reviews. Beament, Marg; Goulet, Linda and Dorian, Anne. *The Northerner* 8 Sept. 1978.

[170] Pinay 27.

[171] Ball, Denise. "Play by Oxcart Summer Players said disappointing, inconsistent." *Regina Leader-Post* 18 Aug. 1978: 4.

[172] Russell, Nancy. "Oxcart Players." *The Star-Phoenix* 30 Aug. 1978: 12.

[173] Creswell, Dene. "Pub filming proves challenge: . . . 5 days shooting expected." *The Star-Phoenix* 14 Sept. 1978: 13.

[174] 25th C, I.7. correspondence.

[175] "Post awards recognize business achievements in helping the arts." *Financial Post* 3 March 1979: 3.

[176] 25th C, I.7. correspondence, 19 April 1979.

[177] 25th C, I.7. correspondence.

[178] 25th C, I.7. publicity releases, 16 March 1979.

[179] 25th C, I.7. correspondence.

[180] 25th C, I.7. correspondence, 29 June 1978.

[181] 25th C, I.7. correspondence.

[182] 25th C, I.7. publicity releases.

[183] Pugh, Terry. "25th St. House Theatre: Season Subscriptions Introduced." *The Sheaf* 16 Nov. 1978: 8.

[184] 25th C, I.7. programs.

[185] Russell, Nancy. "Hard Hats and Stolen Hearts." *The Star-Phoenix* 19 Sept. 1978: 18.

[186] Ashwell, Keith. "Sands saga just romance wearing satiric clothing." *Edmonton Journal* 27 July 1978: C10.

[187] Ashley, Audrey M. "Hard Hats, Stolen Hearts: Alberta play a muddle." *Ottawa Citizen* 26 Sept. 1978: 62.

[188] Pugh 8.

[189] Perkins, Don. "Hamlet." *The Star-Phoenix* 6 Feb. 1979: 13.

[190] Perkins, Don. "William Schwenck And Arthur Who?" *The Star-Phoenix* 8 Feb. 1979: 17.

[191] 25th C, I.7. correspondence.

[192] 25th C, I.7. correspondence.

[193] Perkins, Don. "Sneezy Waters–no encore." *The Star-Phoenix* 19 Feb. 1979: 41.

[194] Kelly, Linus. "25th Street House Theatre's The Queen's Cowboy." *The Sheaf* 8 March 1979: 13.

[195] Perkins, Don. "Queen's Cowboy." *The Star-Phoenix* 3 March 1979: 11.

[196] Kerr, Don. "More Mountie Lore." *The NeWest Review* 4.8 (April 1979): 10.

[197] Portman, Jamie. "Grassroots in Saskatchewan." *Edmonton Journal* 7 March 1979: E2.

[198] Perkins, Don. "Troupe offers family fun." *The Star-Phoenix* 30 March 1979: 7.

[199] 25th C, I.7. publicity releases.

[200] 25th C, I.7. Oxcart Summer Players.

[201] Perkins, Don. "25th Street House Theatre." *The Star-Phoenix* 4 May 1979: 5.

[202] 25th C, I.7. correspondence.

[203] 25th C, I.8. correspondence, 23 May 1979.

[204] 25th C, I.8. correspondence.

[205] 25th C, I.8. correspondence, 7 Jan. 1980.

[206] 25th C, I.8.v. correspondence.

[207] 25th C, I.8. correspondence.

[208] *Regina Leader-Post*, 13 June 1979, p. 13.

[209] 25th C, I.7. programs.

[210] Perkins, Don. "Jakob Kepp premiere." *The Star-Phoenix* 15 Nov. 1979: B5.

[211] 25th C, I.8. reviews.

[212] Campbell, Donald. "25th St. House: Powerful Performance: Jakob Kepp." *The Sheaf* 22 Nov. 1979: 9.

213 Perkins, Don. "Queen's Cowboy returns." *The Star-Phoenix* 6 Feb. 1980: C7.

214 Conologue, Ray. "Maggie and Pierre shows power, finesse and insight." *The Globe and Mail* 15 Feb. 1980: 17.

215 Groen, Rick. "Meet Linda Griffiths, chameleon: She changes from Maggie to Pierre and back." *The Globe and Mail* 16 Feb. 1980: E1.

216 Czarnecki, Mark. "You've lost that Sussex feeling." *Maclean's* 17 March 1980: 44c.

217 Perkins, Don. "Maggie and Pierre." *The Star-Phoenix* 19 March 1980: C13.

218 Fogel, Earl. "Maggie and Pierre." *The Sheaf* 13 March 1980: 12.

219 Tahn interview, August 2009.

220 25th C, I.8. reviews.

221 25th C, I.8. reviews.

222 25th C, I.8. reviews.

223 Perkins, Don. "25th Street's Matonabbee." *The Star-Phoenix* 19 April 1980: D3.

224 25th C, I.8. correspondence.

225 Over thirty years later, Tahn has not wavered from that viewpoint. "It's a brilliant play," Tahn said in a 2009 interview. "It really is. I've had occasion to re-read it since then."

226 25th C, I.8. correspondence, 22 April 1980.

227 25th C, I.8. reviews.

228 Perkins, Don. "Boom opens in Saskatoon." *The Star-Phoenix* 8 May 1980: B5.

229 Paddy, Victor. "Boom finally ignites after a slow start." *The Globe and Mail* 12 June 1980: 15.

230 25th C, I.8. press releases.

231 Tahn interview, August 2009.

232 25th C, I.8. press releases.

233 Perkins, Don. "Coleman relishes new role in Saskatoon theatre group." *The Star-Phoenix* 26 Aug. 1980: D3.

234 Perkins, Don. "Coleman challenges 'grassroots' image." *The Star-Phoenix Accent* 4 July 1981: 10.

[235] Perkins, Don. "Players feel facilities pinch." *The Star-Phoenix Accent* 18 Oct. 1980: 13.

[236] Perkins 13.

[237] Johnsrude, Larry. "Committee report endorses professional theatre facility." *The Star-Phoenix* 14 April 1981: D2.

[238] Perkins 13.

[239] 25th C, I.9. correspondence, 17 Sept. 1980.

[240] 25th C, I.9. correspondence.

[241] "Prelate Ursulines relive history in commissioned play, Sisters." *Prairie Messenger* 31 Aug. 1980: 6.

[242] 25th C, I.9. playscripts 3.

[243] 25th C, I.9. playscripts 87.

[244] 25th C, I.9. playscripts 88.

[245] 25th C, I.9. correspondence, 20 March 1981.

[246] Macpherson, Rod. "25th Street House Theatre: Ziggy Effectiveness on Display." *The Sheaf* 23 Oct. 1980: 11.

[247] 25th C, I.9. reviews.

[248] Perkins, Don. "25th Street's Ziggy Effect." *The Star-Phoenix* 18 Oct. 1980: 9.

[249] Czarnecki, Mark. "The sway of paper dollars over the paper wheat." *Maclean's* 24 Nov. 1980: 70.

[250] 25th C, I.9. correspondence, 20 March 1981.

[251] 25th C, I.9. reviews.

[252] email from Layne Coleman to Dwayne Brenna, 20 Sept. 2010.

[253] email from Layne Coleman to Dwayne Brenna, 20 Sept. 2010.

[254] 25th C, I.9. reviews.

[255] Perkins, Don. "Conversations With Girls in Private Rooms." *The StarPhoenix* 6 Dec. 1980: E1.

[256] 25th C, I.9. correspondence, 20 March 1980.

[257] 25th C, I.9. playscripts 7.

[258] 25th C, I.9. playscripts 29-30.

[259] 25th C, I.9. reviews.

[260] Perkins, Don. *The StarPhoenix* 31 Jan. 1981: C1.

[261] Portman, Jamie. "Good grief! Love and bondage emerge in Prairie theatre." *Calgary Herald* 6 Feb. 1981: C11.

[262] 25th C, I.9. correspondence.

[263] 25th C, I.9. correspondence.

[264] 25th C, I.9. reviews.

[265] 25th C, I.9. reviews.

[266] 25th C, I.9. reviews.

[267] <*the star*.com> 25 Oct. 2007.

[268] Powers, Ned. *The StarPhoenix* 24 Feb. 1981: B3.

[269] qtd. in Powers B3.

[270] email from Layne Coleman to Dwayne Brenna, 20 Sept. 2010.

[271] 25th C, I.9. correspondence.

[272] 25th C, I.9. correspondence.

[273] 25th C, I.9. correspondence, 6 March 1981.

[274] 25th C, I.9. programs.

[275] Perkins, Don. *The StarPhoenix* 21 March 1981: C1.

[276] 25th C, I.9. correspondence, 20 March 1981.

[277] Perkins C1.

[278] 25th C, I.9. correspondence, 20 March 1981.

[279] 25th C, I.9. correspondence.

[280] 25th C, I.9. correspondence.

[281] Tahn interview, August 2009.

[282] email from Layne Coleman to Dwayne Brenna, 20 Sept. 2010.

[283] 25th C, I.9. correspondence, 20 March 1981.

[284] 25th C, I.9. school workshops, report.

[285] Sanderson, Vicky. "Prairie bondage gripping." *The Globe and Mail* 15 May 1981: 15.

[286] Mietkiewicz, Henry. "Superb horror story puts chill on laughs." *Toronto Star* 14 May 1981: E8.

[287] Adilman, Sid. "Stratford interested in festival shows." *Toronto Star* 18 May 1981: D1.

[288] 25th C, I.9. correspondence, 20 March 1981.

[289] Crew, Bob. "Prairie boy kicks up dust with impressive directing." *Toronto Star* 22 May 1981: C12.

[290] Crew, Bob. "Punk play packs a punch." *Toronto Star* 24 May 1981: F15.

[291] Corbeil, Carole. "Play about punk tries to breathe." *The Globe and Mail* 23 May 1981: E7.

[292] email from Layne Coleman to Dwayne Brenna, 20 September 2010.

[293] Perkins, Don. "Cold Comfort popular at theatre festival." *The StarPhoenix* 25 May 1981: D1.

[294] 25th C, I.9. correspondence.

[295] 25th C, I.9. reviews.

[296] 25th C, I.9. correspondence, 15 March 1981.

[297] 25th C, I.9. correspondence, 15 March 1981.

[298] 25th C, I.9. correspondence.

[299] 25th C, I.11. correspondence, 3 Sept. 1981.

[300] 25th C, I.11. correspondence.

[301] 25th C, I.11. correspondence.

[302] 25th C, I.ii. correspondence, 16 July 1981.

[303] Tahn interview, August 2009.

[304] email from Andy Tahn to Dwayne Brenna, 3 March 2010.

[305] 25th C, I.10. publicity releases, 21 Aug. 1981.

[306] 25th C, I.11. correspondence, 25 Jan. 1982.

[307] 25th C, I.11. correspondence, 25 Jan. 1982.

[308] Conologue, Ray. "Moments of truth mixed in with theatrical fireworks." *The Globe and Mail* 12 Oct. 1981: 15.

[309] Czarnecki, Mark. "Swords crossed on the Prairies." *Maclean's* 26 Oct. 1981: 7.

[310] Conologue 15.

[311] Czarnecki 77.

[312] Czarnecki 77.

[313] Conologue 15.

[314] qtd. in Conologue 15.

[315] qtd. in Conologue 15.

[316] Conologue 15.

[317] 25th C, I.10. playscripts.

[318] Macpherson, Rod. "A Very Modest Orgy." *The Sheaf* 15 Oct. 1981: 9.

[319] Thompson, M.A. "Three Plays." *The NeWest Review* 7.3 (Nov. 1981): 5.

[320] Lawson, Catherine. *The Star-Phoenix* 9 Oct. 1981: B6.

[321] Ball, Denise. "Artistic colonialism reflected in Saskatoon group's play." *Regina Leader-Post* 9 Oct. 1981: E11.

[322] Whittaker, Herbert. "Not-so-new playwrights get share of spotlight." *The Globe and Mail* 21 Oct. 1981: 21.

[323] Brennan, Brian. "Sex farce sizzles, rig drama fizzles." *Calgary Herald* 10 Oct. 1981: D7.

[324] Tahn interview, August 2009.

[325] 25th C, I.10. reviews.

[326] Dales, Janice. "Wolfboy." *The NeWest Review* 7.4 (Dec. 1981): 6.

[327] Perkins, Don. *The Star-Phoenix* 7 Nov. 1981: C1.

[328] Macpherson, Rod. "25th Street's Wolfboy: We're not in Kansas anymore, Toto." *The Sheaf* 12 Nov. 1981: 9.

[329] 25th C, I.10. publicity releases.

[330] 25th C, I.10. playscripts 56.

[331] Perkins, Don. *The StarPhoenix* 9 Jan. 1982: D1.

[332] Marken, Ron. "Feast of Fools at 25th." *The Sheaf* 14 Jan. 1982: 10.

[333] Dales, Janice. "Playing the Fool: Reds, Pinkos, and True Blues." *The NeWest Review* 7.5 (Jan. 1982): 8.

[334] Interview with Kate Young. CFPL Radio, London, Ontario, 7 Jan. 1982.

[335] Ladner, Peter. "Maggie and Pierre: the Oatman version." *Vancouver Sun* 25 Sept. 1981: G1.

[336] Perkins, Don. *The Star-Phoenix* 5 Feb. 1982: B1.

[337] Robertson, Sheila. *The StarPhoenix* 9 Feb. 1982: C5.

[338] Conologue, Ray. "Too many characters spoil Griffiths' play." *The Globe and Mail* 2 March 1982: 15.

[339] 25th C, I.10. reviews.

[340] Conologue 15.

[341] Lawson, Catherine. *The StarPhoenix* 20 Feb. 1982: C1.

[342] Czarnecki, Mark. "An illustrious stage in transition." *Maclean's* 24 Jan. 1983: 54.

[343] Conologue, Ray. "Paradise closer to perfection." *The Globe and Mail* 17 Jan. 1983: 15.

[344] 25th C, I.10. press releases.

[345] 25th C, I.10. reviews.

[346] Perkins, Don. *The Star-Phoenix* 11 May 1982: D5.

[347] 25th C, I.10. playscripts 80.

[348] 25th C, I.10. reviews.

[349] 25th C, I.10. publicity releases.

[350] 25th C, I.10. publicity releases.

[351] 25th C, I.10. correspondence.

[352] 25th C, I.10. correspondence, 25 Jan. 1982.

[353] 25th C, I.10. reviews.

[354] Ferguson, Derek. "Culturescape claimed key to city's development." *The Star-Phoenix* 18 Jan. 1982: A3.

[355] Powers, Ned. "Theatres voice concern over facilities." *The StarPhoenix* 16 Jan. 1982: D1.

[356] 25th C, I.10. reviews. Macpherson, Les. *The StarPhoenix* (Feb 1982).

[357] 25th C, I.10. publicity releases.

[358] 25th C, I.10. reviews.

[359] 25th C, I.11. correspondence.

[360] 25th C, I.11. correspondence.

[361] 25th C, I.11. Canada Council.

[362] 25th C, I.11. correspondence, 27 July 1982.

[363] 25th C, I.11. correspondence, 15 Nov. 1982.

[364] The standard royalty rate is 10% of the retail cost of the book which would have meant that 25th Street must sell 5,000 copies of a $20 book in order to receive $10,000 in royalties. In Canada, a book that sells 3,000 copies is considered a bestseller.

[365] 25th C, I.11. correspondence.

[366] 25th C, I.11. correspondence, 15 March 1983.

[367] 25th C, I.11. correspondence, 17 Nov. 1982.

[368] Powers, Ned. *The StarPhoenix* 7 Oct. 1982: B7.

[369] 25th C, I.11. correspondence.

[370] 25th C, I.11. correspondence.

[371] 25th C, I.11. correspondence.

[372] 25th C, I.11. correspondence, 15 March 1983.

[373] 25th C, I.11. correspondence.

[374] 25th C, I.11. correspondence.

[375] 25th C, I.11. correspondence.

[376] 25th C, I.11. correspondence.

[377] 25th C, I.11. correspondence.

[378] 25th C, I.11. publicity releases.

[379] 25th C, I.11. correspondence, 15 Feb. 1983.

[380] 25th C, I.11. correspondence, 15 March 1983.

[381] 25th C, I.11. press releases, 8 March 1983.

[382] 25th C, I.11. press releases.

[383] 25th C, I.11. reviews.

[384] Perkins, Don. *The StarPhoenix* 25 Sept. 1982: B7.

[385] 25th C, I.11. playscripts.

[386] Griffiths, Linda and Maria Campbell. *The Book of Jessica: A Theatrical Transformation.* Toronto: Coach House P, 1989 17.

[387] Griffiths 29.

[388] Griffiths 50.

[389] Griffiths 55.

[390] Griffiths 10.

[391] McDonald, Madeline. "Jessica explores power and oppression." *The Sheaf* 11 Nov. 1982: 17.

[392] Lawson, Catherine. *The Star-Phoenix* 6 Nov. 1982: D13.

[393] 25th C, I.11. reviews.

[394] Ball, Denise. "Bunch of ideas strung together." *Regina Leader-Post* 19 Nov. 1982: C11.

[395] Czarnecki, Mark. "Cultural schizophrenia." *Maclean's* 15 Nov. 1982: 78.

[396] 25th C, I.11. publicity releases, 3 Feb. 1983.

[397] Lawson, Catherine. *The StarPhoenix* 14 Feb. 1983: B1.

[398] 25th C, I.11. correspondence, 4 May 1982.

[399] 25th C, I.11.x. correspondence, 21 May 1982.

[400] 25th C, I.11. correspondence, 23 March 1983.

[401] 25th C, I.11. correspondence, 4 May 1983.

[402] 25th C, I.11. correspondence, 1 March 1983.

[403] Lawson, Catherine. *The StarPhoenix* 26 March 1983: A17.

[404] 25th C, I.11. reviews.

[405] Heath, Caroline. "Laffin' Jack River Show." *The NeWest Review* 8.8 (May 1983): 19.

[406] 25th C, I.11. correspondence, 26 April 1983.

[407] 25th C, I.11. correspondence, 11 May 1983.

[408] Powers, Ned. "Tahn quits as 25th Street artistic director." *The StarPhoenix* 31 March 1983: B1.

[409] email from Andy Tahn to Dwayne Brenna, 3 March 2010.

[410] 25th C, I.11. publicity releases, 30 March 1983.

[411] 25th C, I.11. correspondence, 8 April 1983.

[412] Perry, Leslie. "Council rejects bid to deny theatre funds." *The StarPhoenix* 3 Aug. 1983: A3.

[413] Perkins, Don. "25th Street Theatre will woo audience." *The StarPhoenix* 27 Aug. 1983: D10.

[414] 25th C, I.11. correspondence.

[415] Ball, Denise. "Minor miracle puts Persephone into new home." *Regina Leader-Post* 17 Nov. 1983: D1.

[416] 25th C, I.12. publicity releases.

[417] Tahn, Andy. "Christmas memories." *The StarPhoenix Accent* 22 Dec. 1984: 3.